Calcutta

Two Years in the City

Amit Chaudhuri

Union
Books

First published in Great Britain in 2013 by
Union Books
an imprint of Aurum Press Limited

7 Greenland Street
London NW1 0ND

union-books.co.uk

A catalogue record for this book
is available from the British Library.

ISBN 978-1-90-852617-5

1 3 5 7 9 10 8 6 4 2

2013 2016 2015 2018 2017 2014

Printed and bound in Great Britain by
MPG Books, Bodmin, Cornwall

Calcutta

For my father

Think of the long trip home.
Should we have stayed at home and thought of here?
Where should we be today?
Is it right to be watching strangers in a play
in this strangest of theatres?
What childishness is it that while there's a breath of life
in our bodies, we are determined to rush
to see the sun the other way around?
The tiniest green hummingbird in the world?
To stare at some inexplicable old stonework
inexplicable and impenetrable,
at any view,
instantly seen and always, always delightful?
Oh, must we dream our dreams
and have them, too?
And have we room
for one more folded sunset, still quite warm?
   Elizabeth Bishop, 'Questions of Travel'

By 'modernity' I mean the ephemeral, the fugitive, the contingent, the
half of art whose other half is the eternal and the immutable.
   Charles Baudelaire, 'The Painter of Modern Life'

Contents

A Purchase

It was probably three years ago that the poet Utpal Kumar Basu reported to me a couple of observations he'd overheard in the nocturnal din of North Calcutta. They both came from the same source, an old woman whom Utpalda calls, with some irony, *khurima* ('aunt') and *gyana-bhandar* ('treasure trove of wisdom'). The woman, herself homeless, would cook for the homeless on a porch near Sealdah Station. The memory is from circa 2003, and Utpalda is pretty certain that the group of people he saw that year must have moved on. Utpalda possesses a context for Khurima's first observation: a man had once come to the group of destitute and desultory wage-earners looking for someone – say, Nipen – with Nipen's address (probably a landmark and directions) on a piece of paper. Khurima had responded dismissively: *'Thhikana diye ki hobe? Soye kothhai seta bolo.'* That is: 'What good is an address? Tell me where he rests his head.' Utpalda had found the remark 'illuminating' (his word): 'Quite true,' he thought. 'For the homeless, an address has no meaning. What's far more important is where they find a place to sleep.'

Her second remark was probably made in self-defence and with pride, though Utpalda can't remember whom it was directed at: *'Amra bhikeri hote pari, pagol noi.'* Or: 'We may be beggars, but we aren't mad.' This may well have been addressed to a policeman. Utpalda reminded me that, in the conditions in which people like Khurima found themselves, sanity must be a prized asset. To be homeless, destitute, *and* mad meant you were totally defenceless. As an afterthought, Utpalda recalled that there *was* a mad person in the queue of people who came to her for food. Khurima's aphorism made me wonder about this city in which the difference between the beggar and the madman was near invisible and also immensely wide.

This, then, is the city as it is now: not its only incarnation, certainly, but one of several. It is always possible to glimpse it – through a car window at night – or to walk through it; it is possible to absorb it without being wholly aware of it. For a long time, I didn't see *this* city – so formative, probably, were the impressions of the Calcutta I'd visited as a child to me.

'Erai amader nagarik,' says Utpalda to me gravely, as we discuss Khurima. 'Nagarik' means, at once, city-dweller and citizen. '*These* are our citizens.'

My parents, after living in Bombay for twenty-seven years, moved to Calcutta in 1989. During that period – from the early sixties to the late eighties – people had been steadily departing Calcutta: middle-class people, of course, but also workers. My father had arrived into, and left, the city twice. Once, in the early forties, he'd been a student here at the Scottish Church College, an institution then favoured by East Bengali migrant students for its boarding facilities. Another Chaudhuri, Nirad C, had studied history at the same college, about twenty years before my father. The fact that my father and the great memoirist shared the same initials sometimes led people to ask him with a disarming innocence, 'Are you two related?' or even, 'Do you come from the same family?' Not the same family, but the same part of the world; subject, eventually, to the same shift in history: the older Chaudhuri from Kishoreganj, my father from Sylhet, both bits of Bengal that would go with Partition. My father claims that the present spelling of his surname was given to it by a registrar's clerk in Calcutta University on the day he enrolled there. This standardisation of the spelling of that variously spelt surname at the university might have been a practice at the time, and would explain why the spelling is common to alumni from two or three succeeding generations. The story has had the effect of making me feel I don't know my father very well; neither does he have a very clear idea of how he became who he is.

From him, I got a fleeting sense of North Calcutta as it was. Those anecdotes, related intermittently over decades (he doesn't repeat stories, as my mother does), weave into what little I know of the East Bengali scholar's Calcutta – of the 'mess', the hostel room, communal meals, cheap restaurants, and 'cabins' – from the writings of Nirad Chaudhuri and Buddhadev Basu. He lived in the Hardinge Hostel, which, when he pointed it out to me for the first time (seventeen years ago), was an unremarkable run-down brick building, surrounded by numbing but entirely expected traffic on its way to Sealdah. But, already, things had moved on to such a degree – not just for me and my father, but for Calcutta itself (which had changed not visibly, but in every other way) – that I found it difficult to make a connection with what was just a building. Yet there used to be a romance in my father's allusions to the northern and central parts: whether this was retrospective, or whether he'd brought this romance to the city when he'd arrived here in 1941, I don't know. Some of this romance is difficult to disentangle from remembered sojourns to eating places, and private, momentous discoveries of food.

Most of those eating places and discoveries, once removed from the forties and that romanticism, are disappointing. In the late seventies, my father, executing one of his childlike plans that now and again inflected his very successful professional career, took my mother and me, in Calcutta on a visit from Bombay, to the famous Anadi Cabin to taste its *kasha mangsho* (traditional dry mutton) and *Mughlai paratha,* an oily, flattened piece of bread fortified by egg which always impressed my cousins and me when we were children for its royal provenance. This crowded cubbyhole with damp tabletops alienated us; and I remember the other customers had their eyes averted but were curious. My mother was uncomfortable, and her bright sari probably made her very visible; but she tried to be fair-minded about the kasha mangsho, and judge it on its merits. Actually, it was not so much the food: the Calcutta of today was already upon us – the one without space, without a past, and, as in our case, without a real appetite.

My father left twice – before returning here for what seems now the final time. In his memory – as in any memory – national and world-historical events are indistinguishable from personal detail. The year he joined Scottish Church College, 1941, was also the year the poet he and his friends adored died; and I already know that he became a part, for a while, of the great crowd accompanying the body. Although it's a struggle for him these days to articulate sentences, he still informs me indignantly – as I attempt doggedly to ascertain the year – of, at once, Tagore's death and the abrasion on his calf that led to some bleeding, the result of a poke from someone's umbrella in that suffocating crowd. It's a detail I haven't heard before; and, for a moment, I'm unsure, as he lifts the bottom of one pyjama leg, whether he's speaking of something that happened yesterday – because he's now prone to accidents. But it's the crowd he's thinking of as he passionately stutters the words.

4

From the other snatches of stammered speech, I learn that he withdrew from the city for a year (a third departure, then, of which I knew nothing) to Sylhet, after the Japanese dropped a bomb on Hatibagan in North Calcutta. Maybe he thought they'd blow up the whole place. He came back gingerly the next year, and began an articleship in incorporated accountancy – as he'd been advised to, shrewdly, by his best friend and still-to-be brother-in-law, because salaries in this line were said to be generous, and prospects generally excellent: because, whatever the fate of engineering companies and medical research, people would always need accountants. Unobtrusively, irrevocably, an important development took place: incorporated accountancy and chartered accountancy merged into one body. After being a relatively unemotional witness to the inevitable moment of Independence, shocked at the nights of post-Partition violence in the city, but recouping and resolving to travel towards becoming a chartered accountant, he made his first, official egress from this metropolis in 1949, sailing to England.

He was there for twelve years. My mother, who knew him since childhood, and was taken by surprise by his proposal of marriage before he left, was reconciling herself to his never returning – when he invited her to join him in London. She flew in 1955 from Shillong to Calcutta – with her mercurial younger brother, Dukhu, who was going on a training course for civil engineers in Germany. Customarily, it's the bridegroom who makes the journey from his town or village or neighbourhood to the bride's home to marry her; this was an eccentric, but unavoidable, inversion. My mother's never been one to romanticise Calcutta – as I, for instance, have – but her first and brief impression of the city was one of beauty and clean air – the latter, if it lasted for more than two or three days that year, is not something that Calcutta has possessed for several decades. Perhaps it's because it was a first encounter, or a transient acquaintanceship, or because she knew it would be her last vision of India for a long time, that my mother's memory of Calcutta in 1955 is like a personal intimation.

My father, at last a full-fledged chartered accountant, with other professional qualifications like useful appendages, returned, with my mother, to a job offer in Bombay in 1961. Soon after, she was pregnant, as an Indian doctor in London had predicted she would be: 'Childbearing has a lot to do with happiness and mental peace.' Coming back to India, at least in those days, was a matter of fulfilment, an occasion for optimism – something we tend not to remember or acknowledge. Dukhu had returned earlier from Germany, and had a job in Calcutta; he insisted my mother come to his house to have the child. The reason for this was a combination of practical need and common sense and the precedent of tradition, the last anyway being a consequence of the first two, not to mention economic hard-headedness. Tradition asks the childbearing woman to journey temporarily to her father's house before giving birth. In this way, the nuisance of birth is wished away and literally transported to the 'other' place. Importantly, the psychological closeness between mother and pregnant daughter is seen to be a necessary condition for the birth – a small bending of a regulation to briefly replace the mother-in-law's vigilance with maternal attention; and the general support and care of her own family is essential to the mother-to-be. My mother had no in-laws to escape from; my father was an only child, displaced by Partition; both his parents were dead. So she kept putting off the journey to Dukhu's flat on Fern Road, where their mother lived with him and his new wife. She knew it was going to be intolerably hot by the end of April. Still, because there was no family at all in Bombay, she arrived in Fern Road early that month. By temperament a nervous insomniac, she found sleeping difficult because of the yowling of street dogs at night and the passage of traffic at the Gol Park roundabout. My grandmother contributed to her well-being by knocking firmly on her door at around 6 a.m., just when she'd embarked on her first slumber, so she (my grandmother) might walk to the adjoining balcony and receive the city's sounds and sights. As a result of decisions taken without conviction, and slightly regretted in retrospect – all, of course, is transmogrified by a mother's eventual joy – I happened to be born in Calcutta in the middle of May: a difficult time of year to be here.

My father changed jobs. Leaving Bombay, he took up a position at the head office (which was then in Calcutta) of Britannia Biscuits. We lived, for a year and a half, between 1964 and 1965, in a recent suburb, New Alipore. I seem to summon, without too much effort, a memory of a veranda or porch, and the courtyard and the main road beyond: it could be, of course, that I'm imagining I remember these things. Their shapes and unremarkable colours, and the daylight they inhabit, are pretty consistent, though. This is the time that my mother is jotting down, in a book with a white hardback cover, all the relevant information concerning 'Your Child's Name' and 'Your Child's First Word'. I would see this solemnly inscribed book after growing up, but I think it is finally lost. I could have grown up in Calcutta, and had a very different relationship with it, but I am a Bombay person. By just a few years, I missed the trauma and the impress of change that would come upon this city. Britannia, anticipating labour unrest in the wake of radical left-wing politics, relocated its head office to a more amenable metropolis. What remained in Calcutta was a husk called the 'Registered Office'. It was the usual story of the time: this gradual emptying of the city of commerce; the absolute reign over it of what it had always harboured – politics. My father, on the ascendant, left it for the second time.

◆

It takes a while to understand that a city has changed, and that change, like most change, is irrevocable. By the time my parents moved back to Calcutta from Bombay in 1989, roughly seven years after my father's retirement, the city itself had traversed a great distance from where it was when he'd left it in 1965. Besides clearly being in decline, it had the strange air of something that's been a symbol of the zeitgeist for more than a hundred years, and now embodies nothing but its severance from what's shaping the age. It had become a city that was difficult to connect with in an emotional and intellectual way. For me, in many ways, it was not the 'true' Calcutta.

What was 'true'? Throughout my childhood, I'd encountered Calcutta during the summer and winter holidays – as a place of freedom from school and a realm of childish anarchy. My uncle's house – Dukhu's house, now no longer in Fern Road, but further south, in petit bourgeois Pratapaditya Road, in a lane lined with two-storeyed, different-shaped houses – was my playground. I've written about that house and that Calcutta in so many works of fiction and essays that, when someone suggested I write a non-fiction book on this city, I put it off for years, because I felt I had nothing more to say about it. The Calcutta I'd encountered as a child was one of the great cities of modernity; it was that peculiar thing, modernity, that I first came into contact with here (without knowing it), then became familiar with it, and then was changed by it. By 'modern' I don't mean 'new' or 'developed', but a self-renewing way of seeing, of inhabiting space, of apprehending life. By 'modern' I also mean whatever alchemy it is that changes urban dereliction into something compelling, perhaps even beautiful. It was that arguable beauty that I first came across in Calcutta, and may have, without being aware of it, become addicted to. I ran into it again in New York in 1979, on my first American trip, after a stifling ten days among the monuments of Washington and the sweet prettiness of California. Walking in Manhattan, I was reminded, at once, of Calcutta. New York was in economically troubled times, and still possessed – even for the short-term adolescent visitor – an air of menace and fortuitous unpredictability. The addict of that particular strain of modernity, to whom noise and stink are oxygen, and odourless order death, can sniff it out quickly in foreign places, and swiftly connect it to their own history. 1979 was probably the last year of its reign. New York no longer reminds me of Calcutta; with globalisation – maybe even before it happened – the paths of these cities diverged. With Giuliani, New York famously gentrified its seedy areas; while Calcutta became one of those strategic, deceptively populated outreaches that the wave of globalisation has never quite managed to reach.

The 'modern' is man-made; but it's also a way of conferring life upon things. These things, as a result, enter your world organically. What I remember from the Calcutta of my child-hood has that living quality – a neon sign over Chowringhee, of a teapot tipping into a cup; tangled clumps of hair – wigs – at the entrance of New Market; the judiciously dark watercolour covers of my cousins' Puja annuals. To these man-made objects, modernity, as it governed Calcutta, gave an inwardness and life. This extended to elements of architecture, elements I thought were essentially Bengali – never having seen them anywhere else – but which must have arrived here as Calcutta grew through its contact with Europe.

The most ubiquitous of these are the French windows that are a feature of the older residential and office buildings of North and South Calcutta; unless the house belongs to North Indians and Marwaris, in which case the architecture often echoes the ancient, and even more foreign, *haveli* style. (I'm talking of the older Marwari buildings. The new ones can echo everything from Roman villas to a Disney illustration.) The French windows are, for some reason, always green. My uncle's house had them; if you parted the slats using the spine (in Bengali, the onomatopoeic word for this lever is *kharkhari*), the street would flood in through the crack, without any part of you seeping out. This was another feature of this city's modernity: the importance – for no discernible reason – of looking. The windows were foreign and yet part of my conception of Bengaliness – and they possibly conveyed what I felt about Calcutta intuitively: that, here, home and elsewhere were enmeshed intimately. Subconsciously, I may have presumed the windows were part of Calcutta's colonial history; but, since they were hardly to be seen in England, this explanation didn't hold.

The windows probably came here in the late seventeenth century. In 2007, I'd been invited to preside over a prize-giving ceremony in Chandannagar, where, in 1730, the French general Dupleix had set up his grand colonial headquarters in what was already then, for almost sixty years, a French colony. Power – and the struggle for malarial Bengal – was poised tantalisingly between the French and the British, until it tilted decisively towards the latter in 1757. However, Chandannagar remained a curious and remote French outpost until recently – not so much a quasi-colony, like Pondicherry, but imprinted distinctively with a Franco-Bengali ethos. The prize-giving, ironically, was for excellence in the English language. It took place in the lawns next to Dupleix's beautiful, sepulchral house.

It takes about three hours of breathing in dust and smoke, then gazing in resentful wonder at the new Indian autobahns that are replacing the old alley-like 'highways', then turning into one of those highways and travelling vacantly past small towns and countryside awash with plastic bags, tarpaulin, fields, and crushed mineral water bottles, to finally enter this bit of French history: a beginning on the banks of the Ganges, a hazy but still-indelible sketch. The promenade, which surprises you as you enter the town, is still very French, as is the jetty that hangs like a promontory on the river; the Ganges is pure Bengal, but the jetty is elsewhere, and one can imagine a young Frenchman and his fiancée standing on it, absorbed in each other, more than two hundred years ago, feeling 'home' revisiting them, dizzied and dwarfed, at the same time, by the East.

Not so with the French windows: they are French only in name; they've become indivisible from what Calcutta and Bengaliness mean.

Do we actually see these windows – through whose slats I looked out at the world as a child? Can the windows begin to look back, as if *we* were on the outside?

They inserted themselves in Calcutta's consciousness very subtly. Testament to this are some extraordinary, but rather odd, paintings. As Calcutta began to grow from clusters of neighbourhoods into the monstrous, unprecedented metropolis it would become, with teeming settlements and certain luminous landmarks – high court, hospitals, jailhouses, university – a new kind of city type began to emerge from every kind of social class, a little before the advent of the *bhadralok* – the genteel Bengali bourgeois – and his suddenly all-encompassing way of being. ('Bhadra' means polite and 'lok' is person; this polite person's culture, books, and way of approaching things would reign over Bengal from the late nineteenth century to the 1970s.) The *patuas* belong to this nineteenth-century churning (when the British had already been entrenched in the city for a hundred years): anonymous painters, some of them Muslims, working on Hindu devotional themes outside the temple of Kalighat, selling their products to the common-or-garden urban devotee. Their work is associated with watercolour and with economical but emphatic outlines, as well as the styles of the metropolis: Shiva and Parvati and Ganesh looking like contemporaries of their worshippers, the embarrassingly handsome Lord Kartik (Parvati's son) appearing up-to-date and fashionable, in buckled

shoes and a Prince Albert haircut. This is not to mention the
secular scenes depicting Calcutta – of lascivious babus, their
mistresses, and their domineering wives. None of these pictures
exhibit the obliqueness or psychological realism of bhadralok
modernity: only the vivid footprint of a new, impatient, march-
ing being – the common man.

Although, for much of the late nineteenth and early twentieth
centuries, the work of the anonymous patuas was done in
watercolour, there is an aberration, an experimental foray,
maybe in the early nineteenth century, when their counterparts
in Chinsura town outside Calcutta tried out a new medium: oil.
These paintings are astonishing: they have the resplendence of
oil painting but none of the gloating that oil brought to a great
deal of the European Renaissance – where it coincided with the
new supremacy of perspective, with a manufactured realism,
and the world, henceforth, condemned to becoming a spectacle
in every gradation of colour. These Chinsura oils are like secret
visions of an ancient mythology, brought to light in a moment
of change; most of them are owned by the newspaper magnate
Aveek Sarkar. They are displayed not in his drawing room, which
is populated by other artefacts, but in the dining room – which
means people must access this inner sanctum, and partake of
the ritual of dinner, to view the pictures. During dinner, they
are illuminated by overhead lights; if, turning your attention
from the orchestrated courses and movements through which
dinner unfolds, you glance at them, you'll see that their subjects
are epic or devotional. There is the mystic Chaitanya, in an
ecstatic, free-floating dance, with his entourage; there, and
there again, is the god Shiva, with his family and a group of
tranquil stragglers – presumably followers. The oils glow and
simmer in, and reflect, the electric lights: you have to squint
to catch all the activity and nuances. Behind these figures, you
may, one day (looking at a reproduction, or if you're lucky
enough to be invited to dinner a second or third time), notice

the French windows – so unobtrusively have they become a part of our lives that there is no context in which we might find them incongruous, or even worthy of comment. The French windows are attached to colonial-style buildings. Has Mr Sarkar stopped in his dining room to look at them? I'd been unaware of them until, almost by chance one day, they inched into my field of vision; there to stay. Part of the difficulty of noticing the windows is the relative abstention from perspective in the paintings, so that they are not so much in the background (they can't be, as everything, in a sense, seems to compete equally for the foreground) as self-contained and iconic: among the magic points of focus and revelation comprising the scene. Once you see them, you realise what you're looking at is the emergence of a metropolis, with its eccentric visual field – something that hadn't existed a few decades earlier. In front of the slatted windows and those colonial buildings, Shiva – unsurprisingly louche, but unexpectedly pot-bellied – and at least some members of his party begin to resemble what they were probably modelled on: the common people of the day, the ones who entered, irresistibly, the city's spaces without really owning them, and surge into them still. The bhadralok is nowhere in sight. In fact, now that he's departed (this time, surely, forever) after that unique interim of more than one hundred and fifty years (during which his imaginary universe was all that was real), Shiva, his family, and his gang seem, once again, very close. They occupy and visit the public spaces of our persistent city. They are, as Utpal Basu said of the old woman in Sealdah, our 'citizens'.

In mid-2007 I saw that another one of the genteel bourgeois houses of South Calcutta, this one in a frequently used by-lane in Ekdalia, had come down. Nothing unusual about that; it's been happening for twenty-five years, and, these days, this destruction is almost a daily occurrence. In fact, though I must have passed this particular house a hundred times, I hadn't really noticed it until now, when it was already demolished – that, too, wasn't wholly surprising. What caught my attention, as the car went past, were the French windows that, loosed from their original locations, had been stacked vertically against each other on one side. They'd been left facing the pavement; I got out of the car to look, never having seen the windows like this, out of context, before.

That night, I had a brainwave – that I would buy one of the windows. What I'd do with it I still had no clear idea. Was it part of some incipient project I'd been half-heartedly entertaining for the past two years – another flabbergasting branching out, moving from novel-writing to music-making, from music-making to musical composition, from composing to collecting? Whatever the reason, I wanted to acquire that window.

When I told my wife the next day, she didn't throw her hands up in despair, but nodded in a way that suggested that what I'd said made perfect sense. That evening, we took a detour – because Ekdalia is both near her parents' flat and near Gariahat Market – and entered the by-lane to see those windows. She was transfixed by them. We wondered what would happen if we just lifted one and took it home, except that would be stealing – besides, it was too big (and dirty, the frame covered in dirt) for our car. A watchman at the shop opposite and a boy observed us, but no one could give us anything but vague advice about whom to contact if we wanted to buy a window. A few days later, half-expecting them to have gone, I convinced myself and my wife to visit the lane again – but during the day – to make one last effort. The windows were there; this time my wife, more curious and more of an explorer than I am, slipped into the site, lost to her own speculations, and called me after a few minutes. 'Look at that,' she said – a door from the same house was leaning against a wall. It was painted a green – the generic colour of the French windows in Calcutta – which was still bright in patches, though much of it had peeled off in scabs. What was striking – at least to us – about the door, which comprised two doors contained within a doorway, were the rectangles on the upper halves, which themselves framed two nubile lotus-shaped iron grilles. These would have been inner doors then, but not the main one (given their slightly decorative and pervious quality)? It was difficult to be certain.

The family – like the house – had vanished. Everything pointed towards them being Bengali: the location of the house; the kind of house it was; their inability, or desire, to hold on to it. Possibly West Bengali – that is, people from these parts; it was unlikely (but not impossible) that a displaced East Bengali family could, after Partition, have afforded property in this area. The house might well have come up before Partition, of course; its remnants, the door, especially, reeked of bygone bhadralok respectability.

It was proving difficult to contact them now. Neither the watchman at the shop nor the boy nor any of those who hung out on the pavement had any idea how to, nor saw it necessary to have any idea. Someone on the site finally gave me a mobile number and a name – not a Bengali name – and told me to call this man if I wanted a window. He was neither the builder nor the contractor, but had something to do with the construction of the new building.

At least two kinds of migration have shaped Calcutta in the last thirty years. The first has to do with the flight outward of the middle and upper middle classes, which began close on the heels of the flight outward of capital – leading, eventually, to the sale of houses like the one in question. You can wager that the story behind the sale is simple and typical. The younger generation is elsewhere: New Delhi, or even New Jersey. The ageing parents (or parent) live in the house, which they may or may not have built, but where the children were born. Upkeep is difficult.

One day, their secret wish comes true – a 'promoter' makes an offer: a large sum of money, and two flats in the building that will come up where the house was.

The second type of migration has been taking place within the city itself, feeding the property boom of the last decade, in that false dawn of investment in the state. Although people woke up from that dawn in 2009 to find things reverting to a stubborn, paradoxical, politics-induced changelessness, that migration – and, to an extent, the incongruous boom – continues. It involves Marwaris who've been moderately successful as traders and who've lived traditionally in the North, moving to the more desirable South, where the boxwallah, or corporate employee, once lived – not to mention the bhadralok, and, long ago, in places like Alipore, the old colonial rulers, and, even today, the great Marwari industrialist families (Birla, Goenka, Jalan, Khaitan), who are to be found behind immense gates, in serenely ensconced estates. The other principal candidates for buying up flats and condominiums in the new buildings are the dreaded NRIs, who are of the city and yet not of it, who are Bengali despite being something else. These are people who left thirty years ago for Michigan, New Jersey, or Atlanta – the ugly acronym stands for Non-Resident Indian, and encompasses movement, desire, pride, memory, and, plausibly, disappointment. The NRIs are not necessarily coming back; against their better judgement though, they do want to keep one foot planted in the city in which they grew up.

The two- or three-storeyed bhadralok houses of South Calcutta, with their slatted windows and floors of red stone, their rooftop terraces, are less valuable than the land they stand on. In London, the prices of the narrow Victorian houses with their dark facades go up and up because the affluent want to move into them. In Prenzlauer Berg in East Berlin, inaccessible to West Germans until the wall collapsed, the bohemian and artistic set pushed property prices upward because they wanted to occupy those mysterious, socialist, pre-fabricated apartments. People in South Calcutta shake their heads when an old house comes down – but are also plotting, of course, to move to a better city. When I was last in Berlin three years ago, the memorialisation of the past was relentless, but the attempt, by Berliners, to embrace and re-inhabit the city's troubled post-War history was striking too. Calcutta has still not recovered from history: people mourn the past, and abhor it deeply.

'Kaun baat kar raha hai?' *Who's this?*

Every time I called the number the man on the site had given me, I got to speak to Ram Singh's brother or brother-in-law. Ram Singh was either at the site or having lunch. Two days later, he answered the phone himself.

'Hello – haan – kaun?'

'Ram Singh?'

'Haan, Ram Singh' – a distant concession, coming from one distracted all day by construction work – now in Ekdalia, where he was never to be seen; now, as I was told, in Dover Lane – and unscheduled lunch breaks in the afternoon.

'Woh jo Ekdalia mei khidki hain, main ek kharidne chahta hoon.' *Those windows in Ekdalia – I'd like to buy one.*

There was nothing at the other end except the silence of prevarication – as he tried to piece together what I was on about.

Then, quite patiently, he repeated, 'Khidki?'

Yes, one window – and the door.

In a business-like way, he told me (as if he were inured to this kind of query) that they'd cost me three and a half thousand rupees; this excluded the price of having them delivered in a tempo. Although I didn't know what the market price of used windows was – my guess was nothing – I thought the offer reasonable. I immediately asked him to take down my address, and provided directions.

❖

For three days, the door and the window stood parked against the wall outside our flat, while I worried if they'd outrage the neighbours. I still hadn't any notion of what to do with them. I called Mr Mitter, who has a carpenter's workshop on Rafi Ahmed Kidwai Road, and who often gets shelves and fittings done for us. I asked him if he'd take them away for a while. Mr Mitter didn't waste time asking questions; he was gracious enough to insist he'd take no rent; to a storage space near his workshop went the window and door.

After a year, Mr Mitter informed me that he was short of space; and that the door might be destroyed by termites. So the two objects returned to where they were previously – the corridor outside the door to our apartment. It was unlikely I'd find a way of exhibiting them; or, more problematic still, find a context for that exhibition. The context was a city in which things were being disinterred and dislodged from their moorings, and being washed ashore by an invisible tide.

My wife said we must bring them in, hang up the window, fit the door – but where? The flat was already colonised by furnishings; each object had its immovable caste and assignation. Firstly, a door was discovered, behind a cupboard stacked with vinyl records, which had been doing nothing in years; it was a connecting door between the drawing room and the guest room that was never opened – and couldn't be because of the cupboard, and the objects on the other side. This door had to be de-hinged, and the corners of the two doors with their rusting lotus-shaped grilles planed for them to be fixed to that frame. That left the French windows: some impulse in me militated against them serving a window-like role in the flat. After much scouring, I found a space in the tiny passage between the front door and the entrance into the sitting room: the wall on the right was vacant. No matter that it's always in shadow and obscured by an inner door: we put the windows there.

As a result of their positioning, neither the doors nor the

windows are noticed by visitors. Once their attention is drawn
to them (by me), people are always too polite to make anything
but approving noises. Whatever's in their mind – obviously,
I can't really know – it gives me an excuse to study these
purchases again: self-indulgently, maybe, but also, now, with a
sort of recognition.

Chandan Hotel

Ramayan Shah has a pavement stall selling food on Free School
Street in front of a sign that says Sarabhai Chemicals. The
building behind him is Karnani Mansions, and the look of the
sign suggests superannuation, an office boarded up. Ramayan
Shah and two other low-level entrepreneurs – the always-absent
owner of Chandan Hotel, which roughly occupies six by six feet
on the pavement, and Nagendra, with his heavy iron and board
– have appropriated the terrain here.

I can remember a time when these businesses didn't exist
in this location, and one could walk from Park Street up Free
School Street without any interruption. At a glance, the stalls are
squalid, a small universe of cooking pots, potato peels, benches,
and a few people absently lolling under the shelter of tarpaulin. They comprise an island with no apparent connection to the
Free School Street of the seventies and early eighties, with its
rare second-hand vinyl records and its second-hand bookshops,
which even now sell everything from horoscopes to Leon Uris
to Salman Rushdie to old copies of *Time*. In 1982, before leaving

for England, suddenly disenchanted by Western popular music, I remember bringing with me from Bombay some of the priceless records in my collection (among them Janis Joplin Live), to either distribute gratis among friends who were still under the spell of that music or permit the more mercantile among them to sell the records to the vendors on Free School Street. One of my friends earned six hundred rupees from the sale (some of these records were rare, bought in a London Our Price shop by my father), a small fortune at the time. I took nothing of the proceeds, a measure of my new high-minded propensities. It was a way of washing my hands, with violent symbolism, of my Western-music past. Yet how alive Free School Street was, still busy with transactions between bourgeois and punter, coursing with some of the sensuousness of the seventies! The second-hand bookshops are still there, as are the vendors of the vinyl records, but it isn't clear who the customers are. There's more activity in the recent Bangladeshi restaurants, and in the small shady foreign exchange outlets at which Bangladeshi tourists can quickly change takas into rupees.

Just here, not far from Ramayan Shah's business, is one of the city's nerve-centres. Downtown is one name for it, I suppose, but that term with its hint of sleaze doesn't capture the melee of this intersection, where people are forever waiting to cross at the traffic lights. You have Free School Street on one end, Middleton Row, narrower and shorter, on the opposite side, and, at a right angle to these two, Park Street, this long road finally opening out on to the chaos of Park Circus, and, nearer this end, to the once-imperial artery, Chowringhee. Park Street is neither Oxford Street nor the Champs-Élyseés, but here, in the stretch between Chowringhee and the junction of Free School Street and Middleton Row, it has an energy comparable to no other downtown district that I know. Although Calcutta, with its colonial buildings, was so Bengali in its metier, just here it is like nowhere else in the city, for the Chinese and the so-called Anglo-Indians (or Eurasians) used to live on Free School Street, and a few still do, and down Middleton Row are the inaccessible precincts of the Loreto College for Girls, with its calm but admonitory gates. As a child from Bombay, walking up Park Street and approaching this junction, I knew – without quite knowing why – that I'd never, elsewhere, had such contradictory impulses converge around me.

Uniquely placed, over the decades, to at once view and receive these drifts and convergences, is Flurys, at the corner of Park Street and Middleton Row. Flurys is a tea shop. Once created by a Swiss confectioner, it's now owned by the Apeejay Group, who made their money in tea. If, upon entering, you turn left and occupy one of the tables overlooking the new large glass windows, you can partake of the astonishment of this area, as hoards of pedestrians, with an odd urgency about them, wait, some distance away, to cross to the Free School Street side. You order your coffee and cake, or rissole, and, every five or ten minutes, see the scene repeat itself: the current of passers-by advancing aimlessly, then beginning to congeal at the traffic lights, and finally dispersing, scattering, and temporarily losing form. It seems to you that there are all kinds of people in that crowd visible from the Flurys window – office-goers; wage-earners; youthful groups in jeans; tourists; people who have returned to these parts for tea or coffee; Europeans, in their loose handwoven clothes, with bare white arms showing. They all seem to have arrived from, or to be moving towards, some landmark: New Market, further up, off Free School Street, or one of the half-lit restaurants on either side, or St. Xavier's College, or Chowringhee. When you look up from your cup, you're struck by this mixture of unpredictability and purpose.

I probably first saw Flurys when I was five or six years old. My earliest memory is of going with an older cousin (my aunt's son) and a cousin around my age (a maternal uncle's son, in whose house the older cousin was staying as a lodger) to Flurys on a Sunday, and finding its interior humming loudly. The older cousin, a migrant from Assam, was an exceptional student, and was studying for his chartered accountancy while working at Guest Keen Williams. He – despite his meagre means, and perhaps in anticipation of the success he'd one day have – made at least one extravagant gesture a week, which included buying us books or comics; that day, it was a trip to Flurys. I say 'earliest memory', but that doesn't mean it was my first visit; I remember a sense of recognition on entering the place. Certainly, the Bombay I knew had no venue for such focussed congregating, where every item on the menu – baked beans on toast, sausage roll, scrambled eggs, pineapple pudding cake, buttered toast – had an idiosyncratic pedigree. That day was the first time I had a chicken croissant – croissant-shaped bread sliced through the middle, buttered, patted with mustard, and filled with shreds of roast chicken. This slyly unprepossessing confection was always a little too expensive to order (when a cousin was taking you out) without embarrassment, and often it was in short supply (a fact conveyed to you by an unrelenting shake of the waiter's head), maybe because the croissant-shaped bread was produced in small quantities; until, about fifteen years ago, it fell off the menu and disappeared. My memory of its taste is a reminder that, in Calcutta, in a sort of ritual transubstantiation, you were constantly consuming the flesh and blood of urban modernity; that modernity was, at least until the moment I'm thinking of, the city's bread and butter. The general high spirits (despite the surly waiters) in Flurys that afternoon is also my one memory of a city that still had no inkling of Naxalbari, and the lust for revolution.

Naxalbari is not far from Darjeeling in West Bengal; still obscure, it would be fair to say, despite its mythic elevation since 1967, as few people seem to know anything about the actual place. The 'actual place' is yet another Indian village, with the characteristic vulnerability such villages have had, over several centuries, to the brutal mastery of the landlords and the state. In 1967, two radicalised communists, Charu Majumdar and Kanu Sanyal, of bhadralok origins (admittedly, bhadralok has all sorts of contradictory registers: 'bourgeois', 'elite', 'educated but not necessarily propertied petit bourgeois' – indeed, the whole cultured ethos of liberal modernity), organised a peasant rebellion there; in doing so, planting the seeds, firmly, for a movement whose long-term aim was not a series of local rebellions, but total revolution. From Naxalbari, the forgotten village, sprang an adjective, 'Naxalite', for a movement espoused by the Communist Party of India (Marxist-Leninist), a radical Maoist breakaway faction of the more mainstream Communist Party of India (Marxist), which would be elected to power in West Bengal in 1977, and still rules it – precariously – as I begin writing this book. 'Naxalite', however, is more commonly a noun, describing an adherent of the movement; a noun that, until six or seven years ago, defined a type that had been consigned to Indian political history just as princely states and the British Raj were: a romantic, probably bookish, university student from the late sixties, ideologically transformed, or seduced (according to your vantage point), by Maoist rhetoric, or even coerced by circumstances into a movement that believed in nothing less than an apocalyptic reordering of the system. The type disappeared in the early seventies. After committing several of what Auden called 'necessary murders' (of landlords, policemen, corrupt professionals), these proto-Bolsheviks were rounded up, imprisoned, and broken, or – more often – killed during the time of the arraigned Congress government. No modern middle class – this one was very much, in a sense, of the sixties – has responded to Marx in quite this way; and comparisons to early-twentieth-century Russia and mid-century China don't hold, and not only because of the failure of the Naxal revolution. That generation – literally 'lost' – has certain correspondences with the one apostrophised by Ginsberg in *Howl* a decade earlier – 'I saw the best minds of my generation destroyed by madness' et cetera – though, here too, despite the ritual invocation of 'best minds' in both cases, there are differences: between madness and ideology, self-destructive ecstasy and utopian rage. Nevertheless, the cliché goes that a generation of the 'best minds' in Calcutta more or less vanished in the early seventies, in the manner Charu Majumdar, one of their leaders, did: in captivity.

The Naxalite, as the Maoist, has made a comeback – for, in the midst of the supremacy of the free market and the march of industry, and with corporate power and political interests converging, and land being wrested from local people for 'development', there has been unrest in the countryside. Calcutta, today, is surrounded, from its outskirts onward, by unrest. But the word 'Naxalite' has a slightly different resonance now from its earlier one: of the bhadralok radical, destined, in a sense, for failure. The Naxalite or Maoist today represents not so much a romantic transgression as a genuine, probably unbridgeable, rift. In 1967, the independent nation state was still young and relatively untested; but the revived movement puts the great myth of Indian democracy, which – according to its apologists – has worked for sixty-five years in spite of itself, in doubt. It clearly doesn't work for a very great number of people.

With the emergence and then the crushing of the Naxalites, Flurys went quiet in the early seventies – as did Christmas in Park Street. Until, say, 1969, Calcutta had the most effervescent and the loveliest Christmas in India – probably, I'd hazard, based on my experience later of Christmas in England, the loveliest in the world. Warm, convivial, unfolding in smoky weather, it had the vivacity of a transplanted custom that had flowered spontaneously, but still retained the air of an outing, of an encounter with the strange. Its beauty and atmosphere derived not only from the Anglo-Indians, or the last of the English living and working in Calcutta, but also from a certain kind of Bengali who had embraced the festival. I was reminded of this Bengali type when walking through the Jewish Museum in late 2005 in Berlin, a striking building in an area called Hallesches Tör. Our straggly bunch had followed the guide irresistibly until we came, on the first floor, to a rather sparse reconstruction of an educated Jewish household from the twenties with a piano at the centre. On a sort of noticeboard was a newspaper cutting from the time, with a satirical cartoon recording the stages through which a Hanukkah transmogrified into a Christmas tree – clearly meant to poke fun at the new secular Jew. Although I'd been silent so far, I couldn't help interjecting at this point (the guide encouraged dialogue): 'This was happening in other parts of the world as well – it was happening in Bengal.' Two or three people in my group nodded, as if they knew exactly what I meant; and, perhaps, for a moment, they had an intimation that the story of change that had taken place in Europe had also occurred further afield.

There were certain tables in Flurys at which you could reliably expect to see an Anglo-Indian customer, and tables at which large, imposing Chinese boys would be seated late in the morning, when business was slow. They'd get off their motorcycles on Park Street and walk straight in. There was a clear division to Flurys then; on the left-hand side of the main door was the vaguely horseshoe-like space in which people ate; on the right, the confectionary, where people crowded to buy, in a constant obstreperous stream, bread, cakes, muffins, sausage rolls. On this side of the division were two large rectangular tables for customers, and I'd see the young Chinese men in possession of one of them whenever I went to Flurys in the morning. Near an aquarium at the other end – frugally populated with unremarkable fish – I also remember spotting many times an Anglo-Indian regular, who, with his light eyes, looked something like the Mussoorie writer Ruskin Bond. This was after the other Anglo-Indian families who ate there – 'Dings', as they came to be known superciliously among the children of the Calcutta rich – had disappeared without our quite noticing their disappearance. The story was that the Anglo-Indians left for better jobs and better lives in Australia; also that, being neither one thing nor the other (neither Indian nor European), they felt underconfident in independent India. There was also the old allegation, that they were sympathisers in secret of our erstwhile rulers. However, the Ruskin Bond lookalike persisted at his table by the aquarium. Those large boys also vanished from their table; some of the Chinese had anyway started gradually departing India after the 1962 war (it clearly wasn't pleasant being of the victor's kin in a country that had lost a battle), and some left presumably as Calcutta's fortunes declined. This is to say that being inside Flurys doesn't cocoon you from history – instead, it eddies around you, as the waiters with their trays and teapots do. History in here is circular and repetitive and, in a way, enervating, as it is in the restaurants in Buñuel's films, with their pointless conversations and white-liveried waiters constantly hovering; which is to also say that, although one might not see the Chinese boys sitting casually at their tables, they continue to occupy the corner of one's eye.

On Sunday, emerging from lunch at the plush and largely septuagenarian Bengal Club, I walked towards Park Street, and turned right towards Flurys. Here, abandoning my family for the afternoon, I had a cup of coffee, and then set out without intention to Free School Street, thinking about this book which I had taken upon myself to write. How would it start? I had the opening paragraph; where would the rest of the chapter go? It was while thinking of these questions that I came upon Ramayan Shah's 'hotel' on the pavement, in front of the peeling wall that said Sarabhai Chemicals. It being a Sunday, the few people there seemed half-asleep, and Ramayan Shah, as usual, was away somewhere. Earlier, I would have denied this place its existence, would have seen it but shut it out, would have looked upon it as a stubborn aberration while my mind pieced together, image by image, the 'real' Free School Street as it had existed twenty-five years before. Now, for the first time, I studied it properly, not for the sake of ethnography, or from a sense of duty, but to experience again the ways in which people belonged to the city I lived in. As I said, the two or three casual itinerants on the bench were half-asleep, though Nagendra – flanking with his ironing stand the pots and pans of Ramayan Shah's dubious retail and those of the six feet of space enigmatically called the Chandan Hotel – was pressing clothes. Also, a boy was squatting by the gutter, scouring a pot with what looked like mud. It was a little island of desolation – an island, but still very much of the city I now live in nine months of the year – and I sensed how it was almost an address, a port of call, to its patrons and even its proprietors. I walked onward, passed another bunch of seemingly homeless people, bored, doing nothing, but intimate with the piece of pavement they possessed, towards where the many second-hand record stalls and bookshops – quiet on a Sunday – faintly echoed the Free School Street I'd known. I was trying at once to remember and quickly, involuntarily, forget, forget the pots and pans; to inhabit, as I walked, both the 'real'

Calcutta I'd visited as a child, and which had touched me significantly, and the city in which I found myself this afternoon. I returned along the same pavement, and saw that the boy who'd been scrubbing the pot was now lying on his back on a large table – something like a pantry shelf – apparently asleep from fatigue. Then I noticed he was twitching, and crying out in pain, his body racked by angry tremors when he sobbed. He seemed to be in emotional distress; the pointed way in which Nagendra was ironing suggested he'd decided the boy should be left alone – that this was some private agony. 'What's the matter with him?' I asked Nagendra, though I still didn't know any of the people in this space. 'Something wrong with his arm and fingers,' he said, looking up, his expression humane and approachable, without either any sign of undue concern or of taking offence at my question. 'They get stiff,' he said in Hindi, 'and he can't move them.' When I went up to the boy, I saw his fingers were clenched oddly. 'Have you had an illness?' I asked him; he looked at me calmly, though his face was tear-stained. 'I had *peela*' – jaundice – 'a month ago.' I gave him fifty rupees, for some reason checking once again to see that he was genuinely suffering. 'Is there a pharmacy nearby?' I asked a man in pyjamas and vest who was sitting upon a bench – the customers' bench in the stall. He nodded and got up and pointed to a lane on the right: 'There's one over there. It has a doctor.' Then he offered a piece of information: 'In fact, the doctor prescribed him some medicine but he hasn't bought it.' The boy was still miserable, but distracted; as if he were realising, again, that the world was composed of other things besides the immediacy of pain. 'But you must spend the money on medicine and nothing else,' I remonstrated with him sternly.

Ever since I was a child, I've loved going to Park Street, and still do: and not just for Flurys. Once there was the legendary Skyroom to step into, among whose loyal clientele were not only the gregarious Punjabi and Marwari ladies who all sat at one long table and would then, post-coffee, presumably advance to a kitty party, but also the reserved, extraordinarily tall filmmaker Satyajit Ray. Typically, the space that Skyroom occupied remained, till recently, unsold and unconverted; if you looked closely at the facade, you noticed the remnants of the red lettering with which the relevant trade union first inscribed its discontent and threatened closure. It was a bit of Park Street that had survived the early seventies and, even ten years later, when most of Bengal had shut shop, contained some of the discredited magic you could once breathe in within these restaurants. So my friend P, working for his articleship for the chartered accountancy exams, already making his way in his gentle but focussed manner towards success and the wider world, came here on one appointed day a week with a girl whom he was desperately trying to court, while combining that courtship with some elemental form of happiness: which is why they always had the prawn cocktail, and sometimes nothing else. The silver goblet in which the prawn cocktail was served, the bottle of soda with gleaming balls trapped and dancing inside, the cabbage-shaped-and-painted pot of coleslaw, the rectangular glassware in which 'continental' dishes were baked and which, peculiarly, you were asked to eat straight out of, the long, flat box of post-meal spices: these special rituals and accessories of service at Skyroom survive, in memory, the food itself.

This bubble-world – so real it seemed – couldn't but vanish with the changes. Today there are other places to go to in Park Street. There's the Oxford Bookstore, which had a makeover about fifteen years ago, turning it from a fusty behemoth – I used to go there as a child to just sniff the piled books – into a sort of bright retail site that symbolises the liberalised Indian's lack of interest in any one thing; selling stationery, DVDs, CDs, and tea upstairs. It's a so-so bookshop but a better meeting-place;

somewhere you can retreat to from the fumes and activities of Park Street, touch the books and magazines, and get acquainted with their covers, as you wait, without getting overly dispirited, for your appointment to crystallize, or without being overcome by anxiety if they are late. Further on, across the road near the traffic lights – next door to Flurys – is Music World, the main outlet for CDs in Calcutta. Musicians are keen that their products are stocked here if nowhere else; in the evocative jargon of marketing, Music World has 'maximum footfall'. This, too, is a good place to retreat to, especially just after a meeting, after you've parted ways; to withdraw into yourself after a spell of human interaction, and, fundamentally, switch off as you're faced with a range of decisions. All this holds true as long as you're indifferent to the largely senseless music that's played in Music World most of the time, from all the latest releases.

The rise of stores like Music World is related to the decline of shops like Melody. The latter still exists and does business – in Gol Park and near Lake Market – but has become at one, as it were, with the old market ethos of those areas: of traders and workers; of bargains argued on the pavement; of fluctuating, fitful sales; of being indistinguishable, in a sense, from the sweet shops and flower shops next to it. There was a time when it exercised a sort of bureaucratic control on customers; when, behaving freely in a record shop in Calcutta (and, to a certain extent, in India), you risked censure from the proprietors. At the Melody in Lake Market, I recall from the late seventies, I had a heated conversation with one of the staff; a small, myopic man who used to be consistently taciturn and rude. 'Do you have any records by Bade Ghulam Ali Khan?' I asked. Without a word, but clearly unhappy to receive my superfluous request, he took out three LPs. I chose one and said: 'Could you play this one?'; knowing, in doing so, that I was inviting turbulence. The shop had a turntable on which records were played for customers; but only with reluctance, and a fine sense of discrimination about who was deserving of this favour. 'What for?' he said. 'What's there to listen to in a Bade Ghulam Ali record? Everything he sang was superlative.' This – what I saw to be the worshipful, mean Indian attitude, where some artists were simply placed beyond criticism, while ordinary people were snubbed – outraged me; I also thought these words to be in the tradition of a specifically Bengali mode of daily interaction: *'gyan deoa'* – 'imparting wisdom' – a common form that the put-down took in Calcutta. I replied with a blasphemy: 'This is not the response I would get in a shop in Bombay.' The man lost his moribund equilibrium. 'Don't give me that Bombay-Fombay stuff. That doesn't work over here!' I descended the two steps out on to the pavement in a huff.

That's from more than twenty years ago, but the injustice of it is still fresh. It embodies the way time, and everything in time's continuum, behaved, and in many ways, continues to behave in Calcutta: as if there were always a slight excess of it, in which to have a pointless encounter, or to exchange an unnecessary word or two. But today, there's the alternative of slipping anonymously into the shiny Music World – as long as you can avoid stumbling on to, or hearing, the new releases.

Cross the road from Music World and you are in Free School Street – now called Mirza Ghalib Street after the great nineteenth-century Urdu poet who lived here for a few years and witnessed, bemused, the advance of the British Raj – and then, going past a petrol station, you are, in a minute, in front of Mocambo. Always, there are people – often couples, often small families – loitering before the door and the saluting watchman with no noticeable aim except, as it turns out, to get in: fair-eyed, starved Europeans, who cultivate a look of simplicity and subsist largely on sex; the well-to-do, smart Marwari families, who rally around each other (their great strength and cause of success) even when standing on the pavement; the solitary bohemian or the left-wing Bengali couple who, like their radical nineteenth-century precursors, sometimes still make a point of eating beef steak; the ordinary, young Bengali customer, motor-cycle helmet in hand (for he can't afford a car), who knows no home or horizon but Calcutta, yet is entirely dispensable to its fortunes, and who experiences a sporadic passion for drinking beer and eating out. The group gathers here because Mocambo takes no reservations. Inside, where not a table is empty (thus, the apologetic crew that waits outside, bearing the brunt of the heat or absorbing what's left of the evening breeze), is a scene of murmuring incandescence. The lights are low; but, to make up for it, the upholstery is red, as it must have been in the fif-ties, when the restaurant opened: you feel, when you step in, that you're back in the singular world created by the Cold War, when one half (a fraction greatly exaggerated, of course) of the people of the world was eating out, and the other half standing in queues. Red, in that epoch, signified not only revolution, but, depending on its context, was also a constituent of psychedelia: and it's as a remnant of the latter, with its subterranean glow, that it resurfaces here.

Again, the prawn cocktail – that most debased of starters – is, here, justly famous. It is part appetiser and part dessert; the generous pink sauce that drowns the prawns is not Rose Marie, but almost a liquid confection – as it was in the Skyroom; but thicker, like melted ice cream – something that's sweeter than Rose Marie, but also sharper, with suggestions of Tabasco, black pepper, and – as the black-suited steward once told me in private – mustard. It's something with which to disarm and surprise a hostile party. There's a sinister undercurrent to Mocambo – 'sizzlers', fizzing chunks of meat on hot plates, is the other, more audible, speciality – perfectly in accord with what was once the infantile quality of the bhadralok's fantasy life. On the left of the entrance, the wall is divided into four sections with gigantic dancing girls from Degas, the blue having been retouched and paled again, once painted with a mixture of gaucheness and zeal by Shiv Kothari – the restaurant's late owner.

Further up from the entrance to Mocambo, thirty or so steps away, is where Ramayan Shah has his pavement stall, if one could call it that. These days when I come to Park Street for some reason – to superficially browse at the Oxford Bookstore or spend time at Mocambo – I'm usually off in that direction later, and the people there must view me approaching with mixed feelings. As ever, Nagendra is ironing clothes, in pyjamas and spotless white vest, his hands moving automatically and swiftly. I've never seen him stubbly or unkempt; his clean-shaven cheeks have the enviable green halo of one who is meticulously, and naturally, clean. His thick hair is perfectly combed and immovable and, since it's jet black, I suspect he dyes it. Later, I found out that this is where he lives and sleeps – here, next to the ironing stall, on one of these benches – but I still haven't asked him how he manages to look the way he does: transcendental and not of his surroundings. On the other hand, Ramayan Shah is hardly ever in his surroundings when I am there – he's gone again to the market to buy stuff which he'll later cook for his customers.

The second time I went looking for this stall, I was hoping to see how the boy was – the one who'd been lying on what seemed like a pantry table, his arm stiff and fingers clenched, sobbing. Had the medicines brought about an improvement; was he OK? In fact, he was nowhere to be seen – I turned to ask Nagendra where he was, but the man had as good as forgotten him; I had to reconstruct that episode, while he listened to my inelegant, rambling sentences, for him to get a sense of what I meant. Light glimmered: 'Woh ghar chala gaya' – 'He's gone home' – 'Home', as I began to realise from these encounters, being most often some place in Bihar. The unperturbed tone of

voice told me that no emergency had made the departure necessary; that toing and froing between Bihar and Calcutta was
unremarkable, and happened repeatedly.

Because Nagendra is so perfect and unflappable, I realise I've
stopped short of interviewing him. However, I've had desultory
conversations – conversations that I imagined were going to be
at once rigorous and illuminating, but have turned out to be
desultory and opaque in retrospect – with the interlopers who
hang about in Ramayan Shah's little space (or shelter, since
part of it has a tarpaulin roof). Although the interloper might
look as if he's been sitting there permanently, or that he's a
stakeholder in the business, or a regular, or family, he may be
none of these, and it is likely you will not see him a second
time. What seems certain is that Ramayan Shah's eatery is not
an eating place in the way we middle-class people understand
that entity; that is, you don't actually have to partake of the
food to while away hours over there, or to even go to sleep
on the furniture. On the other hand, I've occasionally noticed
(and in this, too, it differs from, say, Mocambo) people freely
access food without paying for it, even when the proprietor is
away – which, observation tells me, is a great deal of the time.
I'm assuming that there's some local system of scrupulousness
and credit to keep this trade alive for so many years, which is
not comprehensible at first, or second, glance; some notion of
spontaneous self-service which allows people from time to time
to take advantage of the place, in keeping with its ramshackle
do-it-yourself ethic.

A man was crouched in the centre, next to where it said
Chandan Hotel, peeling potatoes. He was in his late twenties,
slight, small, but fit, with a thin moustache; I wondered for a
second if he was Ramayan Shah's family, or an employee – in
which case, he would be serious labour. It turned out he was

just part of the constant drama of the place: he was helping out. He cast, naturally, a wary and resistant look on me; he didn't hugely mind answering my questions, but wanted to know *why* I was asking them. Indeed, my hovering presence there was mysterious, if not a downright nuisance. I explained I was writing a book on Calcutta; this sort of satisfied him – he went back to peeling and slicing the potatoes, and to receiving my questions without any flicker of interest. No, he didn't work here; he merely lent a hand sometimes in exchange for a plate of food; his work, in fact, was issuing parking stubs when cars parked themselves on Free School Street, and collecting money from them when they departed. He was, in other words, one of those inevitable parking attendants with whom no driver in Calcutta, as they start their engine and manoeuvre the car out of the parking space, can escape reunion – they materialise instantly without a hint of being caught unawares, and have already begun counting the change. At this moment, though, the man was entirely settled, poring over the potatoes; when I quizzed him about this, he reassured me that there was no car in peril of leaving – as if his intuition were generally dependable. His name, he told me, was Inder Kumar, and he ate both lunch and dinner (usually) at Ramayan Shah's. What was the fare like, I asked, because I was interested, and, like anyone else, possess a streak of romanticism that wishes street food were more unexpectedly delectable than what you order in restaurants; and, yes, there is street food that seduces you as your eyes skim over it, but the slop I see people hungrily consume in pavement stalls like Ramayan Shah's has never stirred, but in fact only repelled, me. Rice was served during the day, Inder Kumar said, or roti (chapatis) if you preferred; and *sabzi* – cooked vegetables – and a choice of either *rui* fish (carp, most beloved of fishes in Bengal, most prized as well as the most humble and readily available, whose white flesh tastes to me similar to what I imagine blotting paper would taste like if you prepare it to the same recipe) or egg, which is, everywhere in the nation, the human being's cheapest source of protein. The rate was thirteen rupees a plate if you had the egg slop, and fifteen if you chose the fish, which looked – especially the chunky *gaada* piece chopped from the middle of the carp – like a small but solid piece of wood.

Inder Kumar informed me it was seventeen years since he left a place called Mohammedpur in Bihar; that he went back monthly to be with his family; that he had two children in school, a son and a younger daughter; that he was employed by a contractor, who presumably let him keep a fixed amount of his parking collections and pocketed the rest. During this staccato construction, another was listening, someone unlike the people here (who avoid my glances in case I start to pry). He, instead, was more like one of those figures on the far edge of the screen when a random 'member of the public' is being interviewed on a news channel – the one with the restive expression, as if he has a vital opinion to add. This man was, it turned out, Mohammed Khan; excessively wiry and red-eyed, though he clearly wasn't ill. That much was certain because of his manner (physically, he might have fallen down any minute), which was, in contrast to the others, vociferous and ironic. Some part of him viewed the street, even himself, at one remove, and that made him more demonstrative and engaged – over-engaged, almost – than either Inder Kumar or Nagendra. The conversation, now, quickly and without warning, veered towards politics; how exactly this happened I don't know, though I think it had something to do with Mohammed Khan's wide-ranging passions; his candidness; his loose-cannon manner. 'You can call me Mataal,' he added matter-of-factly; and, soon, I found that everyone knew him by this name. He said it without embarrassment – the word means 'drunk' (and now his red eyes and frail outline made sense), but it also has positive connotations: in devotionals, mystics will often refer to themselves as 'matwala' – inebriated in soul and spirit with God. Mataal said he was definitely voting Trinamool – the main opposition to the ruling Left Front – when the time came. This set off an echo in the group, and everybody around us, including Inder Kumar and Nagendra, confirmed that it would be Trinamool for them too.

I wasn't shocked by this absolute consensus; the historical moment (August 2009) was one in which the tide appeared to have turned after thirty-two near-unchallenged years of the Left-led government. Still, I was a bit surprised. After all, the Left Front had largely created the improvised universe in which Nagendra and Inder Kumar and Ramayan Shah survived, and I mean this on several levels. There was the pro-poor, pro-labour rhetoric of the Communist Party of India (Marxist), of course, heard until recently from a megaphone on every street corner; and the preponderant ideology of hammer and sickle that made this gradual colonisation of pavement and bus stop as potential shelter or spaces for trade possible. The fact that this ideology had once been embraced by almost every intellectual as well as moral person in Calcutta meant there could be no viable protests against these conditions, in which, through low-level corruption and a peculiar notion of patronage, generosity, and humanity, homeless families and illegal businesses were allowed to proliferate in various available public spaces. Perhaps that notion of humanity wasn't so peculiar really; one felt its deep pull as one walked on the streets and sat among their unexpected range of inhabitants. But the ethical person, the intellectual, who wouldn't say a word against these conditions in public, cultivated, actually, a hypocrisy that was apparent everywhere. Still, the middle class had swung decisively towards the Trinamool Congress long ago, and each time been disappointed by its volatile leader Mamata Banerjee's endemic mood swings, her violent unpredictability of policy, her missionary populism, the way she frequently threatened, out of a sense of sheer pique, to self-destruct. Gandhi had perfected the art of fasting, emaciation, and self-flagellation as a tool; Mamata Banerjee, to the nervousness of her supporters, was on her way to becoming the mistress of self-destruction, of swiftly attacking the nose because of a perceived slight from the face. Still, the state of the state of West Bengal was such that it was ready to have her as its leader; not just Nagendra and Inder Kumar, but even the members of the Bengal Club and the diners in Mocambo were in unison on this. Worryingly, there was no clarity, about not only what to expect from Ms Banerjee, but whom she represented – was it the masses, or the middle class, or industry, or, impossibly, everyone and everything? The answer was elusive. That she's single, and always wears a simple white cotton sari – a sign of abnegation – perhaps denoted she would take everyone, from Inder Kumar to the man ordering chicken Tetrazzini in Mocambo, under her wing. Revulsion against the Left Front had permeated everything; Mataal and Nagendra and Inder Kumar gave their assent to this feeling. And yet the Front had created the mood in Calcutta that greeted the largely unskilled labour such as themselves, arriving here daily from a neighbouring state – what might have been a mood of parochial animosity was, instead, one of absorption and, to a certain extent, of abetment. But, whether you live and sleep and dream in a condominium in South City or on a bench on the pavement, you feel unsafe when you begin to sense that an epoch is dusted and finished. I turned to Mataal after everyone had expressed their unequivocal opinion, and asked my stock question – 'What do you do?' – for it combines sociological rigour with an assumption of concern and friendliness. For the first time, he prevaricated; but his acquaintances were ready to help him out. 'He supplies women,' said one of them; and others found other words to describe his profession. 'Really?' I said, 'Achha?', because the pimps of Free School Street used to be well known; but I'd presumed that in a post-HIV world

Mataal's trade and the core trade of prostitution itself would have suffered, here, a terminal body blow. I was told otherwise. 'I have many parties,' Mataal corrected me, making me catch a glimmer of an unknown world. 'All kinds of people.' He looked vacant, for our conversation had abruptly come to an end. 'In fact, I have to meet a party right now.'

Finally, one afternoon, I got to see Ramayan Shah: he was squatting near the edge of the pavement, not far from the gutter, surveying his world – the pot and its ingredients – with a masterful but concerned air (a gaze like a chemist's) before embarking on the cooking itself. I, in a sense, already knew him; he, of course, not only didn't know me but, as I stood behind him, showed no awareness I existed. He'd created his own universe, like a spider makes its web, and – though that universe may be invisible to the passer-by – he was far more centred in it than anyone I'd met over here. 'Is this your shop?' I asked – how easy it is to assume the role of a questioner as long as you look the part – and, 'What is your name?' He seemed vaguely startled; then, his consciousness quickly recovered its continuity with its surroundings, and I didn't really matter. The way he said his name softly made me think he was Muslim, and when I repeated what I thought I'd heard – 'Rahman Shah' – he nodded in unworldly agreement, as if names and identities and details itself were dispensable. Only later did I guess – from talking to others – that he'd said Ramayan, not Rahman. He seemed older than his years: I presumed he was in his mid-fifties, but he looked closer to his early sixties. He had a thin grey moustache and a forbearing face; in his much-worn dhoti and kurta, he was like the North Indian peasant he was probably meant to be, resilient, adaptable. Agreement with everyone and everything, I sensed, was his tested strategy for survival – no wonder he'd let my mispronunciation of his name go; no wonder he hadn't acknowledged I was standing behind him – it was not so much out of a wish not to be encroached upon as to not interfere, to not encroach upon. And this air of ready-made agreement gave Ramayan Shah a quality – perhaps deceptive, perhaps not – of innocence. It strikes me now, as I think of him, diligent on his haunches, that Gandhi's mass movement must have been full of recruits exactly like him. How that galvanisation had once occurred was now mysterious.

Whenever I'm in Ramayan Shah's stall in the afternoons – and it's invariably afternoon, as I've used up my morning writing or practising music and then come straight here after lunch or a coffee at Flurys – I'm hot, and I'm also subtly aware, despite the heat, of the ebbing of the light. Afternoon's the most dreamless and introspective time of day, a sort of midnight of the day-time, though you wouldn't know that from the activity on Free School Street; but its span is also the shortest I know anywhere (as Calcutta is in the east), and, by half-past five, you're really preparing for the sudden advent – always unexpected – of even-ing. As I stand at Ramayan Shah's, there's a steady – and noisy – flow of congestion towards Park Street, and, even now, when it's supposed to have been phased out of the city's traffic, the hand-pulled rickshaw rolls onward, with an imperious shopper afloat. The rickshaw-pullers were said to be pimps and touts, and the way they made their function known to young men was through hungry eye-contact, and the muted clink of the bell in their palm. Further up, if you turn left after the second-hand record stalls and bookshops, you'll come to New Market, or Hogg's Market, for me, with its inexplicable and largely purposeless maze of shops, still the most enchanting covered market I've walked around in and, for short spells of time, been frustrated by. Free School Street is an old, important road; opposite the opening that leads to New Market is Calcutta's main fire station. Further up, as the road ends, are the desper-ately impoverished Muslim families who live among debris and garbage, seemingly the preferred habitat of the swaggering, hirsute pigs they nurture. But parallel to Lindsey Street, on which New Market is situated, are the skeletal lanes with either quaint or seedy hotels in whose rooms European backpackers curl up, and who march in the short-lived afternoon (as transitory to Calcutta's day as summer is to England's year) towards Park Street, or march back from it, glancing momentarily in our direction as Ramayan Shah's clientele and staff and neighbours and I exchange small talk cautiously.

Mid-December, and I was back in Park Street, having spent two and a half months in England, in Norwich. So I was doubly glad to be back in the setting I'd fantasised about there – 'fantasise' may not be the right word, because it involves a degree of volition; while I suppose I'm talking about a random and involuntary yearning that would come to me during my stay in England. I don't know where it came from, because I don't actually *like* the Calcutta of today (of that, more shortly). Could it be a residue from my childhood, when, in Bombay, returning from the school I hated to the lovely, shining flat that was home, I thought constantly of Calcutta? These days, certain places and activities revisit me momentarily when I'm away, and, whatever I'm doing, I'm sucked into their memory: walking down Park Street, past Magnolia (a restaurant I couldn't be persuaded to be caught dead in) and the stalls selling chewing gums and condoms, is one of them; settling down at a table at Flurys is another. Actually, I long for Park Street even when I'm not away; just now, as I write these words in my flat in Sunny Park, I feel a desire, like a muted undercurrent, to go to Park Street. In England, other pictures flash upon my eye, as part of that assortment that draws me homeward, towards Calcutta – which, as it happens, was never my home, and, I often feel, never will be. At least one of them is inexplicable: a spontaneous memory of The Good Companion, a spacious air-conditioned shop selling, mainly, frocks and dresses for children made by destitute women, managed by upper-middle-class ladies who want to do a bit of charitable work. What the particular pull of this memory is, I can't tell; it could be that the shop has an unusual amount of space, and, invariably, relatively few customers, besides a society lady you might know vaguely, positioned behind the desk, speaking in perfect, commanding English; the juxtaposition of these elements might make it seem attractive and impossibly far in Norwich.

◆

I was back in Park Street, and was buoyant for two reasons: first, for my proven ability to materialise yet again in the world that I (for some obscure but dogged reason) love. Second, I was irrationally, almost spitefully, cheered by the fact that I was back when it was increasingly going to be the best time to be in Calcutta (a week before Christmas) and, coincidentally, the worst time to be in Norwich. Decades of dispiriting travel between the two countries have made my experience of place not just comparative, but, occasionally, vituperative. Before the England–India divide that's defined my life in the last twenty-five years, there was the Bombay–Calcutta one. When visiting Calcutta from Bombay, I would actually think to myself, 'How glad I am not to be at home!', while, back from England, I over-hear myself exclaiming in the first few days: 'How glad I am to be back!' – literally, at intervals, congratulating myself. In other words, the associations of 'home', 'away', 'return' are quite hopelessly mixed up in my mind.

As I stepped out of Oxford Bookstore, my pace quickening as I turned in the direction of Music World, I found myself accom-panied by a girl who'd been sitting on the pavement (there are always one or two people domiciled just outside the book-store). I'd noticed, without paying attention, that she'd been sitting with an infant, a boy, both diverting themselves with what looked like a large, flat bottle meant for storing mineral water – a curious plaything. Seeing me come out of the shop, the girl immediately abandoned the infant and hurried after me. I thought I'd end her pursuit by giving her a few rupees; then it occurred to me that, since I was writing about the city, I may as well have a conversation with her. The thought, a con-trived and implausible one, became more and more natural and plausible in a few seconds, when we began talking.

'Naam kya hai?'

She was briefly confused, and then probably made an assess-ment – that this man would be worth cooperating with in the

interests of getting a few more rupees later. We kept up the conversation while steadily approaching the traffic lights, where
I'd cross to Music World. She was anxious and waiflike, and
wouldn't have looked out of place in a page inside the *National
Geographic*.

'Pooja,' she said.

'Do you live here?' I asked – meaning this area, Park Street;
more precisely, the pavement outside Oxford Bookstore. She
shook her head. She told me her *des*, her native place, was
Uluberia – not a village or town at all, but a downmarket
locality on the outskirts of the city, near Howrah, which can be
classified as the beginning of the end of Calcutta. Did she live
there with her parents?

No, she lived in front of Forum, the big mall that had come
up on Elgin Road and altered that historical area (the mall,
awash with radiance and activity till nine in the evening, was
one of those locations I suddenly caught myself thinking about
in the solitariness of Norwich). By now, Pooja – whose real
name, I found out, was Shabnam (many poor Muslims, as we
know, instinctively take cover under neutral-sounding Hindu
names) – and I had crossed and reached Music World; here,
sitting on a parapet before a Mama Mia stall – which claims to
sell not ice cream, but 'gelato' – I clumsily opened a notebook
which I was carrying in case I encountered Ramayan Shah, and,
glanced at by the beady-eyed magazine-sellers opposite and the
slinky college kids who always gather here, taking stock of the
situation or romancing, began to scribble Shabnam's replies.
Her brother – whom she'd left alone, daringly, in front of the
bookshop – was called Nasir; she earned between ten and forty
rupees each day; she (who was just ten) didn't like her parents
so much, preferring her grandparents, with whom she lived on
the pavement outside Forum. Our conversation had made us
conspicuous: not just to the magazine-sellers and the smarter,
uniformed men behind the Mama Mia counter, but to other

beggars, whose numbers had grown startlingly, in a matter of minutes.

'I have to get back,' she urged. 'My brother . . .' Yes, to leave an infant alone in front of Oxford Bookstore . . . I'd put that thought out of my head. How would she go back to Forum later? On foot, she told me. Other beggars were listening; and, when they saw me fish in my pocket and give Shabnam her reward for humouring me, they advanced in a proprietary way, demanding money.

It was a lovely afternoon, of course, and an excellent time to be in Park Street – seven days before Christmas, which, with New Year's Eve, would transmogrify the place with its paraphernalia and magic and leave its unmistakable trace there for pretty much the rest of the year. As for the beggars (mainly children and women), I knew they drifted around Flurys and Music World and the traffic lights as a matter of course – I felt I'd seen them before. This, though, was an illusion. Like everyone else on Park Street, they too were part of a whirl and itinerary of arrival and calculated lingering. People come to Park Street for a reason – to have a cup of coffee and forget the world; to try out a restaurant; to keep a business appointment; to become a couple; to study girls; to be a consumer – and once they're done, they're gone. The beggars, too, had their reasons for being here – they didn't actually belong to Park Street. With the destitute, whom you hardly notice, you invariably make an assumption that they're integral to the milieu and landscape they inhabit; as they don't have a home, you presume their home is where they are. This wasn't true of the beggars in front of Music World – like everything else (cars, shoppers, students, coffee drinkers) that made up the strange energy at that junction, they were ephemeral. Chance had brought me and them together, but, actually, there was no guarantee I'd run into them at this spot tomorrow.

I discovered this while talking to them. One woman in particular stood out: sparse-haired, large, in a colourful rag of a sari
she'd wrapped round herself, she sensed why I was here and
promised me a story. 'Listen to me, dada!' she cried. 'Not now!'
I said, 'tomorrow!' She made a sign of disgust. 'I won't be here
tomorrow!' she said, and walked off.

The reason I was distracted was the other woman I'd begun
to talk to over the din. She was plain-looking and reticent, and,
in her way, I thought, lovely. She had a small boy with her.
While the others asked for money, she asked for money to buy
medicine – 'Dada, oshudh kinbo': a well-worn ploy. I countered
this with, 'I won't give you money, I'll buy you the medicine,'
to which, to my surprise, she nodded faintly and said, 'All right.'
Around this time the other woman warned me, 'I won't be here
tomorrow!' and walked away, while I gestured to this young
woman – she'd be in her late twenties – and her son to follow
me to Free School Street, because there was a pharmacy there;
as we waited to cross at the lights, and the other beggars quickly lost interest, I sensed that Park Street is, essentially (even for
the destitute), a place of brief acquaintances and meetings – no
one has too much time for anyone else, you yourself are part
of a web of motivations that are fading and resurrecting – and
you must be on the move constantly to be in the street's ebb
and flow of traffic.

We crossed the road – Christmas preparations were already on,
and, at the turning of Free School Street, opposite the petrol
pump, I saw a man walk past carrying a large cotton wool beard
and an immense red suit: bits that would coalesce, at some
point, into a figure of Santa.

At Ramayan Shah's, I asked for the nearest pharmacy,
as I had months ago when the boy had been lying on a shelf
with clenched fingers, and, once again, someone pointed
peremptorily ahead – 'Aagey, aagey' – towards the right.

I had thought the woman was Bengali – she fitted perfectly with my childhood notion of the Bengali woman: pretty, intelligent-looking, fairly small, an embodiment of puritan dignity, with the straight hair combed into a bun on either side of her parting – but she was, to my surprise, originally from Bihar, and her name was Baby Misra. She said she was thirty years old; and she'd shown me a prescription on a doctor's letterhead to vouch for the authenticity of her plea. I was right to think, though, that she wasn't a beggar – she lived just outside of Calcutta, in Howrah – the graveyard of Bengal's industry – and there she was a part-time domestic help, washing dishes and cleaning up at two homes in the morning, earning two hundred rupees monthly at one house, three hundred at the other. That left her afternoons free, and she'd embarked for Park Street at 1 p.m.

Marvelling at the journeys that had brought us to the front of Music World and the large glass windows of Flurys, I asked her, crudely, why she wasn't begging in Howrah. She admitted, without any of the pride that was implicit in her simple appearance, that she didn't want to be spotted by people she knew. Her journey to Flurys seemed to me, then, both entirely understandable and slightly mad; given she wasn't so well – and despite her deceptive air of reasonableness.

Her husband, Munna, was now far away; he'd gone back to his des, as labourers in Calcutta do frequently, to a place that sounded – on Baby Misra's tongue – like 'Raksaul'. Jitinder, who was five years old, was clearly on an outing; he carried a little stick, probably to entertain himself or, in his own made-up universe, to protect himself and his mother. Like him, I too was not immune to the charms of Free School Street in December – a poor, dirty, congested road, with an open gutter on either side, but busy with insignificant enterprise, and with residues, everywhere, of an earlier bohemian life. I crossed the street and soldiered on – the pharmacy was not where I'd expected it, and bystanders kept promising, 'Just there – further on' – while, doggedly, Baby Misra followed, with her son, confidently brandishing the stick, unimpressed by the crows and stray dogs. I was thinking that there was something else I was supposed to be doing, which I was being kept from, and my stride became more urgent; and then realised that this – whatever it was I was doing now on Free School Street – was exactly what I'd set out to do. 'What is it that's troubling you?' I asked her; she said, quietly, that she had a shooting pain in her right leg, a pain like a 'current'.

Bihar, Bengal's neighbour, has one of the grandest histories of all Indian provinces; home to India's first great empire, to two great and austere religions, Buddhism and Jainism, and to the ancient teeming city of Pataliputra. It's a world that the Indian child knows from comic books – the kingdom of Magadha; the resplendent emperor Chandragupta Maurya on his horse; the tonsured sages gathered round a holy tree; the sensuous women that the artists of the Amar Chitra Katha comic book series drew with lascivious satisfaction. While you glimpse that dreamworld of eternal India, you don't make the connection, either as a schoolboy or as an adult, with Bihar, byword for abhorrent ministers and bureaucrats and police-men, minor warlords and ignorant peasants, whose once-poetic tongues – Bhojpuri and Maithili – now, spoken by the likes of Ramayan Shah, make people laugh. There's no reason to think that the Biharis, who constitute a substantial percentage of the floating population of Calcutta, like the pompous remnants of the Bengali bourgeoisie at all, flattened by decades of left rule, or that the Bengali thinks of the Bihari as anything other than a rickshawalla. It's a testament to Bengali self-absorption that the city is still fundamentally thought to be a Bengali one – although grudging concessions are made to the fact that the economy, now, is almost entirely controlled by Marwaris. But what of the Bihari? On Park Street and Free School Street, and in other parts of the city, he is everywhere; leaning out of a taxi window, eyes glazed, buying gutka from a vendor (who's also, possibly, Bihari) to keep himself going for the rest of the day; or selling chanachur masala in front of a mall; engaged in small trade or the perennial construction work; living apart from his family, then mysteriously withdrawing to his des for a month.

J.P. Medico.

Here was the pharmacy! But the corrugated shutter was down three quarters of the way. I bent down and could sense there were people there; I was told from within that they'd reopen at five o'clock. Yes, I think it's true that some pharmacies – and maybe pharmacies alone – take a long siesta in Calcutta. Do they do such bad business in the afternoon that even keeping the ceiling fan and tube light on makes little sense? 'Open up please! We've come a long way!' I said, taking on the moral tone of my class, the educated class, impatient with the laxity of the poorly educated. Baby Misra seemed quietly relieved and respectful upon seeing me in this incarnation. To my surprise, the shutter went up with a juddering clatter, and the three of us stepped into a small space that, here and there, displayed cheerful signs for shampoos and ointments. One of these showed a radiant little boy with a bottle saying HORLICKS, and, soon after the two men (a younger and an older) had glanced at the prescription (Baby Misra's treatment was very simple: calcium tablets and vitamins), young Jitinder pointed to the sign and, charmingly, without the pressing ways of other children, indicated he wanted the Horlicks. The wisdom of asking for Horlicks rather than chocolates or lozenges was interesting: did he know the former had greater nutritional value – or did he like the picture of the child? The two men, who were giving us the vitamins – annoyingly, they'd run out of calcium tablets – smiled without, however, being certain of how much to smile; they could tell Jitinder wasn't my son and were balancing a demand from an undeserving down-at-heel boy (albeit decently dressed in white shirt and shorts, armed with a tiny stick) with the possibility of a further sale. Baby Misra was having none of this; unimpressed by Jitinder, she collected him from the shelf she'd allowed him to perch on, and placed him on the ground unfussily, as if they had to be on their way. The manner in which she did this acknowledged to me: 'I know your patience is wearing thin.' I paid for the vitamins without a word.

We walked back some distance towards Park Street, and, near Ramayan Shah's 'hotel', where I thought I'd stop for a chat, I bid the lovely Baby Misra and her handsome boy farewell. On our way, while passing a dingy-looking eating place, Jitinder, with the candour of a child, growing gradually familiar with me, had expressed an interest in chow mein. This time, with the inexorable softening of the maternal heart, Baby Misra looked at me – in expectancy and faith. I felt a small constricting of my own heart immediately, and, for a second, felt this mother and child I hardly knew were threatening to deluge my life. Simultaneously – it was impossible to disentangle it from this anxiety – I thought buying Jitinder chow mein was an excellent idea; only the fact that he'd asked me made me resistant to it. We went in, and Jitinder had vegetable chow mein – 'chow', as it's called in Calcutta, the commonest, most munificent street food, limp white noodles tossed around in oil and soya sauce with gratings of vegetable or chicken (I myself have never tasted it) – and then, deliberately to disarm me, said, 'Thank you,' in the way of one who knows only those two words in the English language, and uses them at moments such as this one.

'You shouldn't have given her the money,' said Munna moodily. 'She'll never spend it on medicine.'

By now, I'd seen the back of Baby Misra; we'd had a final conference near Ramayan Shah's. I'd offered to drop her at a 'free' hospital near Number 4 Bridge, for treatment and X-rays, and she'd refused. Maybe it was time to get back to Howrah. She, in turn, had asked me if I knew of any jobs going; 'You can always tell these people if you need me,' I said, pointing my chin towards Ramayan Shah's ramshackle world, as if it were an institution I'd have an enduring association with. She tilted her head sideways – our sweet Indian gesture of assent – and asked if she could have money to buy the calcium tablets.

Soon after this, Munna (clearly a popular Bihari name) passed his remark – he'd ignored me before, absorbed in his aluminium platter of rice and vegetables, but now was unexpectedly, if intrusively, interested – with the air of a persecutor who turns out to be menacingly concerned about your welfare. What do you care? I thought. A mistake one makes constantly is to judge people by their looks – it's the infallible urge to stereotype, conflated inextricably with the urge to fictionalise – and Munna had the large, moustached, glowering features that convey, and incite, animosity. But, as you grow older, experience tells you to distrust your first impression (this can be fatal when it comes to people who have an aura of villainy, and very useful in connection with those who have an air of 'niceness'); so I thought I'd engage with Munna in spite of not wanting to.

'That boy's half-mad,' he said, as he scooped up rice from the dented plate. The boy he'd described smiled enigmatically. He was too busy to be bothered: splashing the utensils, dicing the aubergine. He turned out to be Ramayan Shah's son; he said he was 'fourteen or fifteen' years old, but looked younger – small, enigmatic, and spring-like. As I took in his features from different angles, I did see that he looked a bit like his father; but lacked, naturally, his air of calm acceptance. Clearly, Munna and he didn't like each other. The boy was cheery but homesick (he missed the '*khelna kudna*', the abandon, of his village); and Munna was a bully.

'He eats a kilo and a half of rice every day,' said Munna, rapidly consuming rice himself. 'He doesn't eat food: food eats him.'

The boy's name was (probably appropriately) Hridayanand – 'joyful of heart'. His response to my queries was one of gob-smacked (this ugly English word is the only one that comes readily to mind) disbelief; he'd never encountered such a specimen before. Munna's was supercilious distaste and suspicion. He wasn't sure if I was a scam-artist who was going to exploit him, or whether I was an imbecile up for exploitation – the perpetual and urgent Indian dilemma. Nevertheless, as if he were reluctantly doing me a good turn, he volunteered a potted life history. He had been 'here' – the word could have meant anything – since 1986. That was in one of the worse decades in Calcutta's history, even worse in some ways than the Naxal years, when middle-class children, like the children in Victorian novels, read for their finals by candlelight, when the city seemed to implode and the interminable power cuts earned the chief minister Jyoti Basu – whose first name means 'light' – the nickname Andhakar or Darkness Basu. Since such was at least the middle-class perspective on 1986, it made me wonder how much worse it would have been in Munna's home town to make the move. Everyone around 'here' was Bihari, he proclaimed: a generalisation, of course, but with a germ of truth in it.

They – four of them – slept on these latticed string cots and narrow benches – the rudimentary furniture that occupied the pavement at various angles. He cleaned cars and earned one hundred and fifty rupees a day (almost double the minimum wage in this country of starvation deaths and millionaires); and sent back two and a half thousand monthly. At home in Munger zilla, he had two daughters.

'Police cause trouble,' he said, with the wariness of one whose domain depends upon offering small bribes to the law.

No, I didn't have a great deal to learn from Munna – nothing that, by now, I didn't already know. But Munna was aware of the value of his time and information. 'Arrey, at least give me something for a cup of tea!' he said as I got up to go – careless of the decorousness that had characterised the others I'd socialised with till now at Ramayan Shah's. Nagendra was ironing away within earshot, and his expression could have meant anything: 'I wish I was somewhere else', or 'Serves him right!'

25 December 2009: the Bengal Club Christmas lunch menu had lobster bisque as usual. Then there were the other things – fish buried under almond sauce; roast ham with a sort of dark twinkling lacquer veneer; turkey, of course, most unexciting of meats. But how could you have a Christmas lunch without turkey? And Christmas pudding in brandy cream. It was the sort of weather in which a jacket and tie – the club's dress code for men for the event – is just fine. Most people were into their mid-fifties and beyond; and there was a lot of sipping of cocktails and mocktails, donning of paper hats, a mild, unselfconscious, bravura indulgence in silliness. The club was once designed to keep natives at bay – 'Dogs and Indians not allowed' – but now, I'd say hesitantly, it's old-fashioned, yet lacking in hauteur. We were here en famille; with my wife, my daughter, who, with a friend, ate separately from us in the Oriental Room, my parents, parents-in-law, my sister-in-law and her husband, Kabir (who live in a remote London suburb). Kabir had retrieved a pale khaki linen suit for the afternoon.

After occasions like this, we generally scatter. My father is no longer clear about what his intentions are, and seems ready to be led almost anywhere; my mother isn't certain why my father has changed in the last two years into this indeterminate human being. My daughter is easily bored; barely eleven years old, she had, that day, some tantalising rendezvous to keep at home – it made her restless. My parents-in-law are excessively polite, as almost all Bengali in-laws are if they're in the disadvantageous position of being of the daughter's family: they convinced me (as they do each year) of the exceptionally good time they'd had. Kabir looked as if he'd had enough of wearing his khaki-coloured linen suit.

And so they dispersed, one by one, from Russell Street, which opens at this end on to Park Street. And, as on our wedding night, my wife and I were eventually left alone with each other – but on the compound of the Bengal Club. I didn't want to leave the neighbourhood; I'd half-succumbed to the same wishful enchantment that I do when I'm here. Besides, I'd eaten too much; the residue of the piece of Christmas pudding saturated in brandy cream not only didn't fit in with my experience of Christmas Day – it felt out of place in my stomach. My arteries were, predictably, asking for caffeine.

'Let's go to Flurys,' I said, knowing fully we'd have to wait to get in. In my mind was the undeniable realisation, 'Christmas comes once a year', uttered by the angel floating ministeringly at one shoulder, with the devil at the other shoulder adding, 'And you're half a minute away from Park Street.' Perhaps they were both angels? And in which part of the world could you have such a Christmas afternoon, with its special aimless anticipation – except in Calcutta, and here? People were at large. They looked unaware of various things, of the complex history that killed Christmas on this street and now for whatever reason had resurrected it. There's something almost miraculous about the continual return of Christmas to Park Street; it's a miracle that (despite the fact that all miracles are apocryphal) I didn't want to miss. As with all festive occasions these days in this city, what had once started probably in the nineteenth century as part of a secular metamorphosis (the emergence of a new, busy, pleasure-loving middle class; a fresh air of celebration) is now woven into a cheery provincialism, of a city no longer emblematic but ordinary, yet uncannily lit by its past. The strollers on Park Street seemed as unmindful of yesterday as they were of history: Christmas Eve didn't survive even as memory. They were on their way somewhere, for no good reason, as we were, to Flurys; the hawkers were selling the little clay Santas with the mildly nodding heads and parsimonious beards, as if Christmas Eve were still a few days away. It didn't occur to them, or to the passers-by, that you mightn't want anything to do with Santa – clay or otherwise – once Christmas Eve was over. I had once bought one for my daughter, a few years ago, and she didn't want anything to do with it then; it stood on a shelf for two weeks, its head vibrating every time you struck it with your finger, and then its one colour began to fade, the already faint red ebbing into something like an impressionist's wash. Its inside was white, and hollow like a bell. As with such objects, they become hand-me-downs to the less privileged, and a maid took it for her daughter after I reluctantly consented to part with it.

Flurys was full of afternoon revellers. We would need to wait for fifteen minutes to enter; I had a sudden urge – not so sudden, the thought was at the back of my mind – to check out Ramayan Shah's. 'Could I . . . you could come with me' – but my wife shook her head and indicated she'd wait for my return *here*, in the small queue keeping vigil outside Flurys, 'OK – back in ten minutes – we should have a table by then' – and I went down the steps and past the magazine vendors and across the road, having loosened my tie, folded my jacket (the last sign of the Bengal Club luncheon) on the crook of my arm. There was activity at the petrol station and in front of Mocambo, of course, but, coming to Ramayan Shah's, I found an odd solitude, a release of purpose. A strange cessation reigned here. This wasn't only because Ramayan Shah was missing again (did it really matter if he was there or not? – more and more he seemed a symbol of elusiveness, like Godot), but that the inner rhythm here was different – from the rest of the neighbourhood and from its own incarnation on normal days. Right next to Nagendra's ironing stand were two figures asleep on string beds, covered from toe to head in sheets keeping out, in the shroud-like form of rural Indian sleepers, what this country has in such abundance and what makes it so attractive: sound and daylight. They were still, but crawling with flies; Christmas, possibly, had given them justification to withdraw into this cocoon. 'Where's Nagendra?' I asked; thinking, too (Fitzgerald once defined the writer as one who can harbour two incompatible thoughts in the head simultaneously), that our table at Flurys might now be available. A man dicing vegetables gestured towards one of the motionless figures on which dozens of Christmas flies had alighted – alighted, it became clear in a second, with no long-term commitment to the venue. A little further off, Ramayan Shah's son Hridayanand was scouring a pot with a dreamlike containment, neither happy nor unhappy. I think he was probably incapable of being unhappy, or, like most children, was unhappy about immediate rather than overarching matters. Right now he was more bored than unhappy. Since sociological rigour is essential when you're writing of a city, I asked the man dicing vegetables who he was and, intrusively, what his earnings were like. He said he was Gupta, proprietor of the Chandan Hotel (I'd noticed the unostentatious handwritten sign long ago and had been cautioned that it was *not* the name of Ramayan Shah's outfit). This neglected space, this bit of nothing, left for future use between Nagendra's stall and Ramayan Shah's stove, I'd always presumed 'belonged' to the latter, that it served a function in his two-decade-old enterprise; but on meeting Gupta the Chandan Hotel acquired, for me, a tenuous territorial shape. Gupta, in reply to my socio-economic query, said he earned a hundred and fifty rupees a day (this was odd, because I'd never seen him plying his trade; but it was clearly either the average on the pavement near Mocambo, or a number that tripped easily off the Bihari tongue). On Christmas Day, he admitted he made less. I would've questioned him further about this disappointing dip in his income, but wanted to get back to Flurys while I still stood a chance of getting a table.

At the traffic lights, I saw a deeply familiar figure on the opposite side, sitting, amidst the concourse of motley people any festive day in Calcutta comprises, on the white parapet outside the large window of Flurys, studying me with a mix-ture of distant empathy and interest. It was my wife, R. She'd abandoned the queue and opted, as she often does, to sit down. She looked at me as if she'd never expected to see me again. I was simply surprised to find her where she was. But the queue had dissolved, and we got into Flurys almost instantly. 'Did you notice the woman beside me?' she asked when we were seated. Although I do notice women, I often find that I don't notice the same kind that R does. She'd been sitting next to a small family on the parapet. Now that she mentioned her, I *did* recall some-one at R's side – 'The person in the green salwaar kameez,' she said exasperatedly – but the colour of the clothing hadn't regis-tered itself on my mind's eye. What *had* imprinted itself there was that she was, for the want of a more delicate expression, someone from a different class background, someone with a very different horizon, someone ordinary and well known and yet, at the same time, little known. All this, as it were, I knew, although I hadn't noticed the colour of her salwaar kameez. It was she, on seeing that R wanted to sit down, who had invited her to: 'There's space here.' And there was; the parapet distends just there like a swelling lip, and becomes ample. R told me how this woman came here with her family at this time of the year, annually, because the ledge outside Flurys provided her with a view of an incredible stream of life on the 25th. 'She spoke to me first in Bengali and then in Hindi,' R said, and this was worth remarking on because, only a generation ago, Bengalis spoke a risible, embarrassing Hindi, and even looked down upon that language. In the last thirty years, not only had Bengal fallen, but so had the once-vaunted Bengali language; and, in the meanwhile, a new kind of Bengali person had come into being and increased in small towns, suburbs, outskirts, and even in the metropolis (which these days felt as if it were on the outskirts of somewhere itself, or like an agglomeration of little towns), in which people watched Hindi films on DVDs, and a daily ration of Hindi reality shows and Bengali soaps. Most of this audience couldn't but be proficient in Hindi. The woman in the green salwaar kameez was one such Bengali, while R and I had a foot sufficiently planted in a superannuated Bengal for us to find this unselfconscious lapsing into Hindi worth commenting on. Streamers hung from the ceilings of Flurys, as it always does during Christmas. After ordering the menu's relatively recent 'brewed filter coffee' (earlier it was simply 'coffee'), I apologised to my wife and said I'd like to step out for ten minutes and speak briefly to the woman she'd been sitting next to. Clearly, I'm not good company these days; R sees me not so much as a person occasionally seized by inspiration or curiosity but by inklings of excitement. Either it has to do with music, or a particular sound, or idea; or, as was the case now, with Christmas and the city. 'Go,' she instructed me. 'The coffee will take at least fifteen minutes.' Like me, she too was vaguely stirred by the notion of a family sitting outside Flurys on the ledge, looking at the same world that we were from behind the window, but at greater proximity.

So as not to unduly alarm the woman in the green salwaar kameez, I introduced myself as the husband of the person who'd been keeping her company five minutes ago. She was cautious but not hostile; she made room for me in the space R had just vacated. I'd seen faces like hers before – in Northern Spain; in China: a new kind of provincial who populates the globalised world, who changes with its changes without ever travelling outside of the country, even beyond their city or town. This lady, for instance – she lived in Salt Lake, a suburb created in the late seventies not far from the airport, and she'd come here to Park Street to spend the afternoon. She introduced me to her son, a shy boy of seventeen or eighteen, who she said studied at 'Something Institution' (I couldn't catch the name), and to her sister, who resembled her, but was older, less pretty, and seemed to know it. She was waiting, she said with a tremor of humour and anticipation, for her husband to return from the KFC on Middleton Street. The only false note occurred when I asked her what he did; withdrawing a tiny bit, she said, prevaricatingly, 'Service'. This could mean any kind of regular employment: an ordinary white-collar job. Anything grander, and she'd have been specific. I felt, again, that I'd seen people like her in other parts of the world, out on a walk, going down a promenade or past some shops, entirely of a locality, a place, but also entirely of the present, the here and now. Sitting next to her, waiting for her husband to return, I thought I could have been, and probably was, anywhere.

'Could you go and see your bara mamima this evening? She might die any time now.'

So my mother to me, before Christmas Day was over. Those childhood visits – now translated into belated deathbed visits! Never to see bara mamima again – my late maternal uncle Jyoti Prasad Nandi Majumdar's wife – to allow her to sneak away without so much as a greeting or a sighting!

She lay, that Christmas evening in Golf Green, very still on the divan in the little sitting room in the one-bedroom flat. We'd heard for about a week that she was fading. R and I sat talking with her daughter and sole companion Rini. Golf Green is an odd colony that came up next to waterbodies and wilderness in the mid-seventies, its blocks of apartments divided candidly into 'lower income group' and 'middle income group', perfectly capturing the prudent ambitions of a new generation of Bengali homeowners. My aunt, all these years, had been here, in MIG. Childhood flooded back, mainly because of the stillness that I only ever used to encounter in this city in December. The temperature falls to a level that makes the fan unnecessary. And the child in me begins to attend to details – the pinpricks of sound, of voices and televisions in other apartments, for the rest of the year made fuzzy by or mediated through the fan's shuttling. Even now, I noticed that the decorative peacock feather on top of the fridge was still. That stillness comprises, for me, an inalienable continuity with the child who first observed this world of relatives in Calcutta.

'Have you noticed who's come?' said Rini didi, as, on our way out, we stood at the door. With an effort bara mamima opened her eyes and nodded – barely.

A friend visiting from London tells me how he likes the Calcutta Christmas much more than he likes the English one. I do too; but he has specific reasons. And he has no memory of a Calcutta Christmas to refer back to; Calcutta, in effect, has no past for him – he's only been here once before.

'There's not much sign of the crucifix here,' he says. 'You don't have that awful mournfulness of Christianity. It's all about Santa,' he concludes, nodding. He has seen gigantic simulacra of the bearded gift-bearer in shopping malls; in front of restaurants. Although globalisation, in its full-blown form, is yet to reach Bengal, its apparitions, this December, are clearly visible: thus the striking Kumbhakarna-like dimensions of many of the Santa Clauses. 'And there aren't that many nativity scenes,' he says. 'In fact, I haven't seen any.'

He's right; it's an absence I hadn't noticed, perhaps with good reason. In Aparna Sen's lovely first film, *36 Chowringhee Lane*, the director almost forces an analogy when she plays a recording of a tenor singing, stratospherically, 'Silent Night' over visuals of destitutes sleeping on bridges and pavements. To find a representation of the nativity, one might need to go to a church; but, on the whole, the miraculous birth is unremarked upon. The predominant atmosphere of Christmas here has never been one of solitary stocktaking or of the notion of the return of God to earth, but of make-believe.

For me, the principal emblem of Christmas in Calcutta is neither Santa, nor the nativity, nor the Cross, but the Christmas tree. Almost no one in Calcutta has seen a real one. It enters certain spaces – the middle-class living room; the showroom and shop; the cafe – but it's we who, with its seasonal proximity, are travelling inadvertently towards the faraway. With its fake, shiny bristles, it represents a journey. It's also a reminder that the faraway can be manufactured – perhaps is *always* manufactured. No one misses the actual Christmas tree; to eventually see one is not so much a disappointment as a matter of slight puzzlement. I saw real Christmas trees again recently, being sold on a pavement in the Angel in London, unloaded from a truck, arranged, and covered in gauze, so that they resembled, somewhat, the inert botanical figures in *Invasion of the Body Snatchers*. I was fascinated by them, but received no final illumination, as they seemed a bit off the point; as Christmas outside of Calcutta seems generally. Once you've experienced a genuine transplantation (a genuine fake, as it were, an offshoot that takes on its own life), you lose, strangely, your appetite for, and your capacity to recognise, the original. This might explain, from more than four decades of living memory, the historical radiance of the Christmas trees of New Market.

What do people in this city, now that it's neither moored to its past nor part of a definite future, do as the new year approaches? They celebrate; they eat out. The rich and well-to-do have an internal map (mostly of avenues and lanes in South Calcutta) of houses and parties they must visit or avoid; or they'll romp in a club, dancing on a lawn to a band as the old year dies out. Others go to Park Street.

This New Year has probably been around in Bengal for two hundred years. The Bengali new year, which might be more than a millennium old, is the first day of the month of Baishakh, in early summer, usually the 14th of April, give or take a day for the variations in the almanac. Once, the New Year must have been a curiosity, a strange, amusing diversion to be smiled at, neither comfortably of this place nor to be wholly ignored (what *was* this thing?); but now it's the Bengali new year that's become ceremonial and arcane, part of a continuity that's even more make-believe than Christmas. On the first day of Baishakh, at least some men dress up for a day as 'Bengalis', wearing the intricately pleated cotton dhuti that was, even until the sixties, the most elegant attire a Bengali man could be seen in, horribly difficult, like the sari, to master, but worn always with a suggestion of casualness. Such were the contraries of the bhadralok.

My wife, who works as a scholar on the nineteenth century, has pointed out a poem to me called 'Ingraji Naba Barsha' – 'The English New Year' – by the (she thinks underrated) poet Iswar Gupta. It first appeared in 1852, a time just preceding the tumultuous change of 1857 (when the Sepoy Mutiny led to colonial power passing from the East India Company to the Crown, and formalised the Raj), and is canny and mildly satirical; R reminds me it's also deeply attentive to the real, in the way it captures that occasion with the urgency of a bulletin. Iswar Gupta was a tremendously popular poet in his time – perhaps *the* Bengali poet – but, after the preponderance of the new bhadralok humanism from the 1860s onward, after the ascendancy of the 'new' Calcutta (which, one hundred and fifty years later, is old, ruined, maybe even dead), he was no longer deemed a serious poet, and then ignored and forgotten. Iswar Gupta is not a poet of 'emotion recollected in tranquillity', as Tagore, at certain moments, might seem to be.

Bankimchandra Chatterjee, the first Bengali novelist, called him 'jaha achhe tahar kobi', or the 'poet of what's at hand' (for his subjects included pineapples and goats); my wife, echoing D.H. Lawrence, says he's a 'poet of the present'. Iswar Gupta is not a poet of memory, or the personal or historical perspective; but that doesn't mean he's ahistorical. History is not the annals; it's what happens around us when we're unaware it's history. It's Gupta's unawareness of himself, his subjects, or of Calcutta as something separate called 'history', in a static, retrospective sense, that makes them all bustle with it. As a poet, he has recourse to devices common to traditional Bengali poetry – such as onomatopoeia – that later poets would use temperately, if at all, in a more Sanskrit-derived, literary manner, but which he employs shamelessly and with a radical outrageousness, as a response to the odd transitory society he inhabits. R writes that, in 'Ingraji

Naba Barsha', the poet 'initially describes a white man . . . joyous and indulgent, well-dressed in his well-decorated home. At his side, his wife looks "fresh" in a "polka-dotted dress" (*"maanmode bibi shab hoilen* fresh / Feather-*er folorish phutikata* dress").' The English words dropped liberally in the two lines – 'fresh', 'feather', 'dress' – aren't really comparable to the comfortable melange-like contemporary chatter of the globalised Indian middle class; they're used in the way the lower classes traditionally use English – to pepper a sentence; to mutter a jocular barb; to pass a sexual insult about an upper-class woman. Midway into the poem, 'the poet imagines himself to be a fly accompanying these two' – the Englishman and his polka-dotted wife – 'on their carriage to church' (all these churches still exist mysteriously in different parts of the city), 'sometimes sipping from their glass of sherry, sometimes sitting on her gown or her face and happily rubbing its wings'. In what incarnation but that of a pest would the man on the street partake of the slopes of a memsahib's breasts? For Iswar Gupta, at this point, 'poet' and 'pest' seem interchangeable. The next scene describes the astonishing dinner back at the Englishman's house, 'evoked almost entirely and only through sound':

> *Very best sherry taste merry rest jaté*
> *Aage bhage den giya srimatir haaté*
>
> *Kot kot kotakot tok tok tok*
> *Thhun thhun thhun thhun dhok dhok dhok*
>
> *Chupu chupu chup chup chop chop chop*
> *Shupu shupu shup shup shop shop shop*
>
> *Thhokash thhokash thhok phosh phosh phosh*
> *Kosh kosh tosh tosh ghosh ghosh ghosh*

Hip hip hurré daké whole class
Dear madam you take this glass.

As R points out, this doesn't, largely, need translating, 'except the framing couplets, of which the first one says that the very best sherry that makes the rest merry is to be given to the missus before anybody else, while the one at the end is almost entirely in English except for the word *daké*, which means calls'. A great deal of movement and physical activity is captured from that New Year's Day – '*Kot kot kotakot tok tok tok*' probably the sound of heels ascending the steps and then authoritatively hitting the floor of the drawing room; '*thhun thhun thhun*' the pitch of the cutlery; '*dhok dhok dhok*' the sound ascribed usually to the rapid drinking of water, but here, almost certainly, of alcohol. The particular shape and form of these sounds were still unexpected to the Bengali ear. The terse, consonantal sound of English is also probably being alluded to, and mocked. Indians who didn't and don't know English, and want to mimic the way it's spoken, make brief plosive noises: 'phat', 'phoot', 'phut'. So there's a belligerence to Iswar Gupta's poem, the petulance of the poet / pest; it bubbles with resentment and energy.

Some of these sounds are audible in the Bengal Club as 2010 arrives, as they are in other clubs and residences – the '*thhun thhun thhun*' of forks, spoons, and knives, the '*dhok dhok dhok*'. Then, on Russell Street, there's a great deal of what was absent from Iswar Gupta's time: the honking of horns. These are the cars that have queued up, in futility, for Park Street. In the Bengal Club New Year's Eve garden party, meanwhile, they're playing 'Scarborough Fair' and 'Blowin' in the Wind'. R writes, of the onomatopoeia in Iswar Gupta's poem, that its 'sheer presence of being' turns the poem into a 'live playback recording of the changing shape of the everyday on New Year's Day, 1852 . . .' Tonight, too, is noise.

We're foolhardy to be in Park Street. We've eaten at a Chinese restaurant, and my parents and daughter have gone back home – the press is daunting as my wife and I make our way towards the traffic lights. We shouldn't be here (because, really, we have nothing to do) and never are at this time of the year (except in a car, in crippled transit), but I'm drawn to it for many reasons: for the narrative I myself have woven around it in the course of writing this book, and am now entangled in; for the people themselves – those who've gathered here and of whom Utpal Basu said to me gravely in a different context: '*Erai amader nagarik*' – '*These are our citizens.*' This wasn't an admission of defeat; it was an assertion that you can't deny change or say it has nothing to do with you. Young men in mock-leather jackets swarm the pavements; the street pulsates with excitement as the year dies. Park Street isn't their natural terrain; out of a suppressed sense of exclusion, maybe, and from genuine excitement, they walk about in proprietary groups in front of the famous restaurants of the middle class – Bar-b-que; Moulin Rouge; Peter Cat. A resentment simmers, which somehow gets channelled into the celebrations.

We cross the road to Mocambo; from a distance I see someone at the ironing stall, not Nagendra, but a deputy – the figure is diligently pressing clothes, now, at 11.15 p.m. On his haunches, Ramayan Shah is flattening dough for puris; some he has compressed into pastry-like shapes. A kadhai reveals the filling – tiny cauliflower florets, their tips rusted like dried blood. This snack costs a paltry two rupees a plate.

Back in Park Street, we are stranded in front of the erstwhile Skyroom. Motorbike after motorbike passes down the road, two men on each one, and, as midnight approaches, the men at the back raise both arms, in a strange symbolic gesture, and roar; the crowd in leather jackets streaming behind us roars in response. It is like a victory lap.

The couple standing beside us clearly don't belong: a dark, distinguished-looking man of South Indian origins in a blazer;

his slight, unobtrusive white wife. We are nervous, and are undecided about whether or not to be participatory; 'It's like Times Square,' she says in an unidentifiable American accent, smiling, 'except Times Square's worse.' Their daughter and their adopted son (who, it emerges, was born here) are partying at Park Hotel further up; while they're awaiting their hired car, which is clearly stuck in the slow rerouted traffic inching into Park Street, to pick them up. They live, says the slightly harried gentleman in the blazer, in Philadelphia. I'm interested in his wife's remark about Times Square; I believe there used to be genuine concordances between New York and Calcutta – of mood, atmosphere, ethos – but it never occurred to me to compare the drifting menace of Times Square with what used to be the enchantment of Park Street. Yet I also recognise this habit, of making comparisons under duress. Edward Said had written in an essay that '[m]ost people are principally aware of one culture, one setting, one home; exiles are aware of at least two, and this plurality of vision gives rise to an awareness of simultaneous dimensions, an awareness that – to borrow a phrase from music – is contrapuntal. For an exile, habits of life, expression or activity in the new environment inevitably occur against the memory of these things in another environment.' I understand this completely, except that I balk at the bathos of the 'exile'. I prefer 'traveller', with all its contemporary associations of banality – duty-free shops; frequent flyer miles; waiting for a car. In the midst of the ordinariness and exasperation of travel, it's certain – or at least possible – that the past will come back to you. And, unbeknownst to us, midnight has crept upon us. There's an unsettling roar, pre-verbal, vociferously threatening – intended not so much to express as to drown out. 'Happy New Year,' insists the woman, to which I hastily add, 'Happy New Year.' 'Happy New Year', 'Happy New Year' concur, on the kerb, R and the distinguished-looking gentleman.

Names

Naturally, I'm queried sometimes about why I returned to India – and why to Calcutta. Although India, in the so-called boom, might be a place for a certain kind of professional to come back to, Calcutta, on that boom's outer reaches, with its precipitous political future, is a curious place to make a home. Unless, of course, you belong to that species condemned, all over the world, to uniqueness – I mean the only child – and you have ageing parents. Only recently, a woman whom I know slightly told me on the telephone that she was going to leave Bonn and her thriving career in the UN in Europe and return to New Zealand. 'I worry about my parents, especially about my father, these days,' she laughed with some embarrassment. 'It's the curse of the only child.' If not the only child, then, in India, the sole male offspring. Not long ago, my wife met a young, good-looking, clearly successful couple in a friend's house for tea. She heard the man had relocated from an enviable position in a foreign bank in Bombay to a similarly responsible position in what is, however, today's Calcutta. Was it disaffection that

had caused the move? Not really. It was something that's older
in this part of the world than disaffection, and more obstinate:
the sense of familial duty. The father had aged, and the son
decided (after discussions with a tolerant wife) that he should
be nearby.

Yet living in Calcutta is hardly to live in Kabul or Baghdad or
even Johannesburg – nor is it comparable to inhabiting a suburb
in Atlanta, or moving to Ipswich. As a city, it's neither too threateningly alive, nor too defunct (if extinction can be measured
and graded). Anyway, if Calcutta today suffers in comparison,
it's not really to other cities, but principally to itself and what it
used to be. Anyone who has an idea of what Calcutta once was
will find that vanished Calcutta the single most insurmountable
obstacle to understanding, or sympathising with, the city today.

I had several reasons for coming back; some of them emerged
without warning in the late nineties, and others had been with
me for as long as I could remember. For instance, homesickness. I couldn't recall a time when I hadn't been homesick and
lonely in England. Partly, this had to do with my own – as I discovered, very human – need for light. I was impressed when, in
the early eighties, I read a report in an English newspaper about
how people in the north of England wilted, psychologically and
spiritually, as plants do physically, from an absence of light in
the winter. To this lack, I'd add my abhorrence of silence – a
high-pitched pressure on the eardrum clearly audible to me in
an English room.

Connected to this is the often problematic fact that I'm a
musician. I turned, in the late seventies, from what had been
till then my favourite form – American folk-rock – to Indian
classical vocal music. The regime of classical music – practising
with my teacher and with accompanists; picking up new
bandishes and compositions and ragas – ensured I spent several

months a year in India even when I was a student in England. To be in India – in Bandra in Bombay after my father's retirement – was to be reborn, to experience sunlight, stillness, birdcall, morning, evening, for a limited duration only, to realise it was possible to revisit some of the first experiences of your life as if they were new. Those student years consisted of a series of such rebirths, because of the end-of-term breaks in British universities, and the cheap flights (when my parents moved to Calcutta, I began to fly Bangladesh Biman and Royal Jordanian) out of London. But there were the flights back. If I got to know birth, I also got to know death. There's no rationality to this – to why I'm possessed by posthumousness, uselessness, torpor – all symptoms and traits of dying – before I leave. But who ever said that clinging to life could be explained rationally? I suppose what I mean is – India, for whatever reason, is synonymous to me with life; and you don't love life by weighing its advantages.

The Bengali poet Joy Goswami saw me in the doldrums, in my Calcutta flat, on the eve of yet another departure to England in 2002. A meeting had been arranged by a journalist from the *Statesman*; Joy and I were to be in conversation, covering, randomly, a range of interests. The *Statesman* would transcribe and publish this conversation. The only available time in our calendar was this afternoon prior to the flight early the next morning.

Generally, on the day before I leave – sometimes, even two or three days before departure – I stop doing anything; I stop moving. I don't like engagements on the day. I'm giving myself completely to the time left me – in the process, becoming a bore. I go through the motions, inwardly disengaged; I'm convinced I have no right any more to be here. Dusk is the worst time – the closing of the day, which is as beautiful a time as the day's beginning, because it has its own signals of continuity, gesturing towards return and the day that follows. This is what is most insulting; that none of those multifarious signals – the stripe on a shaalik's wing, a schoolboy's shout on coming home from school – are addressed to me. I am alone in the universe in knowing that this orchestration of the day's close, leading to the new day's arrival, is absorbing everyone else in its rhythm, but that I'm irrelevant to it. Joy is shrewd enough to notice (as he and Chitralekha of the *Statesman* are served tea) my isolation, my disguised posthumousness. He calls it *bishonnota* – 'deep sadness'.

'It's peculiar to musicians,' he says. 'I have a friend who is a musician who's exactly the same way before he travels.'

None of the reasons for my return had to do with Calcutta being what it's still often stubbornly called – a 'capital of culture'. When my parents moved here in 1989, I realised slowly that it had ceased being any kind of centre. Of course, over it (already stunned as it was by power cuts) still hung, like a presence that wouldn't go away, the shadow of the Bengal Renaissance – that is, the great changes that had taken place from the late eighteenth century onward to produce figures like Rammohun Roy and Debendranath Tagore, who created the Brahmo Samaj, the reformist sect that decisively turned away from an 'incorrigibly plural and various' Hinduism towards a unitarian, Upanishadic world view. And this unitarianism, through which, in effect, man discovers he's suddenly alone in the universe (despite a putative God), would have deep philosophical implications for the appearance of liberal modernity in Bengal, with men like Madhusudan Dutt, Bankimchandra Chatterjee, Rabindranath Tagore, and others feeling compelled, as it were, to take upon themselves the hard task of creating a new literature and culture: a new image of man himself. I had no illusions about the present-day inhabitants of the city having any real interest in this history.

The eighties was, as I said, a time of rebirth. There was the actual feeling of being born another time as I stepped off the cheap flight from Heathrow and experienced, in the hour after arrival, the onrush of life and traffic becoming real. Related to these student's journeys was my birth as a writer – or perhaps, again, rebirth, as I'd been writing for more than a decade, trying to be, at different times, Enid Blyton, Rudyard Kipling, one of the anonymous poets of the Bhagavad Gita, T.S. Eliot, Tagore, Samuel Beckett. Then, in London and later in Oxford, I had a deep desire to revisit home, to escape everything dead and still around me – by home I mean India, perhaps even Calcutta (though it wasn't my home), and by India and Calcutta I mean 'life'. I was possessed by a desire, especially when I was reading, to revisit life, and, in Oxford, I found it was possible to do so in R.K. Narayan's stories – a writer I'd earlier dismissed, as D.H. Lawrence said the English once dismissed classic American writing as 'children's literature'. But, in those years, I found it possible to discover Calcutta in the oddest of places – in the mining town in D.H. Lawrence's *Sons and Lovers*; Katherine Mansfield's New Zealand, which she said she wanted to explore to the last detail, including the 'creak of the laundry basket'; the across-the-balcony exchanges in Naipaul's Trinidad; the economically conjured-up neighbourhoods and streets in the stories in *Dubliners*. Calcutta, for me, was a particular idea of the modern city, and I found it in many forms, works, and genres. Why, in 1999, did I move to it? Because I'd been rehearsing that journey for years: as a child, in trips from Bombay in the summer and the winter; and later – in my continual search for a certain kind of city – in my reading. And Calcutta would make its way back to me, unexpectedly, through Irish literature and Mansfield and Eudora Welty and the writing of the American South. There was movement on both sides, or from many sides. Even later, when I finally became a published writer, that city would be given back to me by my readers, from their strange identifications and instants of recognition. My friend Aamer Hussein, the British-Pakistani short-story writer, told me how Mai Ghoussoub, the publisher of London's Saqi Books, had, on reading the section on Chhotomama shaving in the balcony in *A Strange and Sublime Address*, phoned him and laughed: 'It reminds me of Beirut!' I was delighted, like a child, but not surprised. Was this a 'contrapuntal reading', in Said's manner? Or was it evidence of how, even in modernity – perhaps *particularly* in modernity – we have shared, primal memories of the spaces we've inherited and which came to exist in the world in the last two hundred years? When we speak of shared memories, we hint at some uninvestigated, autochthonic past. But what of the world, the cities, that arose in the nineteenth century? Are *we* the exiles and travellers of the last two centuries, or our ideas and visions?

What do I mean by 'modernity', in the special sense I discovered through the Calcutta I knew as a child? Not electric lights, telephones, cars, certainly, though it might encompass these – we had plenty of those in Bombay. I'll keep it brief: by 'modernity' I have in mind something that was never new. True modernity was born with the aura of inherited decay and life. My first impressions of Calcutta from the mid-sixties are of a Chowringhee whose advertisements shone through the smog; and of my uncle's house in Pratapaditya Road in Bhowanipore, which, with its slatted windows, seemed to have stood in that place forever. It was built, in fact, roughly forty years before my first becoming conscious of it. Similarly, the city itself – which is by no means old by the standards of Rome, Patna, Agra, or even London – is, actually, fairly new, its origins traceable to three hundred and twenty years back in time, the groundwork for the Calcutta we now know probably laid no more than two centuries ago. Yet if you look at paintings and photographs, and see old films of the city, you notice that these walls and buildings were never new – that Calcutta was born to look more or less as I saw it as a child. I'm not referring here to an air of time-lessness; the patina that gave to Calcutta's alleys, doorways, and houses their continuity and disposition is very different from the eternity that defines mausoleums and monuments. It's this quality I'm trying to get at when I speak of 'modernity'.

Let me provide an example. In the Courtauld Gallery in London hang several exceptional Cézannes, among which is one of the painter's several viewings of the Montagne Sainte-Victoire, and the fairly empty countryside (barring a few houses nearby) before it. This view is framed by a large pine tree, its branches flailing against space, but not quite obscuring the view of the mountain. On the right-hand side, at the bottom of the mountain, where the empty yellow stretches and rectangular patches of greenery end, you notice something horizontal – except that it's rising very slightly at an angle – with dark arches, like a bridge. It is a culvert. The curator's small note points out that by including the culvert in the scene Cézanne is marking the incursion of modernity into the world of nature, or words to that effect. My first response was to disagree. For 'nature', in keeping with the simmering abandon of the time, and remi-niscent of his younger contemporary Gauguin, is painted by Cézanne with a palette of incongruous colours, with pinks, oranges, and yellows: the scene, far away from the city, crack-les with Parisian newness. The culvert, once you notice it, is the only thing that looks genuinely, deeply, old: instinctively, Cézanne paints it an organic, faded brown. Its colour is identi-cal to the rocks on that side of the mountain; the rest of the Montagne Sainte-Victoire has iridescences of pink. Cézanne is telling us, with great delicacy, that modernity in the nineteenth century is indistinguishable from nature; perhaps it *is* nature – in some ways, the culvert, which has emerged from the rock, seems more of its place than the mountain itself. The shadows etched under the arches are mysterious, like a womb's dark-ness; and since Cézanne himself is a progeny of the modern, how can he not feel that it's older and darker than the earth and the mountain?

I spoke about my rebirth as a writer in the mid-eighties – which would lead me to start writing my first novel in 1986. About this time, India, too, was having a rebirth. But the two births weren't coeval or connected; they took place near each other without being affected by that proximity in any way. I noticed, in a surly, suspicious fashion, the nation's second birth, though I became aware of it as such only in retrospect; the nation, naturally, didn't notice mine.

Mine was a sort of event that's perhaps unsurprising in the lives of poets, but incongruous for a yet-to-be novelist. Allen Ginsberg describes it occurring in his life as an episode – in the late forties, he was masturbating ('jacking off') in Harlem, his life having plumbed a new low, while (speaking of incongruities) he had a book of Blake's poems open at his side. On that page, fortuitously, was 'Ah, sun-flower' – 'Ah, sun-flower! weary of time,/Who countest the steps of the sun:/Seeking after the sweet golden clime,/Where the traveller's journey is done.' Ginsberg had just come, and was lying in a stupor – 'that state . . . of hopelessness, or dead end' – his eyes 'idling' over the poem, which he'd read so many times that 'it didn't make any particular meaning' – when he suddenly understood it was addressed to *him*; *he* was the sunflower. And, almost at once, he heard a 'deep earthen grave voice': 'I didn't think twice . . . [it] was Blake's voice . . . so completely tender and beautifully . . . ancient.' And then a thought arrived: 'I suddenly realised that *this* existence was *it!*' I'm especially struck, in this story, by Ginsberg's account, in the light of this thought that had just come to him, of the view from his window: 'What I was speaking about . . . was . . . that the cornices in the old tenement building in Harlem . . . had been carved very finely in 1890 or 1910. And were like the solidification of a great deal of intelligence . . . and love also. So that I began noticing in every corner where I looked evidences of a living hand . . .' I'm moved by the invocation of cornices; because no sooner had I had my intimation in 1985, when I was twenty-three ('that *this* existence was *it*'), than, for some reason, I thought of Calcutta, a city I had *not* grown up in, and recalled, particularly, those household features that had always absorbed me: the slatted windows, the lintel that came to rest horizontally to secure a doorway, the round iron knocker-like rings that hung from the stone sides of the terrace.

I mentioned that, around then, India too was having its rebirth. My parents had moved from the centre of Bombay to St Cyril Road in Bandra: an idyllic location. I spent a year there between graduating from University College London and going to Oxford as a graduate student. I was thinking about Calcutta, and had no higher ambition than to write a novel about a boy spending his vacations there with his cousins – much as I did when I was a child. The idea of the holiday excited me for some reason: I had no idea why. The book wouldn't have a plot as such, although I was hardly conscious of this, and, anyway, wouldn't have seen that as a problem; what it would have, instead of story, was the boy's sense of escape and freedom.

Change was afoot, and there was more than a hint of danger heralding the nation's rebirth. After midnight, in Bombay, the underage children of the rich would drive their parents' cars at high speed, losing control and running over people asleep on the pavement. I recall the earliest of these calamities took place on Turner Road, which St Cyril Road opened on to; people slept out on the pavement there, and, one morning, we heard how they'd been killed when a young man's car went berserk temporarily. But maybe this wasn't the first of these incidents involving young people and cars: we knew the ghazal singer Jagjit Singh's family, and learnt one day of how his son had driven very fast out of the house, crashed into a lamppost, and died instantly. It's not that there weren't mishaps in Bombay before; they happened all the time. It's just that these accidents had a different ethos; they were marked by a curious impatience and irresponsibility, a mood the country hadn't quite had access to before. When you read about them in the local paper, it was difficult to tell what caused the disquiet you felt – the incident itself, or the sort of energy it represented.

The nation had a second birth, and so did Hinduism. I remember noticing a new slogan on the backs of trucks in Bombay: *Garv se kaho hum Hindu hain* – Say proudly, I'm Hindu. The trucks were full of exultant, huddled demonstrators. Not just India and Hinduism – the world was in the midst of another birth. The moment would reach its apotheosis with the destruction of monuments: the Berlin Wall; the Babri Mosque. All these were events linked to the annunciation of a new order.

From the nineteenth century onward, Hinduism existed, in the minds of Orientalist scholars and tourists of spiritual experience, in connection with slowness, dilatoriness, and vacancy. The annual growth rate of the gross domestic product was called, in a joke that had currency in bureaucratic circles, the 'Hindu rate of growth': this, in the protected economy created by Jawaharlal Nehru. After Manmohan Singh's 'liberalisation' of the economy in 1991, the trade barriers coming down for the first time, and the concerted dismantling of the Babri Mosque by the Bharatiya Janata Party's foot soldiers a year later, Hinduism appeared to embrace velocity and real time; under the BJP government that followed, the 'Hindu rate of growth' became an urgent matter.

Two cities were altered by the alchemy of globalisation. The first one I grew up and was unhappy in: Bombay. By the eighties, it suddenly felt less like a commercial centre, which it had been for decades, than a nerve centre. Its metier – of glitter, movement, reflected surfaces, of existing in a perpetual present – had merged perfectly with the world's new-found metier, and India's. The eighties confirmed Calcutta's economic decline under the Left Front government, its (to use the word Joyce once used of Dublin) 'paralysis'; but they also announced that the sort of lyricism that Calcutta represented, with its central paradox – that life and the imagination would hover most palpably over decay and dereliction – was now unviable. By the early eighties, the death knell of modernity was being sounded everywhere. Calcutta was one of the great casualties of that passing; it's not that it suddenly began to fail, but that its long history and aura of failure, cherished and even metamorphosed into something vital by the Bengali imagination, ceased to be intellectually or artistically instructive or illuminating. Without the transformative effect of the imagination, decay is just decay, disrepair plain disrepair. This is what happened to Calcutta in the eighties.

Like certain genres and styles of writing, certain cities too become unviable at particular points in history: they become impossible to inhabit or use; without our realising it, they grow inaccessible. Look at the career of poetry in the globalised world, for instance; its story of near extinction. To write a poem today sometimes feels like rehearsing a bygone moment of history. To live in Calcutta, to negotiate the maze of its lanes and alleys, almost feels the same. I could still tap the magic of its neighbourhoods when I wrote my third novel, *Freedom Song*, in the mid-nineties; but, after that, I felt I couldn't do so any longer – just as a teenager might outgrow a 'phase' of writing poems, or a writer feel compelled to discard an evocative, fluent style of writing for an intransigent one. And, for this reason, I resisted, for three years, the idea of writing this book, until the poet Utpal Basu's comments made me think again of the 'citizens' who live in the city today – khurima, the old woman outside Sealdah Station; the merrymakers, exuding menace and discomfort, on Christmas Day on Park Street.

The difficulty of evolving as an artist, of resigning yourself to the fact that the styles and visions most precious to you have lost their place and urgency, of accepting that what you once thought was uninteresting is now full of possibility! One can see the photographer Raghubir Singh working his way through this dilemma. Here was a man clearly formed by Henri Cartier-Bresson and Satyajit Ray, by the pursuit of the image in which the random and the everyday, in a lucky moment, come together.

This quiet pursuit marks his famous photographs of Calcutta, in the book *The Home and the Street*. Yet, today, most of those pictures look strangely dated – it's as if Singh can't quite access Cartier-Bresson's aesthetic, and Calcutta's; all the details are there, but something impedes him; Cartier-Bresson and Calcutta, by 1988, are slipping into history, and Singh must have a troubling intimation of this fact.

Then, five years before he died, Singh published, in 1994, *Bombay: Gateway to India*. He came into his own in these photographs – of rich people's villas and drawing rooms; celebrities; handcart pullers; balloon sellers; a glass shop front; the interiors of a jeweller's. The world had changed; Raghubir Singh changed too. He turned from Cartier-Bresson's and Satyajit Ray's provisional and natural movements on the streets; instead, as V.S. Naipaul notices, glass recurs as a motif in these photographs – shop windows; glass doorways; mirrors; chandeliers. Where there was, once, organic colour, light, and shadow, there are now constant hints of refracted, ambivalent, polished surfaces. Singh doesn't become a postmodernist – but he abandons the wonderstruck poetry of derelict modernity to become a formalist chronicler of a new terrain.

This is a little parable about cities and genres; how, while some of them lose their imaginative centrality, others take their place.

I've said that, as Calcutta fizzled out with globalisation, two other cities moved centre stage decisively. One, Bombay, became effectively what Calcutta once had been, *the* Indian metropolis, with the invigorating, defining extremities of experience that great cities possess. But Bombay was always singular. The other city, New Delhi, which had been waiting in the wings in the decades since Independence, was an unimportant, provincial small town. It was bureaucratic, boring, notwithstanding the fact that it was the capital of India. My memories from the late sixties and the early seventies are, however, charming: I had the sense of having visited the distilled, slightly fusty quiet of a town like Poona, or a cantonment area. There were trees and avenues and, since we only ever went in the winter, bare branches against the sky. At least a few people we knew had houses with fireplaces: that was one of the things I liked about Delhi – that, unlike Bombay and Calcutta, people could live there in houses. Many of these had probably come up in the sixties. They had a bare, spacious, habitable air that only just escaped governmental dullness into a post-Independence tranquillity. My New Delhi, in those few visits, was determined by a privileged topography: Connaught Place, Khan Market, the Jantar Mantar, the Ashoka and the Oberoi Intercontinental hotels, the India International Centre, which was then struggling to be born. None of these, however, felt like a hub, and that was what was pleasant about them: it was easy to believe, in Delhi, that life was happening somewhere else. Many of these areas had a weather that was postcolonial, post-Independence, and pre-globalisation: a genuine fragile socialist newness pertained to them, a little uninteresting, but unique, like a rare, carefully tended flower. There was no culture to speak of; instead, there were the state-sponsored museums we visited – an international dolls' museum; a museum of Gandhi's life – cautious places, and, like the textbooks at school, distrustful of personality; but, like the nation state of the time, doggedly uplifting. The nation state, and its great myth, 'unity in diversity', also strongly approached my mother and me from the various retail outlets she visited on Janpath: the national and regional handicrafts stores; and that many-tiered monument there, a paean to the rich layers of Indian identity, the Cottage Industries building.

I encountered the changed New Delhi in Oxford. It had receded in my consciousness. Delhi had been a place of indefatigable parliamentary activity – the politics of India is the politics of survival – of, in the eighties, political murders, Mrs Gandhi's assassination and its violent aftermath. But it was still difficult to experience it, with its India Gates and Avenues of Peace, as a city.

In Oxford, during my first year there, I sensed a change. It was difficult to put one's finger on it; shifts in attitude, in ideas, in power, are felt, in the beginning, as an unease, like a small physical discomfort. Almost all the Indian students I met in my first two years in Oxford – the ones who'd come there on the two or three available scholarships of prestige – were from Delhi, in particular, from St. Stephen's College. A minority of the Delhi students were from the Hindu College. The rest of the Indians were from other places. Everyone in India now knows of St. Stephen's, but, in 1987, it had no special resonance. Its aura and ascendancy as the leading educational institution in India was still in the making, as Delhi, as a centre of power, was also being made. In Oxford, I was a witness to the making, and had my first intimation of power. I remember it taking me a bit by surprise, as if the changes had happened without my knowledge, until I began to become aware of them in the students' rooms.

Most Delhi Indians had come to 'read' either history or politics or economics, or to do graduate work in these disciplines. They may not have been from Delhi originally; but (it quickly became clear) almost all the conduits in India to higher education in

Oxbridge were now in the capital. It didn't matter if you hadn't been born there; you needed to inhale its air, absorb the mood that made your aspirations and the aspirations of the nation state flow into each other. There was no looking back for them. Many were planning for further fellowships – the next stop would be an American university – or to return to India, some to the Indian Administrative Services or one of the other elite and elderly wings of the Indian bureaucracy. And as there was no pause to this onward march, these students seldom felt any homesickness. In fact, homesickness was seen as something ridiculous – a reference to a homesick person was accompanied by giggles. What were you *doing* here, if you were homesick?

The fascination for the Indian Administrative Service was puzzling. I hadn't come across it in Bombay, with its attraction to American business schools, or in Calcutta, with its worship of doctors and engineers. Not even Kipling, with his covert admiration of power, could view the Indian Civil Service – whose numbers once counted among the 'heaven-born' – without irony. And what about the 'idea of India', which I'd encountered as a child in Delhi in those handicrafts shops and in the Cottage Industries building? Could one entertain it without a mixture of affection and deprecation? But the 'idea of India' was no longer, in 1987, an indigenous, handwoven, state-subsidised thing: it was going to be, for the young self-appointed overcoat-and-scarf-wearing vanguard I met in Oxford, a proper vocation. They didn't regard this idea with irony – instead, they viewed it with a sense of custodianship. It was going to be in their safekeeping.

I live in India much of the year – but I can't say I like the India of today. That 'Delhi of the mind', which I first encountered in Oxford, which was then young and tentative, is, in 2011, entrenched and middle-aged. It sits on everything, unbudgeable: on university committees; the civil service; funding bodies; the print and electronic media. And you hear its voice through people who are talking all the time: not in drawing rooms, but on television. The television studio, and, really, the flashing screen itself, has taken over from the drawing room as the venue where the powerful and influential are invited to congregate and chatter.

And Calcutta had become, as the Americans might say, a dump. By the early eighties, Mother Teresa's profile as the face of eternity was so widespread that, in the Western world, this great city (*mahanagar*) of modernity, with its many contradictions and exacerbations, was seen as a present-day Galilee, a place of supernatural cures, of lepers awaiting the miraculous touch.

Within India itself, Calcutta had become a butt of jokes. This slow turn was fascinating; the former centre of 'culture', once admired for its eccentricity and waywardness, being ridiculed by other uppity cities like Delhi and Bombay for being obsolete and out of joint; for its unionised workplace, its permanent go-slow work ethic, its oppositional politics. Resistance to change and, eventually, to globalisation came to be seen as Bengali traits. It was a mood encouraged by the Left Front government, which came into power in 1977 and was never thrown out in a subsequent election: an economic climate within which 'sick' companies owned by the state were kept on life support, and private sector industry and fresh investment frowned upon. No amount of protestations to the contrary, and moves to lure investments, by the chief minister Jyoti Basu and his successor Buddhadeb Bhattacharya could alter what was now an immovable impression in people's minds – because the

Left Front government was entangled in a fiction of its own making.

From the colonial encounter onward, after which he had emerged in Calcutta as an altogether new breed, soon adept at the ways of the English intruder and then overreaching himself, the Bengali was seen as strange, pretentious, and untrustworthy by both the Englishman and the North Indian. Kipling had a savage distaste for him. My uncle, who was a bachelor and lived in London for decades, had, for his neighbour, a Pakistani, Aftab, who was also his closest friend. Once, Aftab, temporarily choosing to disregard my uncle's Bengali identity, cautioned him: '*Agar dekha saap aa raha hai aur Bangali bhi aa raha hai, pehle Bangali ko maro*' – 'If you see a snake coming towards you, and a Bengali approaching, kill the Bengali first.' My uncle took this as English crowds at Hyde Park received the invective poured on them by the speaker on the box: with delighted laughter. For, even in the seventies (from when I recount this snatch of conversation), the Bengali identity was unassailable; it didn't see itself as beleaguered. Besides, my uncle would have agreed that there was some truth to Aftab's aphorism. After all, the main casualties of Bengali pomposity and mean-mindedness had been Bengalis themselves. This generalisation could cover everyone from the man on the street to the highest beacon in the culture: Tagore's hostile treatment at the hands of Bengali critics is part of local cultural legend.

Let's take a brief look at the word 'Bengali' in relation to a prefix and an adjective. Almost every Bengali word has an opposite that can be arrived at simply, by adding a prefix, most often the letter 'a' (pronounced 'aw'): for instance, *manush* (human) and *amanush* (inhuman). I'm reminded that there's probably an infinite list of these, having just revised a chapter on prefixes with my daughter for the Bengali grammar paper in her first annual exams: *abichar*, *asadharan* et cetera, all of which she'd had to commit to memory.

Many of these opposites and negatives are traditional, and common to other Sanskrit-derived languages; but some also subtly reflect history. One such word, I think, must be *abangali*, which would have sprung into being around the time *bangali* did – its English-language equivalent, used almost as frequently as the Bengali word, and as casually, is 'non-Bengali'. It's telling that, generally, Bengalis aren't aware of the peculiarity of this term, or of the innocence with which they use it. It has none of the pointedness, the political crassness (and the datedness), of 'un-American'; it is regally unselfconscious. As the poet and translator P. Lal (whose origins were in North India, but who was domiciled in Calcutta and married to a Bengali) once wryly said to me over a dinner table during a reception at the governor's mansion, just when the occasion had ensured we'd run out of things to say to each other, 'It's a unique category, the "non-Bengali".' He hinted to me that he could think of no comparable way of viewing the world in another culture. Theoretically, it's a definition that encompasses the rest of the world; but it's usually used to refer, in an off-hand way, to the rest of India. What does it signify? A deficiency? An absence? Distance? Or a mode of being, imprecisely acknowledged? Or is it meant to complete and confirm 'Bengaliness'?

The adjective I had in mind is 'honorary'. There was a time, until two or three decades ago, when Bengalis were still regarded with affection and even admiration in the Anglophone Indian elite; and certain 'non-Bengalis' would describe themselves as – or be conferred with the title of – 'honorary' Bengalis. This meant that the person in question had a smattering of this refined language of Indian modernity – an Indian language that was actually used as a first language by a home-grown cosmopolitan elite – enough to say, with or without humour, *'Ami tomake bhalobasi'* ('I love you') or *'Apni kothai thhaken?'* ('Where do you live?'). These stray statements performed an incantatory 'open sesame' – into the bounded, charmed, small-scale world of 'Bengaliness'. The 'honorary' Bengali might be myopic; might be an aficionado of art-house cinema; might be politically left wing; might have taste for lyric poetry; a tendency towards the autobiographical; an appetite for fish; or display none of these traits.

A few days ago, an elderly gentleman, at whose house my wife and I are invited periodically to lavish teas, phoned me about a column he writes for a local newspaper. He expresses his kind esteem of my work by checking out his sentences with me. 'Tell me,' he said, 'does this sound okay? "The cultural scene in the city has been disfigured by the huge presence of non-Bengalis."' 'What do you have in mind?' I asked, wondering if he thought the opinion too strong to commit to print. 'Does the sentence sound portentous?' he said with concern. 'And what about "cultural scene"?' 'You could change it to "cultural landscape",' I said. He made the amendment at once. 'Do you think you might offend those non-Bengalis you mentioned?' 'I *want* to offend them,' he replied. 'I have only a few years left to live, and there's nothing I'd like better.'

The 'non-Bengali', here, is a euphemism for the Marwari; who is referred to slightingly in colloquial Bengali parlance as *Mero*. The Marwaris are from a province in Rajasthan called Marwar, migrants who moved to this city a century ago, and then, in the last twenty years, being naturally migratory, from the north of Calcutta to the smart bhadralok enclaves of the south. They're often traders made good; they're also from a community that has produced some of India's great industrialist families. The Marwari is a mercantile type; much of the energy and activity in this wavering metropolis emanates from him. Although he now largely controls the economy of the city, he's long been the object of satire in Bengali literature – often memorable satire. Rajnarain Basu, who wrote under the pen name Parasuram, and was one of the great Bengali humorists and writers of the mid-twentieth century, has a Marwari businessman in conversation with two corrupt, pusillanimous Bengalis in an early story, 'Sri Sri Siddheswari Limited'. The Marwari observes to his Bengali interlocutors, 'As your Rabi Thakur said so well, *"Vairagya sadhan mukti – so hamar naahi"*.' Parasuram is parodying many things here. Firstly, the Marwari's Bengali – unrecognisable as Bengali and yet instantly recognisable as Marwari Bengali – a mixture of Bengali, Hindi, and even Maithili, the expansive North Indian vowels not only destroying the rounded modulations of the Bengali language (the product of post-Enlightenment polite-ness), but killing a famous line from its most famous poet. The Marwari is (mis)quoting a Tagore poem: '*Bairagya sadhane mukti, sei path amaar noi*' – 'Salvation through renunciation – that path's not for me'. Tagore is making an important anti-romantic, anti-metaphysical statement: *I don't wish to turn away from life. The physical, the earthly, are important. Desire, and the urge for life, are important.* Parasuram's Marwari is, in his droll way, making an equally important point: that desire – albeit of a different kind; desire for material reward and well-being – is his chosen path and avowal. The businessman's interest in Tagore, in Bengali culture, is insincere and even self-servingly creative; and the satire is particularly rich because Parasuram knows the laughter is two-sided – that he's poking fun at the Marwari, and the Marwari is laughing at the Bengali; laughing, as the saying goes, all the way to the bank.

Grudging asides about Meros aren't entirely taboo among Bengalis even today; although, increasingly, they make you nervous. However, in the changed scenario of the present, in the new 'cultural landscape', it's safe to assume that Bengali jokes outnumber the Marwari ones. Yet even – perhaps particularly – genteel, educated Bengalis continue to sometimes make disparaging remarks about Marwaris. Paradoxically, there's been no backlash against minorities in Calcutta since the violence of Partition; the long reign of the Left Front government has, probably, made Calcutta at once the most untenable and the least xenophobic of the major Indian cities – of, possibly, the major cities of the world.

A few years ago, around 2007–08, newspapers in Calcutta announced that Bengali was now spoken by only 37 per cent of the city's inhabitants. People were shocked – or at least taken aback – by the figure. Here, clearly, was proof that Calcutta was no longer a Bengali city. Besides, if ever a city – rather than a nation or state or province – had been synonymous with a language, it was Calcutta. Part of the reason for this was the significant decisions taken in the 1860s by writers – by the wayward (but great) poet Michael Madhusudan Dutt and the novelist Bankimchandra Chatterjee – to abandon English early in their careers and turn to Bengali. To speak and write in Bengali from the late nineteenth century onward didn't, where the bhadralok was concerned, exclude a knowledge of English; it implied it, irrefutably. Speaking Bengali in Calcutta seventy years ago was unlike speaking English in London at the time; that is, it was the tip of a multilingual iceberg, with Hindi, Urdu, and English almost as readily available as Bengali and its Eastern dialects, and the backdrop comprising Gujarati, Tamil, Telugu, Punjabi, Armenian, Mandarin, Cantonese, Italian, Tibetan, Bhojpuri, Maithili, Oriya, Marwari, Assamese. Of course, visitors who've spent a few months in Calcutta will begin to speak some Bengali, because in many ways it's a language of the street and the offices and also of nooks, crannies, and recesses, of tea-tables covered with plastic, of friendships and confidences; and visitors, one imagines, gradually begin to make local friends, have conversations with neighbours, and exchange confidences. And yet, probably because it emerged from and was situated in a multilingual world, there has been no successful chauvinistic movement connected to the language. There was once a political party that called itself Amra Bangali (We Are Bengalis). They could've been something out of Parasuram: for his fictions can be at once dystopian and comical. The Amra Bangali gang went about in the early eighties blackening English-language signboards. Then, before they could mature from being a nuisance into a threat, they vanished.

Their job was actually accomplished in a more organised and far-reaching way by, paradoxically, the Left Front government. In 1983, under the CPI(M), English ceased to be taught at the primary level in Bengali-medium schools, for being an impediment to the progress of the less privileged who lived in a milieu that had little English. This ideological move, thirty years later, was seen to have been misled and not have benefited the disadvantaged classes and areas it was supposed to. It was reversed only in 2009. By then, the city had changed. It had entirely lost its aura of leadership ('What Bengal does today, India does tomorrow': thus the famous but obsolete formula from the nationalist Gokhale, once frequently quoted by Bengalis, and today only invoked with bitterness). The ingenuous Rajiv Gandhi, visiting Calcutta in 1985 as prime minister, had inadvertently informed its inhabitants that it was a 'dying city'. Out of the remnants of that city, and through a simple act of renaming, eventually arose a new one – without pedigree or history; large but provincial; inhabited but largely unknown – called 'Kolkata'.

The Bengali language was at the centre of a moment of sudden self-consciousness in Calcutta in the nineteenth century, the stirring and arms-stretching of individualism, the 'I' waking up from dormancy and sleep and speaking its name. What dreams this 'I' had had in the meanwhile we can only guess at. The 'I' also became the 'eye', open and looking at the world: and so, in Satyajit Ray's film *Pather Panchali*, we're first introduced to Apu, the boy, as an open eye. He's pretending to sleep; his sister Durga shakes him; the eye opens; light floods in. That light is consciousness. It illumined, in nineteenth-century Calcutta, literature; the academic disciplines; the professions; science. And the great names of that era contained radiance and illumination: Rabindranath – 'lord of the sun'; his older brother, the idiosyncratic, gifted, elegant Jyotirindranath – 'lord of light'. My own name, Amit, which means 'endless', has appended to it (by my father) a middle name I never use: 'Prakash' – 'light'. 'Endless light.' Last month, as I write this, I met another Amit, much older than me, who too has a middle name, 'Jyoti', meaning exactly the same thing. 'Amitava' is another name recruited for this purpose, a conjunction of two words, 'amit' and 'abha', or radiance. The names of ordinary-looking middle-class men in Bengal were, for four or five generations, replete with illumination.

When I'd visit Calcutta from England in the late eighties and early nineties, soon after my parents moved there, I'd sense there was something amiss. Even from above, from the aeroplane window, it looked poorly lit at night, with large patches of dark, compared to the bright, intricate city I used to view from the sky as a child. If the plane was landing in the daytime, you noticed that the verdant fabric that surrounds the city, with epic watery inlets – West Bengal is very fertile – was now bereft of the poetry that used to excite me as a boy when I gazed downward. Even the low houses that came closer as the plane descended – entirely unremarkable, entirely mysterious – which once seemed to me as if there was everything going on inside them, now looked part of a location in which nothing happens.

What had changed? I think it's to do with the decline and marginalisation of the Bengali language – through the disappearance of the bhadralok class; through the processes of globalisation – a language which, in its books, its poems, songs, stories, cinema, brought the city into being in the imagination. Calcutta is an imaginary city; it's in that realm that it's most visible and detailed and compelling. I remember the covers of my cousins' Puja annuals and of their collections of mystery stories, and the envy and inarticulate loss I'd feel upon studying them. But today? I turn to a snatch of conversation from the Scottish writer Alasdair Gray's novel, *Lanark*. 'Glasgow is a magnificent city. Why do we hardly notice that?' asks a colleague at art school of the protagonist Duncan; who replies: 'Because nobody imagines living here . . . if a city hasn't been used by an artist not even the inhabitants live there imaginatively.'

And this is largely true of this new, hazy, provincial metropolis, Kolkata, which came into being in 2001 – and explains why we know so little about it.

This city – Kolkata – is neither a shadow of Calcutta, nor a rein-
vention of it, nor even the same city. Nor does it bear anything
more than an outward resemblance to its namesake, Kolkata:
the city as it's always been referred to in Bengali. I myself can't
stand calling it any other name but 'Calcutta' when speaking
in English; just as I'll always call it 'Kolkata' in Bengali conversation. Is this because we – cities and human beings – have
contradictory lives that flow in and out of each other? To take
away one or the other name is to deprive the city of a dimension that's coterminous with it, that grew and rose and fell with
it, whose meaning, deep in your heart, you know exactly.

In 1999, for a number of reasons, I moved to this city that would
soon be without its name: though the official name-change
hadn't taken place. It was, to all purposes, already no longer
Calcutta.

For one, I'd had enough of England – not just its weather,
rain, and loneliness, but the things about it I'd grown to like:
its television, newspapers, and bookshops. I've been discussing
names; and I can say that, in the new Britain of the nineties,
many continued to carry old resonances, while they were actually being hollowed of meaning, emptied of what it was that
made one thing – or name – distinct from the other. The most
famous and striking example of this were the names of the two
major parties, Conservative and Labour, or New Labour. They
sounded like parties historically in opposition to each other;
in reality, of course, they weren't. The last great political war
in Britain after the miners' strike (which I'd watched agog for
hours on television, as one of the first serially televised political
upheavals) was the one between old Labour and New. The con-
frontations in the latter were less bloody; but its outcome was
decisive. New Britain was a country of consensus. Names in
the public domain that had meant different things now denoted
shades of one thing. For instance, I recall a time when BBC 2

and Channel 4 had particular textures and shapes. A time came – I don't know when, but it was in the late nineties – when I realised that, though those channels had the old, prickly names, the 2 and 4 always sticking out like a rebarbative angularity, they'd become no different from BBC 1 and ITV – which themselves had grown indistinguishable from each other, like heavyweight premier league football teams that always seem to be at war.

This happened also to English cities, towns, and villages – even to the distinctive connotations those generic appellations had. Once, on a coach from Oxford to Cambridge, half-nauseous because of the convoluted route, I noticed that every place we passed through (the coach doesn't take the motorway as it winds through the midlands) had a Tesco's in it and a Texaco outside it. This may seem too obvious today to mention, but then, in the mid-nineties, it was still a gradually unfolding realisation: that the idea of town, village, and city had become anachronistic. I felt, during that trip towards Cambridge, I had nothing left to discover in England; not that discoveries were no longer possible there, but that I had little access to them. Around the mid-nineties, I went to a dinner at a ground-floor flat in Southern Avenue in Calcutta in the winter, and was struck by the paintings on the walls. The flat was Ruby Pal Chowdhury's, of the Crafts Council, and her husband's; among the things I noticed in its informal atmosphere was a beautiful clay bust of Mrs Pal Chowdhury's mother-in-law: very lifelike and singular, painted white. The elder, late Mrs Pal Chowdhury seemed to have been, from the expression of the face, a remarkable person. 'But it was made by an ordinary artisan from Krishnanagar – no one famous,' protested Ruby Pal Chowdhury. 'And it's clay . . . very vulnerable. A fall could break it, and a leak in the roof could destroy it.' She seemed suddenly protective, in the midst of that dinner, of the mother-in-law. She showed us a portrait done in oil by an English painter called Harris, who lived in this city for some years in the 1920s: it was unmistakably the mother-in-law again, a young woman, wearing a red sari, gazing into a book. In its stillness, it was less like a picture of a figure than of a vivid cosmological shape: of a new universe that had come into being – which, when you looked closer at it, became a young woman in a sari, reading. I remember thinking that, though Calcutta was now to all purposes dead, it possessed some secrets, and that there were discoveries for me to chance upon here amidst the deceptive nullity – which, for whatever reason, I could no longer in England.

Names . . . Add to this the publishing houses, whose names I'd been quietly savouring like sensations in the late eight-ies as I wrote my first novel. Much glamour accrued to them. Heinemann, which first published me, had those alpine, canonical figures, D.H. Lawrence and Thomas Mann – and two emblems of an India that was fading: Anita Desai and R.K. Narayan. It had that symbol of writerly productivity, whom eve-ryone read and, suddenly, almost no one did, Graham Greene. To be part of this list was to insinuate oneself into a history and what felt like a pre-history. Thomas Mann – almost the begin-ning of the modern novel itself! Just around the corner was Secker and Warburg, where I secretly desired to be, publishing the more recalcitrant, poetic writers: like James Kelman.

Then, irrevocably, these names became interchangeable. As we know, most of them, by 1998 (just a year before I left), were bought over by two German conglomerates. People continued to use the names as if they meant something specific, like a detail in a story. Then they stopped speaking of them in that slightly childish, enchanted way. The world of publishing, and publishers' names, lost its potency or magic. Had I glimpsed them on the cusp of change, glimmering? Or had I just invented that world? Mann, a deceptive experimenter within the near-extinct forms of realist fiction, may have said 'yes' to the second question. Perhaps the meanings of all epochs are unstable, and you need to go on pretending, on some level (as Mann did), that they aren't. But to be *within* that world of publishing, as an interloper who'd gained entry into it eight years before, and to feel that it was now no longer itself, that it was essentially foreign, was hard.

I'd had enough of Britain under Blair. I returned to India.

The New Old Guard

I first met Nirupam Sen at a party. The list of invitees was small; our host was Manoj, a Marwari businessman with a middle-class air. By this I mean he neither looks like a trader nor an industrialist, but a man who has a university background and is in a job. Nevertheless, he *was* a businessman and was proud of it. The pride came from being something of a one-off, of having made of himself a small-scale success (which, in a booming global economy, and even in a resistant outpost like Calcutta, means considerable wealth), and having done it without the immemorial infrastructure of the Marwari business family. He confirmed his maverick status by casually and tastelessly referring to other Marwaris as Meros. Manoj's taste in acquaintances and contacts was eclectic: one could run into business types you'd never see anywhere else at his parties; local industrialists of stature, like Harsh Neotia of the construction business; whoever might be the British deputy high commissioner at the time (Manoj has a business venture in England); and the occasional politician, either from the centre right, like the effusive but slightly furtive-looking Dinesh Trivedi, or the unprepossessing Nirupam Sen from the left. Manoj himself was equanimous about his political affiliations. He spoke of his guests as individuals, enthusiastically, rather than in support of their particular political ideology.

This party probably took place in the summer of 2008. I say this because it happened in Manoj's flat and not on the lovely terraced garden he uses in the winter. I have other means of dating the event. I remember viewing Nirupam Sen as he stood in the distance – the minister for commerce and industry – not as someone on his way out, but one whose task had barely begun. For more than a decade now, the Left Front had been making noises about luring investment to Bengal, of encouraging rapid industrialisation. In the 2006 assembly elections the Front, under Buddhadeb Bhattacharya, successor to the imperious Jyoti Basu, had surprised everyone by returning to power in the state, mainly because the Opposition's Trinamool alliance, led by Mamata Banerjee, had imploded temperamentally. It had seemed that voters had desperately wanted a change of face, but had been obstinately denied it by the Opposition. Nirupam Sen knew this, and it made of him an attractively realistic and uncomplacent figure. Times had changed; the perpetuity of the Left could no longer be taken for granted; but he was still restrainedly upbeat about the job at hand, a job he'd been more or less entrusted: the industrialisation and economic revival of Bengal. It must have been summer, because had the global crash already occurred (once it did, it exposed capitalism's fragility, and gave a fleeting fillip to the Left's vision of the world), we'd have had a different conversation. Also, the great reversals in West Bengal had still not taken place, the developments that would put the Left government in a strange Hamlet-like mood, seeing itself as a caretaker government in 2010, a government that was, after thirty-three undisputed years, in transit, and, by its own admission, only symbolically in power. By 'reversals',

I mean, of course, the series of events through which Tata's Nano project, meant to produce the world's cheapest small car, had to make an ignominious egress from the state; and the general elections in 2009, which saw an alarming, and record, number of Left Front MPs lose their seats to the Trinamool Congress. At that dinner, all this was to come, and Nirupam Sen was characteristically low-key, but, I believe, optimistic.

When Manoj introduced me to Sen, I was already pretty well-disposed towards him. He had a reputation for being unostentatious, serious, and, despite being a hardcore Marxist, an advocate of change. There was an allegation against him – a 'canard', according to Manoj – of being involved directly in the Sainbari murders in Burdwan in 1970: gruesome killings of a family that had strong allegiances to the Congress party. In 2008, the case was as remote from the consciousness as the dead themselves; I myself hadn't heard of it. Anyway, industry in Calcutta had decided it had in Sen a person it could work with. Whatever he might be like with his comrades or to his enemies, whatever he was *really* like, in his conversation with me he was humane and non-ideological. In the end, it's hard to decide about the value of one's own impressions. Still, I realised I could open up with him in a way I couldn't with Bengali Marxist sympathisers – some of whom belong to my extended family. The latter used to be swift to take offence if you breathed any kind of criticism about the party or the state (the two had become conflated in their minds). Sen was easier to talk to; you didn't have to constantly worry about outraging him, as you might have if, for instance, you were speaking with the grand old man of Bengali Marxists, the last chief minister, Jyoti Basu. But this was the new face of the party under Buddhadeb Bhattacharya: less prickly, more approachable; more self-questioning, less defensive; less of a stickler, at least to the naive observer, for the Communist rulebook. So I wasn't wholly surprised when

Sen told me how close the party had been to losing power to Mamata Banerjee. We already knew this; nevertheless, the candid admission cleared the air. We discussed societies in transition; I reflected on how resistant and unionised Britain had become in the late seventies (around when the Left came to power in Bengal), how it took Thatcher to heartlessly, ruthlessly, break the unions, and the Labour Party to respond by mutating into New Labour. The situation in Bengal today was, in some ways, comparable. Sen nodded throughout. This is not to say that I, and presumably he, wanted the Bengali equivalent of Margaret Thatcher to emerge in Calcutta. But it was good to have the freedom to pursue these analogies till they fell apart, without, in Sen's company, having the ghost of self-censorship hover over the conversation. Such was the equable air of the minister for industrial reconstruction.

Almost three years later, in March 2011, I decided it was time to see Sen again. A lot had happened since that dinner; and the state assembly elections – the most important elections in sixty-four-year-old West Bengal since 1977 – would take place in April. After 2009, after the humiliating loss of Tata's Nano factory to Gujarat, and the setback in the general elections, the Left had retreated into a shell. It seemed to be biding its time, going through the motions of governance before its inevitable departure from office. Meanwhile, everywhere there had been talk, for more than two years now, of 'change' or *paribartan*. It originated in a seemingly spontaneous movement that came into being (with a great deal of middle-class support) in relation to the farmers and peasants of two obscure villages outside Calcutta, Singur and Nandigram. After the emergence of this movement, whose rhetoric of resistance and redressal at some point merged into the Trinamool Congress's rhetoric of removal – the removal of the Left Front government – the notion of 'change' in Bengal became a different one from the idea introduced not long ago by the communists: of change within the party and the state; of a calculated embrace of industrialisation, investment, and development. Now, 'change' came to imply the urgency of a change of government; and the Left Front came to be synonymous with repression and fixity. These thoughts had been in the air for a while, but suddenly they rose to the foreground of the consciousness. The mood was like a contagion in middle-class Calcutta and beyond; everyone, even those who didn't want to catch the infection, caught it, and showed all the symptoms. The Left must go.

At certain points in modern Indian history, obscure villages and locations, whose names invoke millennia of stasis, become incandescent with some debate that's central to the nation's consciousness. This happens without the nation necessarily having been aware of that issue's centrality – until the flashpoint, when the unknown place becomes a battleground. After that moment, the location may well enter the history books, while remaining, in every other sense, unimportant.

Sometimes the battle is a real one. For instance, who'd heard of Palashi, or Plassey, in Bengal, before Siraj-ud-daula capitulated to Clive's troops in 1757, opening the door to Empire? For that matter, who's heard of it since?

During the freedom struggle, an outpost called Chauri Chaura became briefly famous when a group of protesters set fire to a police station, causing Gandhi to suspend his satyagraha movement until it returned to non-violent ways.

The peasant uprising in a region called Telengana in the late forties was the first anti-landlord movement in independent India. Its successor, which emerged from the equally little-known Naxalbari in North Bengal, led to the first formal, and violent, articulation of Maoism.

In 1998, the right-wing Bharatiya Janata Party government exploded five nuclear devices at a test range in Rajasthan called

Pokaran. The following year, the Pakistani army, directed in the background by General Musharraf, initiated an invasion into the Kashmiri border, in a mountainous and unheard-of district called Kargil, specifically shelling Dras, a town no one had heard of.

What do these names, otherwise seldom uttered, tell us? Firstly, they resist the banality of the contemporary. We can't imagine mentioning them in the same breath as shopping malls and the new Apple product. We also can't imagine, or foresee, how a place like Dras might one day converge with the known world of malls and Apple products; though it well might. These locations and towns and villages represent a remoteness and inert changelessness; then, briefly, we realise that – beyond the bounded environment of the metropolis – this is precisely the India that is, and historically has been, in a state of siege.

To this roster of obscure names, whose effect on the consciousness is both undeniable and difficult to pin down, must be added Singur and Nandigram.

Nandigram is a village in Purulia district, its inhabitants mainly farmers and mainly Muslim. Like most other villages in the Bengal of the last four decades, it was, traditionally, a communist outpost. The land reforms brought about by the Left Front government – redistributing land controlled by landlords among peasants, ending centuries of oppression – is its single greatest achievement, and one that's not to be belittled.

That trouble began in Nandigram, one of the many villages that had benefited from land reform, was ironical; it also pointed to the compulsions of the Left Front under Buddhadeb Bhattacharya. The state was probably near bankrupt; agriculture was no longer productive; the world had globalised, the Berlin Wall long fallen, a new sort of economic game was being played worldwide, and you needed to participate to be able to generate money. The advent of Indonesia's Salim Group was announced celebratorily in Bengal. Special economic zones were being created throughout India since the early 2000s; land purchased, or even wrested, from peasants to make space for focused development and industry. Nandigram was the first village to resist being transformed into a special economic zone, in the process becoming not only a distinct entity within the state, fortressed, oppositional, neither of Bengal nor not of it, but scuppering both Bhattacharya's and the Salim Group's plans. It was a classic David and Goliath story – with a twist to the confrontation since, here, Goliath, formerly the progenitor and nurturer of David, had sneakily turned upon him.

Nandigram mobilised sections of the Bengali middle class and its media, and it introduced a new, inebriating celebrity activism into Bengal. Among the famous personalities who condemned the government for its approach to this whole matter of special economic zones was the highly regarded poet Joy Goswami; the filmmaker and actress Aparna Sen; and a number of artists, playwrights, theatre people, some of whom were household names in the neighbourhoods of Calcutta because they worked in television serials and soap operas. This was probably the first time in a very long while that public figures had gone public in their criticism of the government. Adding her weight – negligible in literal terms, considerable in symbolic ones – to this outcry was the frail but predominant Mahasweta Devi, seen by many to be Bengal's foremost living writer, a novelist and short-story writer who'd spent her life working with the tribals, and also making their lives and world her subject matter. From a strange but opportune marriage of genuine passion and outrage, sentimentality and self-promotion, individual conscience and an amoral but hyperactive media was born a constellation of what the latter named 'buddhijibi', or 'intellectuals', though not everyone in that group was an intellectual, and not by any stretch was every intellectual or writer or artist of stature in that group. Nevertheless, the buddhijibi were here, a posse of recognisable

faces, and Mamata Banerjee probably sensed that their emergence had a bearing on her political future. No doubt some
of the buddhijibi – that is, those who had embryonic political
ambitions – realised that Mamata's re-emergence would be significant to *their* plans. Who made the first overture to whom is
difficult to tell – but, suddenly, the buddhijibi and the Trinamool
Congress were speaking from one platform.

This is not to say that the buddhijibi became paid-up members
of the Trinamool Congress; though one or two of them did.
But the affiliation was a powerful one. Until that moment, no
self-respecting Bengali artist or intellectual had come out openly
against the Left. The Left was identified with 'the people'; and
no artist – anyway in a vulnerable position in this regard, open
to accusations of elitism and irrelevance – would want to distance themselves from that large, imprecise constituency: the
common man. With Nandigram, and then Singur, the Left
demonstrated it had turned decisively upon 'the people'; and
Mamata Banerjee, who had for years fought the Left not on
right-wing, but on populist terms, attempting to poach 'the
people' from a Marxist agenda and make it hers, now found a
successful formula for making that populism work for her. The
Left Front government had behaved with its usual high-handed-
ness, with a conviction about its own immunity to opposition,
in Nandigram; but Nandigram fought back. A handful of buddhijibi cheered them on. The Left was misled by its own hubris,
and humbled by the treachery of development.

Nandigram was an unexpected setback; but the critical blow was
struck at another obscure village, Singur. Its largely agricultural
land was appropriated for the factory that would build the
world's cheapest small car, Tata's Nano, worth only $1500. This
toy-like ill-fated vehicle, whose destiny it was to look as if it
had been prematurely brought into the world, more foetus than

car, and whose birth was near abortive and then indefinitely delayed, this car, when it finally took to the road, turned out to have an engine that at times exploded mysteriously. Until 2009, it was seen to be Bengal's quirky but irreplaceable mascot for development. But the acquisition of Singur's land had also been thoughtlessly, violently executed: the thoughtlessness of a cadre-based, 'grass-roots' party now inured to the democratic process. The small fortress of Singur – a reminder of how many potential principalities there are in India, of how many conflicting and legitimate desires qualify 'development' – was shored up by the Trinamool Congress, by the media, by the buddhijibi. Just how much Ratan Tata – an ingenuous-looking man, who at certain moments appears deceptively vacant – played the puppet-master to the government is hard to tell. But it's clear that little Singur had taken on not just the CPI(M) or Tata but what the middle class with swelling fondness and pride refers to as 'India Inc.'. For the first time I can recall, Ratan Tata sulked and threatened; then he withdrew the operation. By now, Buddhadeb Bhattacharya's government – always eagerly self-questioning, always openly humane and fallible, the last democratically elected communist outpost in the world – had become adept at embracing defeat. This unique capacity for martyrdom – the martyrdom of both the party and the state of West Bengal – had become its single most striking feature. Singur was decolonised; where did that leave Singur, or, for that matter, Bengal?

I had all this in mind when I decided to meet Nirupam Sen a second time. A few weeks remained until the election; and it seemed like a good idea to gauge his mood and to continue our last conversation. The events I've described have a direct bearing upon two of the portfolios held by this (his detractors would say, deliberately) self-effacing man, portfolios that made him, in effect, the second most important person in the

government: commerce and industry; and industrial reconstruction. Although the spotlight hardly ever fell on him, he'd
have seen those events as a rebuttal of his tenure: neither he
nor Bhattacharya had achieved what they'd set out to do. As a
consequence of Singur, the Left had done poorly in the general
elections in 2009. Then there was another setback. The Left,
at least from the outside, looks like a family, its cohesiveness
augmented by its private language. Its intensity derives from
the fact that it's a family largely composed of, in a manner of
speaking, orphans of bhadralok history (for we hardly hear of
the mothers and fathers of party members), brought together
not by accident but by idealism and its cousin, ideology. Bonds
of orphanhood and kinship are particularly charged (as Kipling
showed us in *The Jungle Book*) when they are self-created, and
each party member is probably a bit of everything – mother,
father, sibling, friend – to every other member. This emotional
undercurrent was revealed whenever older party members –
like, say, Subhash Chakrabarty – died, and Biman Bose, the party
secretary and spokesperson, burst into tears when making the
announcement. When close kinship is forged in this way, the
sense of betrayal is probably more acute as well; one always had
a feeling that the Left's suspicion of the Right had a slightly different, more blithe, tone in comparison to the Left's suspicion
of its own ranks. The days of Party purges are gone, and they
possibly never arrived in Calcutta; nevertheless, the expulsion
in 2009 of Somnath Chatterjee – Speaker in the lower house of
the Indian Parliament (the Lok Sabha), senior CPI(M) member
and protégé of Jyoti Basu – from the Party led many to puzzle
over whether all was well in the family. Chatterjee, among the
CPI(M)'s most urbane parliamentarians, had had a conflict of
interest during a Lok Sabha vote; disobeying a party directive
in his incarnation as Speaker, he found himself flung out by the
politburo in 2008. This couldn't have happened, many felt, if
Jyoti Basu had been in power. And then came another moment

of transition in a time of continual, unpredictable transition and change – this most predictable of occurrences in 2010, the death of a frail, ailing ninety-five-year-old man, Jyoti Basu.

Jyoti Basu, under whom the communists came to power in West Bengal in 1977, and who retired from the chief minister-ship in 2000, remained astonishingly perky and active – and occasionally abrasive – into his late eighties. He was about eight years older than my father, and my mother would look up from the newspaper whenever Basu's age was mentioned in a report, and talk (with my father in mind) about how the process of ageing was obviously slowing down these days. When, by his mid-eighties, my father's steps began to falter and he began to confess, uncharacteristically, even ruminatively, to feeling old, she would reprimand him, reminding him that Jyoti Basu was still ostentatiously ambulant. In no other sense did she much care about the former chief minister. Comprehension had dawned on her when Basu had proclaimed, with his usual unex-citable hauteur, *'Ei rokom to kotoi hoi'* – 'Such things happen all the time' – upon the death of an officer of the state healthcare services, Anita Dewan, who, beaten up along with three oth-ers by CPI(M) goons, succumbed to her injuries. Nevertheless, Basu's continuing capacity to move on his feet provoked in her a grudging admiration.

Basu points to the equivocal bhadralok origins of the Bengali left. Just as many Indians discovered India's civilisation and heritage abroad, often directed to it by some British Indophile, Basu was converted to communism in London, where, studying in the thirties to be a barrister at the Middle Temple, he fell under the spell of the Marxist Rajani Palme Dutt.

He seldom smiled; when he disagreed with someone, or when he encountered any disapproval of his regime, the nos-trils of his thin nose flared slightly. His seriousness wasn't inscrutability or aggression; it was partly, I think, a pose, the

wishful intensity of a romantic. This unadmitted-to romanticism, besides genetic predisposition, might well have been what
kept him youthful. But towards interviewers and journalists, he
could be patrician, as if they needed to be held in check with
steely displeasure. More than ideology, it was Bengali puritanism, which was engendered in the early nineteenth century
through Brahmo unitarianism and Hindu reform, and which
abhorred, at once, religious profusion and bad taste, which
made that face, with its gaunt lines, its air of intellect, its deep
gaze behind the glasses, both charismatic and forbidding. No
wonder he made my mother, who is torn between puritanism
and abandon herself, uncomfortable. By the late 1990s, a few
years before Basu resigned from the chief ministership, and as
he became frail, the skull emerged more clearly, and the face,
now a thin, stubborn covering of skin, still unsmiling, and with
less and less reason to smile, became a mask – an attenuated,
immutable outline of the earlier face.

Under this man, agrarian, rural Bengal finally, and astonishingly, received justice in the late seventies and early eighties, as
peasants and sharecroppers were empowered and accorded the
rights long due to them, and landlords curtailed; under him,
Calcutta became an abandoned and unimportant city. A democ-
ratising neglect, a suspicion of elite institutions, like Presidency
College, and an inexorable winding down, is what Calcutta got
after the trauma of the Naxal uprising and Congress dishonesty
and mismanagement, and in exchange for unshakable Left Front
stability. It was a confusing time. It would take much more than
a decade for people in Calcutta to understand that this period –
the eighties and early nineties – was one in which they lost face,
lost, too, the easy access to intellectual prestige they took to be
a law of nature, and that it was then that Calcutta gave up its
pre-eminence as India's most interesting, pulsating metropolis.
I didn't live here then; from my visits, I recall disorder, extraordinary abeyances in the twenty-four hours that comprise a day

when there was no electricity; and I recall the rise of a busy new saint-at-large called Mother Teresa.

Dourly, Basu presided over this era – which also saw the collapse of the Berlin Wall, the anomalous rise of state capitalism in China, the dissolution of the Soviet Union, and the liberalisation of India's economic policy. Everything he – and, for that matter, any middle-class person from anywhere – took to be eternal and changeless was being dismantled. Basu couldn't have liked that. Momentarily, I remember, he even took refuge in the persona of the bhadralok, when he said of Rajiv Gandhi, 'We understand each other, because we are both gentlemen.' Nor could he have liked the unending power cuts at home, when people began to call him Andhakar Basu. For his name, like the names of many Bengalis carrying the legacy of the so-called nineteenth-century enlightenment in Bengal, means 'light'. That light – of reason, rationality, advancement – always carried with it, as we see from today's Calcutta, its own darkness.

It was Basu's successors – the next chief minister, Buddhadeb Bhattacharya; Nirupam Sen, whom I was about to meet – who had to speak, for the first time, the language of self-criticism in public: 'We have made mistakes; we have to change.' Basu never had to adopt this tone; it wouldn't have suited a Marxist of his generation. The only time he complained about the Party was when the politburo kept him from accepting the offer of becoming the prime minister of India, at the helm of the victorious United Front government in 1996: he called it a 'historic blunder', surprising everyone that a politburo member (such as he was) could actually voice a personal opinion. People had almost forgotten that he was an individual, a human being with desires; yet, on the whole, he was respected for his aloofness. It was better, I suppose, to have a man like him oversee, and in some way facilitate, the decline of Calcutta, rather than a man who was *not* a bhadralok: a semi-literate Bengali, say, with a hustler's background, like some of the politicians today, or

a suburban communist in a hat, like Subhash Chakrabarty. Or
was it?

I was surprised at the bitterness and anger voiced about Basu
after his death. None of it had found expression in his lifetime,
perhaps because people were nervous of his glare. Or perhaps,
by January 2010, when Basu died, people realised what had
happened to Bengal. And they were harsh on the man: but the
harsh words came only when he was properly out of earshot.

Manoj, less like a friend than a man on a stealth mission, picked
me up in his car and took me to a building on Camac Street
which I've often gone past and fleetingly wondered about. It's
relatively new, about ten years old, but it's neither a shopping
mall nor a nursing home. The minister for commerce and
industry had his office here on the seventh floor.

Nirupam Sen sat behind a large desk in a hushed air-conditioned room, his chair swathed, as the chairs of bureaucrats and
ministers often are, in a white towel. This measure is probably
taken to protect the chair from its occupant's unwitting mark-
ings: middle-class Indians can have a touching reverence for
furniture, and will conceal certain presumably treasured objects
with a small piece of cloth from the dust and the environment.
Or was it a kind of official symbolism, the spotlessness of the
towel a kind of moral statement? For the towel to look clean, it
itself must be invisibly tended to.

Sen hadn't forgotten me; he was his usual undemonstrative,
unpretentious self. I was nervous that I was encroaching; a few
days remained until the elections, which would cover Bengal
in phases. Burdwan constituency, of which Sen was the representative, would vote before Calcutta. Yet Sen wasn't hurried
or impatient, and our conversation lasted two hours – probably because nothing of great importance emerged from it.
Mainly, it was a familiar – but no less painful for being familiar
– account of how Bengal had been deliberately marginalised

after Independence by the central government, first of all by the Freight Equalisation Policy of 1948, which involved subsidising the transportation of minerals to any part of India by the Central government, so that a factory dependent on those minerals wouldn't suffer in terms of costs even if it were set up in a place far from their source. The greatest beneficiaries were states like Maharashtra and Gujarat in the West; and Delhi and its environs. The mineral-rich states, like Bengal and Bihar, lost their natural advantage, and their economies were badly damaged. All this was as well known as Sita's abduction by Ravana in the *Ramayana*; but Sen spoke of it and other bygone discriminatory policies as if the wound were fresh, just as devotees can get worked up each time they hear the abduction episode.

He also told me – upon my asking – a little bit of his personal history; how, born in 1946 in Burdwan, one of a family of seven siblings, he grew up in poverty, presumably as the family profession by caste – *kobiraji*, or traditional medicine – became irrelevant. His father, he said, had in fact started out on the path of being an allopathic doctor, been admitted to medical college, and then had to give it up on the death of *his* father. So Sen's father became a schoolteacher, and then joined the Communist Party in the early forties, involving himself in famine relief during that infamous man-made famine in 1943, caused by a combination of food supplies being diverted to Tommies and local wholesalers hoarding grain, in the last years of British rule. Sen, with his dark, long bespectacled face, his expression in turn attentive and earnest, looks like a schoolteacher himself, but, by his own admission, was never interested in academics – probably because of his involvement in politics from 1961. And he may never have got married (he'd decided no woman in her right mind could possibly entertain the thought of such a husband) had not his wife, whom he met in college, taken the initiative and as good as proposed to him. Although Sen isn't the sort of man you'd associate with excitement, you realise from throwaway remarks – for instance, about the 'debate' about various things in the sixties – that he's part of a culture that's quickened by political disagreement and oppositionality. When he refers to the various criticisms now directed at the CPI(M), he refers to this culture in a general, axiomatic way: 'Everyone in Bengal talks about politics,' he says, 'just as everyone here is a doctor.' By this he means that everyone has a ready diagnosis for a problem, or an ailment, in Bengal. He attributes this to Bengal's history of 'social consciousness'. He doesn't add that only in a society in which everyone is a patient – a society of hypochondriacs – would everyone be a doctor; that one must feel constantly victimised and arraigned by politics to be a society of potential politicians. As I listen, I see overlaps with my father and my uncles (Sen's father, too, went to Scottish Church College); but, just as Socrates claimed he was not a citizen of Athens or Greece, but of the world, I can imagine my father and uncles and their friends as people who belong to the world, and not just Sylhet. In Sen, I see the Bengal of the last thirty years more clearly – its smouldering pain; its ordinariness: I can't think of him belonging elsewhere.

Sen, during our meanderings through recent history, could have woven in his swan song, but didn't. In fact, at the end of it we resolved to meet again – as if the more complex issues needed to be addressed later. 'I'm sorry to ask you this,' I said, 'but what do you think the outcome will be?' He'd been tolerant so far, and there was no sign that he'd be less so now. 'You mean the elections?' he asked, regarding me steadily. 'Yes.' 'It'll be tight,' he said. 'Fifty-fifty.' 'Really?' I was surprised: nothing about Sen suggested he was a bluffer or delusional, and all predictions – and the feeling in my gut – said the Left was headed for a crashing defeat. 'What makes you say that?' 'Well, two years ago it was different,' said Sen, referring to the Trinamool's wipe-out of the Left in the general elections. 'But now people have had a taste of their MPs and councillors, and know them for what they are.

It won't be the same this time around.' The trouble was, the electorate had tasted and drunk the Left for three decades; and, though Bengalis prefer an impressive degree of predictability in their diet, they seemed to have reached the limit of their love of the familiar. 'What do you think?' he asked. 'If you don't mind my saying so, people are fed up with the Left Front,' I replied. A look of hurt flickered momentarily on his face. 'They'd even prefer a nuclear disaster, and in the Trinamool Congress they may have found one.' We both laughed aloud at the joke. 'One day, when we have more time, you must tell me *why* people are so fed up with the Left.' He was genuinely concerned and even tantalised. Over our two hours together, he'd conceded failures of foresight and governance. He'd also pointed out that not unless you were in government could you appreciate the exigencies of the scramble towards industrialisation: that neither globalisation nor the big corporations, like Tata, left you with a great deal of leeway for manoeuvre. But he asserted the Left's successes, especially when I raised the question of its policies towards education: more and more children from remote villages were going on to finish school, and perform exceptionally in their higher studies. Why, then, were people fed up? 'We probably need another conversation for that,' I said; and this prompted us to duly exchange cell-phone numbers.

I wasn't certain, though, when I'd be seeing him again.

There had been two personal exchanges in our conversation, in the midst of our back and forth about the days of the Left Front in Bengal, bygone and present. The first was to do with my maternal cousin, Subho. When Sen's constituency, Burdwan, came up at the beginning, I thought I should ask him if he knew Subho, who'd taught mathematics at Burdwan University, and now held a senior administrative office there; and, besides, was a long-time member of the Communist Party. Sen's face softened into a smile and he said: 'He sings beautifully' – my cousin is a singer of Tagore songs, East Bengali folk songs, and political songs. There was an echo, a concordance, in their lives too, that extended beyond the Party: just as my cousin has two children, an older daughter, and a younger son who's mentally challenged, so too does Sen. The term he used, naturally and without self-consciousness, as if news of political correctness had still not arrived wherever he was, was 'mentally retarded'.

The second, very brief exchange had to do with the allegorically named ministry of industrial reconstruction, conjured up in Jyoti Basu's time, inherited by Sen: now particularly Kafkaesque (by which I mean not bizarre, but belonging to a parallel world that possesses its own veracity) since, to ordinary eyes at least, none of that 'industrial reconstruction' had taken place. Yet it was this ministry, I told Sen, that had invited my father, soon after he moved to Calcutta in 1989, to become an advisor to Lily Biscuit. Advice from experts is much sought after in India, and readily proffered; as a result, the post of the advisor is among the easiest to create in a company. My father had reached the zenith of his career selling biscuits, becoming the first Indian chief executive of Britannia Industries in 1979. Britannia was an offshoot of the British conglomerate United Biscuits, under whose umbrella flourished Jacob's, Huntley and Palmer's, and Peek Freen's, whose products had been integral to the English teatime. In consonance with the flight of capital from Calcutta in the sixties, Britannia had re-established its head office in Bombay in 1964. After almost twenty-five years, my father was back in Calcutta. That intervening history – of Britannia, my father's job, and Calcutta – felt as compressed as a fable. In some quarters at least, my father's reputation as biscuit guru must have preceded him (being an unusually modest man, he'd made no overtures himself) and reached Jyoti Basu's ears (the chief minister had met him a couple of times). Lily Biscuit was a respectable indigenous phenomenon – Bengal-specific; a regional quality biscuit brand. Its lore originated aeons ago;

my mother claims, correctly, that Britannia was absent from her youth, and unmissed, largely because the excellent Lily was then consumed with tea. Introduced into the world of the Bengali bhadralok by a Bengali bhadralok family, it finally ran out of steam, as bhadralok enterprise appears to. Will someone in the social sciences write a dissertation on how the rise of individualism in Bengal (in contrast to the West) destroyed rather than energised entrepreneurship, at least on home ground; how, in India, caste and community drive capital and the free market? Every morning in the early nineties, an Ambassador, a state government car, would pick up my father to take him to the Lily Biscuit offices in Ultadanga. By then, he was well into post-post-retirement, and I think he took this excursion – after having recently annexed the heights of the private sector in what was still largely a socialist economy – as a posthumous visit to a hidden underworld: the public sector, whose existence, all these years, he'd had nothing to do with. The daily journey was a journey into the dead. But he brought back tales of life: tea-drinking, laughter, and gossip in limbo. His reports were not unlike the accounts emerging now, in June 2011, of the sort of routines that governed the staff at Writers' Building, the seat of government in Calcutta, in the last two decades. Lily Biscuit was a 'sick' company, bought over by the West Bengal government to ensure there were no job losses – an ingenious form of anti-venture capitalism. Bengali industry was afloat with such vessels: proud barges and liners that were now, not run aground, but mildly stationary upon shallow water. Much the same thing had happened to the actual barges on the Hooghly, which had once made Calcutta a great port: they were sitting there for years.

I told Sen just a little bit about my father's background: enough to hint we were in opposite camps in the class war. Sen looked unruffled. The old enmities have lost some of their edge in the bewildering world we inhabit. Besides, I only meant to register my own amusement that my relationship with the ministry of industrial reconstruction went further back than Sen's.

My father had missed being one of the beneficiaries of globalisation. A student of English literature at Scottish Church College, Calcutta, then briefly a well-wisher of the Marxists while in London, then a nominal follower of M.N. Roy, the 'radical humanist', whose spell on him had never quite worn off, he found his calling at last on the narrow ledge of capitalism in socialist India. By the time India 'opened up' and liberalised its economy in 1991, my father was acquainting himself with 'industrial reconstruction' and the remnant of Lily Biscuit. He was not going to dip into the booty of the new economy; he draws a monthly pension of Rs 6000 from Britannia, less than what a retired government schoolteacher gets, because the new capitalists feel no philanthropic pang towards the private sector's old guard.

In a way, I'm almost relieved he was born fifteen years too late to be where the big money is today. Only recently, I heard of how a biscuit company (unnamed, probably because of a legal injunction) was pressuring the central government to replace the free lunches it gives to poor schoolchildren with biscuit packets. The government would have happily given in had there not been an outcry. I shudder to think of my father involved in such a scheme today, although everything I've known about him makes it seem unlikely. Is it not better that he lived in an age when he could be at once optimistic and righteously angry about the need to deregulate the market? The leisurely progress of his vascular dementia means that he's aware of his family, of Calcutta, of India, and of his Britannia pension, but at several removes. Vascular dementia precludes the absolute blankness of Alzheimer's; it's a gentle slope descending into oblivion.

Universal Suffrage

I arrived in Dubai after midnight, nervous about missing my connecting flight. It would depart at 2 a.m. Passing through security for the second time in nine hours, rehearsing the whole belt-discarding, shoe-and-wallet-jettisoning routine with a bunch of Indians, Bangladeshis, Pakistanis, and Europeans, I plunged into the capitalist wakefulness that's Dubai airport. What was I doing here? Going back to Calcutta, of course. Ever since British Airways terminated its meagre ration of thrice-weekly flights in 2009, travelling back from the United Kingdom necessarily involves a stopover in some part of the ancient world — in some resplendent metropolis in the middle of a desert. I'd been in London, in the South Bank, for a few days of an unusually warm spring; on the third day, I'd just about begun to find my feet in British time, and now, on the fourth, was struggling to rediscover Calcutta time in Dubai. As I tried to follow the clock's forward leap, walking very quickly on the concourse, I made sure to buy some chocolate, and pick up a box of dates.

Assembly elections had been taking place in India during my absence, phase by phase, over April and May, and one of the consequences was going to be new governments in at least some states. Most states changed governments every five or ten years. The non-ideological alliances of compromise and mutual opportunity have proved, since the nineties, to be surprisingly resilient. There has been, famously, a democratisation of politics, an embrace of not only grandiloquent low-caste anarchists like Lalu Prasad Yadav and Dalit dictator manqués like Mayawati, but of an array of disquieting hustlers who are reportedly no less depraved than the polite Nehru-jacketed secular sorts from the Congress. In West Bengal, of course, there had been no alteration for thirty-four years; the electorate, steadfast at first, then increasingly hapless, had voted the Left Front into power seven times. The old bhadralok Marxists had been going in and out of Writers' Building in their white dhutis and panjabis like Roman senators in their togas, casually unmindful of the barbarians sizing up the gates. Although the Front had incurred heavy losses a couple of years ago in the general elections, and Mamata Banerjee's great vision – the vision of decisively booting the Front out – was not just a possibility but the most credible outcome, the CPI(M) was no longer persuaded of the barbarians' success. Even Nirupam Sen, never a toga-wearing type, had, as I pointed out earlier, sounded sceptical about an easy majority for the Trinamool – as the Roman in 476 CE might have been narrow-eyedly dismissive of Odoacer's prospects. It was to this Bengal I flew back on 22nd April.

The London to Dubai flight had been uncomfortably full, despite the aircraft being the gigantic A380. Next to me was an Asian couple of Muslim origin (I could tell from the names by which they affectionately addressed each other, and the repeated use of 'inshallah' in their London English), but British in identity, excited by their journey towards India, where they'd never been, and their imminent vacation in Kerala – a green, water-drenched idyll, but also, coincidentally, a CPI(M) bastion. The woman watched Hindi films, now with indulgent familiarity, as if she were surprised to be reprising her life in her Wembley drawing room, now with proprietary boredom (I had a sense she was viewing some of them a second time), and, whenever she was distracted from the storyline, matter-of-factly consulted the pages of *Hello!* magazine. She nudged her partner and invited his response frequently; he replied with the colloquial immediacy of a man who has an opinion on everything. 'Look, it's *him*,' she said, upon seeing Hrithik Roshan, or 'That's *her*,' on viewing Bipasha Basu, with the intimacy reserved for things one has only ever encountered in books and pictures; while he shared these sightings avidly. She wanted confirmation as to whether Kate Middleton was really that beautiful; on the other hand, she was genuinely astonished at how slim she was. I eavesdropped, read, spied on my neighbours, watched a film, slept a little.

The Dubai to Calcutta flight, in comparison, possessed a dimly lit provincialism you encounter all the time in Dhakuria, Jodhpur Park, Lake Town and Salt Lake. It was a smaller aircraft, three quarters full. My neighbour was a twenty-eight-year-old man. He worked in Leeds for Tata Consultancy Services, which was doing cheap software programming for the British govern-ment. He'd got on to a flight from Manchester, reached Dubai half an hour late at 1 a.m., worried, as I had, about making it to this plane, and now leaned back. Adults, like children, will forget trauma with ease, and live gratefully for the most part in the present. This, at least, is how people who have anything to do with Bengal approach existence: frontally, with a narrow focus. This man's father had had a second cerebral stroke at the age of sixty-four, which is why he was on his way to visit him at this odd time of the year – neither summer nor Christmas – for ten days. It was a relatively early age to have had two strokes, and I quizzed him about it, given my own father's tendency to have 'mini strokes'. But my father is eighty-nine. It turned out that his, among other things, was a schoolteacher. Arriving into Calcutta's heat, he'd take a train to Kalyani, the small town in which his parents lived, on the day, 23rd April, that Kalyani voted. 'What do you think will happen?' I asked him. 'There seems little doubt that there will be a *"paribartan",'* he said, giggling – there was something elusively feminine about him – guiltily delighting in the word that had been put into currency in the last two years.

He not only represented the Bengal of the last three decades, he *was* it. Intelligence and marginality marked him equally – the moderate privileges he'd grown up with in Kalyani, and the most he'd made of them – as well as that delicate, androgynous fussiness. I recalled the Left Front's scrapping of English from state-funded primary schools in 1983, a decision reversed only two years ago. Nirupam Sen and I had discussed this: why the dropping of English at that stage should diminish excellence. After all, Sen himself was clearly from an English-as-second-language background; so was my father and the great memoirist and English prose stylist Nirad C. Chaudhuri – they'd both grown up in East Bengal before Independence, and my father, who would startle me by quoting Eliot's 'Prufrock' and Shelley's 'Ode to a Skylark', began his education in a *paathshala*, an immemorial village school. Class, then, was not a reason for once choosing Bengali over English primary education; nationalism might have been. Tagore too belonged to this extraordinary English-as-a-second-language set, and was always diffident about his command of the language, hated English lessons, and confessed how he found it difficult to distinguish between the pronunciation of 'worm' and 'warm' – a not uncommon Bengali problem. Was it today's state education itself, then, rather than the early absence of English, that was to blame for the working class's sense of deprivation; or was it the encroaching tide of globalisation, which recognised no other language, and to which Bengal had capitulated later than almost anywhere else but Cuba? Anyway, the legacy of that twenty-seven-year-old policy was audible in my neighbour's inflected English speech, which we continued to have recourse to until we gave up the pretence of being generalised, pan-Indian individuals, and confessed to each other we were Bengali. We continued talking of Calcutta, how it made flying hard work. Part agitated yokel, I narrated stories of flights out of Bombay and Delhi, how *two* British Airways planes depart each day from these cities, not to mention competitors like Jet Airways, Virgin, and Air India – and yet the flights to London are always bustling, the business class section not only chock-a-block with the Indian rich and their children but (I've noticed on occasion) their children's nannies, self-conscious and reticent once the infants have gone to sleep. Exhausted, like hitch-hikers on an interminable highway, we fell asleep, dazed by memories of parents and intimations of better places.

Before we landed into the palm and plantain trees and ponds that constitute the outskirts of the city, I ruminated on a final comparison with my new friend. 'Where, after all, was Dubai fifty years ago, or for that matter Hong Kong, Delhi, or Bombay? Calcutta was India's premier city; one of the world's greatest.' Yet we felt a quickening on viewing the familiar scene from above in the morning light.

Growing up in Bombay, I'd feel a mysterious charge of anticipation on returning to Calcutta. I loved the domestic airport in the sixties – an old colonial building with potted plants, like a hospice. And I loved, too, the way from the airport to Bhowanipore in the south, towards my uncle's house: the pastoral scene at the start, ponds and palm trees, giving way gradually to city lanes, and then to the narrow and long Pratapaditya Road, where working women in the porches of the small houses wore a single faded piece of cotton as a sari, but no blouse underneath, just as I remembered them from the last visit. Could a city be a village and a city at once? Could it be both what it had become after Job Charnock, supposedly the founder, had first arrived there – the great metropolis of the East – and still retain to itself the shadows of Sutanati and Kolikata and Gobindapur, the three villages from which it had risen? On the way inward from the airport, it certainly seemed so: not only to me, but, I felt, to the Bengalis who lived here – that they were at once in the midst of the modern and the ancestral and fabular.

My child's excitement had relatively little to do with actually knowing anything about the transformation in the nineteenth century that had made Calcutta what it was when I first discovered it: a perplexing, contemporary thing. The Bengalis had no grand history, in the way the Rajasthanis or Biharis did. '[I]f the sahibs go out to kill a bird, they write a history of it, but the Bengalis have no history,' complained Bankimchandra Chatterjee. 'The people of Greenland have a history, the Maori race too has a history . . . Even the Oriyas have a history,' he concluded, scathingly. Writers don't so much write about their own lives as create them, Barthes said; it's an oddly modern idea. Bengalis, similarly, had to make their own history. They did it in houses, tenements, and in neighbourhoods connected by stifling alleys that are no wider than a small room. This making is what I must have had an intuition of, even as a child. And this is why I feel, even now, that the most revealing places in Calcutta are not the museums or the great monuments (of which, anyway, there aren't many), but the houses and lanes in which people live. 'I like this city,' the novelist Akhil Sharma shrugged and admitted to me on his second trip to it. 'You feel that something happened here.'

Something did. Under the Crown, Calcutta, capital of the new India, became 'second city' of the Empire, till that privilege was rescinded in 1911, and the capital moved to a less political and a quieter place, Delhi, a superannuated historical site, the seat of the thirteenth-century Sultanate, a city that had receded into invisibility since the poet-king Bahadur Shah Zafar's arrest in 1857 for his role in the Sepoy Mutiny. In doing so, the British appeared to turn away from modern man, everyman, the 'little man' of modernity, to what they always preferred in India, even while deriding it: the historical setting, ancient heritage. If that was all there was to it, Calcutta's significance would be the significance of a major administrative port, and Bengal an episode in colonial history, possibly an evocative locale in a period film, like Siam. But other things had happened. The Asiatic Society, where the Indo-European family of languages was first identified, was founded; institutions came into being, including the great educational ones, the Hindu (later, Presidency) College and Calcutta University, the latter for more than a century India's most prestigious centre for higher studies. Well before this, Raja Rammohun Roy, the polyglot Bengali scholar, had, by the end of the eighteenth century, made a career change, unexpectedly making the leap, as the historian Christopher Bayly points out, from being a 'late-Mughal state intellectual' to being the 'first Indian liberal'. If you look at portraits of the man, you see a handsome moustached face under a circular turban, locks of carefully kempt hair on either side, and the figure itself occupying the long robe of the Persian style. The myopic, dhuti-wearing bhadralok – almost always bespectacled, like a Jewish comedian – still hasn't emerged in Roy's time or even, later, in Rabindranath's. Roy's face, in the portraits, is unique, but also generic, like the faces of Elizabethan England – Shakespeare, Marlowe, Elizabeth I herself – which are reported to derive from a single ur-outline. Roy, himself, is just about to leave that world, no sooner has he entered it; he looks busy, as a corporate man might today. Who is this pretender; what is he up to? Engaged in argument with Brahmin pundits and Christian missionaries alike, his legacy is associated with the religious, social, and intellectual reform that began to transform

Bengal by the nineteenth century; but it contains the germ of the most interesting project taken up by this undistinguished lot, the Bengalis: the project of creating themselves. By the 1860s, Bengalis were not only producing the canon – poetry, fiction, criticism – but making their own history.

Naturally, colonial contact engendered some of these possibilities while shutting down others; but what 'happened' can't be comfortably reduced to the notion of Western influence. What's most intriguing is that the British knew almost nothing of what was 'happening' in Calcutta's cultural life; invisibility was one of Bengali modernity's prerequisites and cardinal achievements. It conferred invisibility too; if you read Bengali literature, you won't find out a great deal from it about the British rulers – they generally fell outside the purview of its restively cosmopolitan explorations. Bengali writing, then, was deeply but strategically realist, focusing on certain details, excising others, inventing a world richer than any English-language account of the age. It was immersed in, and excited by, the extraordinariness it was located in; you get the feeling that well before Calcutta was appointed the Indian capital, and well after it had ceased to be one, it was a capital of the nineteenth century and of modernity. Sartre began his essay 'La République du silence' with the provocation that the French were probably most free under Nazi occupation. You feel something similar, but on an incomparably larger scale, surveying the curiously munificent and playful texts and artworks that Bengal produced from the 1860s to the 1970s; that political invisibility can sometimes be a necessity for play. Tagore invokes the word *chhuti* – 'holiday' – repeatedly in his songs and poems, in a magical, talismanic way. He writes in his memoirs of staring out of the mullioned veranda of his ancestral house into the garden; his life as a pupil and student is a narrative of one who's attempting constantly to escape discipline. He can't bear the presence of the English, and, despite his wariness of Indian nationalism, his life is punctuated by both personal and public rebuttals of the British government. And yet if you look at his restless travelling between genres, his experiments in poetry, fiction, art, and even fashioning a persona, you're confronted by a Bengali who is, in one sense, confined and invisible, and who is, in another, at his most free.

If you ask a Bengali today about what happened to this inheritance, he or she, in all likelihood, will blame the Left Front government for its unravelling. Until recently, a range of other scapegoats and factors would have been mentioned. Among them would be the British government, which partitioned Bengal twice, the second time upon Independence, destroying its core industries, like jute, and, before that, in 1943, creating a famine. So would the largely Congress-led central government's puzzlingly stepmotherly economic policies towards West Bengal. (For instance, the infamous 'freight equalisation policy' that Nirupam Sen had mentioned.) The Naxal movement, and its subsequent strangulation by the then Congress state government and the police, would be cited as a further reason contributing to Bengal's present drift.

But now, during the elections, thirty-four years of the Left would have to take the brunt of the responsibility. Among its many transgressions was the politicisation of institutions, their alleged infiltration by party members or sympathisers; the recalcitrant work ethic, encouraged by fostering militant trade unions; the awful reputation, as a result, of the state among investors.

For now, the early triumph of Left rule, the land reforms that led to the redistribution of rural land, Operation Barga (after *bargadar*, or sharecropper), is looked upon with impatience. The Left has trumpeted it too frequently. The Left's other achievement, of creating in Calcutta India's most tolerant, multicultural, multi-religious metropolis, isn't remarked upon. The unspoken thought seems to be – what good is coexistence, when mere existence is difficult?

The competition, as we know, was an unmarried woman of humble means, strident voice, and a bludgeoning style. Once of the Congress, Mamata Banerjee was expelled from it in 1997, when she founded her own party, the Trinamool (literally, 'grass-root') Congress.

For a while, she had a shaky alliance with the right-wing BJP, which fell through. The Left had perfected a style of politics that was populist and oppositional (taking to the street to agitate against the Centre's policies). Mamata borrowed this manner and rhetoric from the Left, and brought to it her own, not always perceivably rational, fervour. In other words, she's a passionate child of Left politics.

When, in 2009, the Left lost a record number of seats in Bengal, people who'd voted in seven assembly elections but had grown sheltered from the very unpredictability of democracy realised, suddenly, that the Left *could* lose. This realisation dawned on the Left too. Mamata, in the meanwhile, was about to forge an alliance with the Congress, the party that had once shown her the door, for the 2011 assembly elections, as, by some distance, the dominant partner. Once derided by the Left and even beaten up by its goons (she'd later appear bandaged on television), she was ready to achieve the impossible. It didn't matter that she had no real policies; a lower-middle-class woman in a white cotton sari and rubber flip-flops (in this guise, she was '*didi*': elder sister), she had vanquished the seemingly punitive patrician system represented both by the Left and the Congress in Bengal. It is, by any standard, an extraordinary feat, turning her, in the most current sense, into a celebrity. McLuhan's tautology about people who are famous for being famous no longer holds; we now want our celebs, whether they're English royals, Hollywood stars, or sportspeople, to suffer publicly, to enter detox and to survive it. By the time of the 2011 elections, there wasn't really a great deal anyone knew about Mamata except, by now, her determination to survive both her outer and, crucially, inner demons; she'd become the protagonist of a great Bengali reality show.

On the 26th, recovered from jet lag, I went out to assess the afternoon preceding the historic event. Not knowing what to do, I made my way to the Institute of Jute Technology on Ballygunge Circular Road, where R and I planned to vote the next day. I'd come here twenty years ago, to vote for the CPI(M) candidate, Anil Chatterjee. I'd had a number of reasons. Firstly, although I was twenty-eight years old, I'd never voted, and felt like growing up. Secondly, there was no alternative in sight. Besides, I was an admirer of Chatterjee's work in classic Bengali cinema. If he was half as good a Member of the Legislative Assembly as he was an actor – mercurial, full of vitality – he'd be a good choice; even if he wasn't, I would support him for the hilarious panache with which he'd played a fashion photographer in Satyajit Ray's *Kanchenjunga*.

In the elections that followed, I went nowhere near the Jute Technology building. I couldn't possibly vote for the Left again simply because there was no other option, like a miserable undergraduate who goes to an awful social gathering rather than stay at home. Now, on election eve, the mood was once more different. It felt like there was an unspoken consensus that people would sooner commit suicide than return the Left to power. There was also an undercurrent of agreement that to vote for the Trinamool was to commit suicide. Yet there was a hopefulness in the air, a cockiness, even: the cockiness, say, of Rowan Atkinson in *Blackadder Goes Forth*, when he's orchestrated events so that he'll be in front of the firing squad in the morning, and receive a pardon just as it takes aim. As I entered the deserted Jute Technology college (devoid now of the usually bustling jute technology staff and students), I knew I faced a quandary for tomorrow's vote. I kept putting off thinking about it; writing about the event was a means of losing my focus on participating in it, in however small a way. But it was my knowledge that I'd infinitesimally influence the event by casting my vote that brought a muted excitement to the idea of writing about it. Yet my plan for voting was depressingly perverse, and deliberately designed to achieve nothing. The CPI(M) candidate in my neighbourhood was the Speaker's son, Fuad Halim, a young, self-effacing doctor who did social work, a man no one knew and who'd for some inexplicable reason decided to join the fray. His main opponent was the former mayor Subrata Mukherjee, who'd jumped ship and changed parties many times in his career, and for whom neither I nor my wife (who was displaying, on election eve, a more carefree, less tortured resolve in this matter) cared to press the button. But to vote CPI(M) yet again? I felt the exhaustion of one who's belatedly understood the illusory nature of choice, and feels bitter. Entering, I was politely asked by a young Border Security Force guard to explain myself. Having fobbed him off with some high-falutin nonsense about writing a piece, I went into one of the two halls that would be used for voting (which were otherwise, I imagined, spacious jute technology classrooms), where three polling officers were seated, shirtless, behind a table. With their consent, I began to ask them – especially (out of a sense of symmetry) the one in the centre – general questions. They were government employees with day jobs (the mild elderly man on the left worked in the main branch of the State Bank of India), and they'd done election duty in previous years; like jury members, they couldn't refuse the job, for which they were paid a modest fee, if asked to do it. The moment I wondered aloud if the elections on the 27th were any different from previous ones, my main interviewee grew unapproachable, bureaucratic, as if he were at a desk in a bank, and clarified tersely that every election, where he was concerned, was exactly the same. When I pressed him, a man who'd been sitting before the vest-wearing officials, myopically going through papers, said firmly I must leave. I'd noticed him, and noticed that he'd noticed me and was pretending, like a consummate actor, to be oblivious; he had a deft, intelligent air, and was sorting out the papers with a ferret-like concentration. 'Excuse me,' I said, not to challenge him, but to satisfy my curiosity, 'who are you?' 'The presiding officer,' he said, not making a big issue about it. An older BSF officer with an automatic gun – moustached, dark, more of a physical presence than the boy outside – took my arm, and, when I respectfully loosened it, very gently escorted me out; in an attempt to be cheerful and subtly difficult, I reminded the three men I'd see them again the next day, and they naturally behaved as if they hadn't heard.

Further up Ballygunge Circular Road is a beautiful colonial building, the David Hare College, named after the nineteenth-century Scottish watchmaker and fiercely non-evangelical educationist, beloved of Bengalis, both privileged and under-privileged, of the time. The place was lighted up, and swarming with convivial-looking policemen. Given the number of plastic chairs and charged atmosphere, it might have been a policeman's wedding. I was seated opposite a man in khaki regalia, with epaulettes and tassels, a cap on his head, who was speaking hur-riedly into a walkie-talkie. It emerged that the policemen were waiting with bated breath for the 'stand down' order, when they could finally go home. It had been a big day. The college not only had a polling booth, but (and this explained the number of policemen congregated there) was a centre at which electronic voting machines were received, and then distributed to ninety-one booths in the area. When I shamelessly informed the busy, nervous-looking khaki-clad man I was a novelist, he said, 'What do you write? Are you addressing society's many problems?' He added, 'Literature is a mirror to society.' Policemen in Bengal once had a reputation for being unusually, perhaps unexpect-edly, intellectual. Monobina Gupta, in *Left Politics in Bengal*, mentions that Louis Malle, in Calcutta in 1968, received per-mission to film a political demonstration from a policeman who was a fan, and who, on meeting Malle, told him he'd 'watched *Zazie* a week ago, at the Metro theatre, barely a stone's throw away from the protest . . . Oh, yes, he had completed a course in French and also translated Louis Aragon's *Elsa at the Mirror*'. 'What kind of problems do you have in mind?' I said, deciding it was best to engage my companion in conversation. 'Problems take three forms,' he informed me, while a policeman of lower rank eavesdropped, agog. 'You can be born with problems. People can *create* problems for you. Thirdly, people can make you *think* you have problems.' He meant me to be perplexed by this last category, and I was. 'This group is the most difficult. It fosters the resentment that leads to terrorism.' 'But terrorism is not a real concern in this city, is it?' I asked. As we tackled these themes, I noticed him glance with alacrity at an urbane-looking bespectacled gentleman who was approaching us, a bhadralok bureaucrat out of a Ray movie. I was momentarily seized by a nostalgia for Ray's world; at the same time, a strange thought passed through my head: 'If this guy doesn't recognise me, I might as well give up writing.' This was followed, swiftly, by the pre-emptive voice, 'There's no reason why he should recognise me.' It turned out he was Mr Chakrabarty of the Calcutta Port Trust. My companion, who, as it happens, was Mr Chatterjee, an assistant commissioner of the police, introduced me affectionately, as if I were a precocious teenager. 'I've been telling him that the writer must deal with society's problems,' he said in English, to which, impeccably, Mr Chakrabarty replied, 'Ah, Mr Chaudhuri has more than fulfilled his responsibilities to society.' I was struck that it was possible to have a brief exchange on the role of the writer approximately twelve hours before what people had once predicted would surely be a violent election.

I made from the David Hare College for Park Street. A young writer friend with two well-received books to his name – I'll call him 'Salim' – had emailed me a few days earlier about visiting

Calcutta; it would be his second visit to the city. Salim lived in Delhi and England and other places, and I presumed he was covering the elections for a British newspaper. But, in the last day, I'd been getting frantic texts about a bad stomach; the messages conveyed the panic of being in a city where one doesn't know anyone who knows any doctors. Then the message language had stabilised; medication had been administered, and, tomorrow (election day), Salim would leave for less unsettling territory: Bombay. I wondered if he were too weak now to meet me; but a text told me that company was what he craved.

Salim was lying recumbent in his air-conditioned room in Park Mansions when I finally saw him; he had a visitor at the bedside – a middle-aged, stocky gentleman, someone who, in his matter-of-fact gentleness, was again out of Calcutta's past, like the Port Trust's Mr Chakrabarty. Salim thanked the man profusely when he took his leave soon after I'd entered the room. Park Mansions was a block of colonial flats with a compound, hidden from the main road (which was Free School Street), very still and charming at this time of the evening. To step on the wooden floorboards at the entrance, walk towards the old lift, and to ring the bell and be let in by the caretaker was, to me at least, full of history and promise.

'It's a lovely place,' I said, to which Salim smiled and said 'Ye-e-s' sceptically, as if he were weighing my remark. We discussed, for a bit, the nuances of a habitation such as this one – what was it that kept it from having a dull, numbed, governmental quality? Past privilege is what it exuded; but present well-being too. There was still money here; it was quietly in possession of the old building. It had the walls painted a white that looked silken in the lamplight. What was it about white walls – here; or in old institutional buildings in London; or nursing homes for the convalescent to recuperate in – that had a safe, patrician glow?

'So what are you doing here?' I asked. 'I'm not actually sure,' he confessed. 'Yesterday, I was following a campaign trail in Barrackpore, asking people questions. Then I began to feel very ill.' 'I wasn't feeling so good myself yesterday – it was horribly humid all of a sudden,' I said. 'Was it something you ate here?' He quickly wanted to absolve the city of guilt. 'You know, I don't think so. I think it's an infection I had earlier that hasn't gone away.'

We had slipped, unbeknownst to him, and without self-consciousness on my part, into what for Bengalis is a returning subject of conversation: the state of their digestion. The English are supposed to open conversations with the weather, and then reference it again as a sort of join or punctuation between one thought and another: it sounds ridiculous, but is largely true. It's their daily, sometimes hourly, reassessment of the fact of existence – something that neither their religion, work, nor education any more expects from them. Bengalis talk constantly about food to express an irrational joie de vivre in the midst of a jaded present; and they speak of their digestion – especially a mysterious complaint called 'gas', or *gash* – to register melancholy, a persistent dissatisfaction with life. This phenomenon, which has been studied by a German sociologist, Stefan Ecks, explains the constant outflow of antacids and cures for dyspepsia, like Gelusil and Aqua-ptychotis, and laxatives such as Isabgol and Dulcolax, from pharmacists' shelves in Calcutta: these are actually a curious kind of mood-enhancer, a crutch to the Bengali mind. Dyspepsia is the curse of the sedentary man, who probably appears in Calcutta well before Macaulay speaks of his intention of conjuring up 'a class of persons Indian in blood and colour, but English in tastes, in opinions, in morals and in intellect'.

'What's the situation out like there?' I asked Salim.

'Not good at all,' he said, shaking his head grimly. 'I had the sense that people are in a state of despair, that they're really between a rock and a hard place.'

'Did you talk to anyone interesting?'

'Well, I was following this guy around – Dinesh Trivedi.' General Secretary of the All India Trinamool Congress, MP from Barrackpore, Trivedi was the Trinamool's conciliatory (and non-Bengali) face. 'I liked him,' said Salim. 'He was open and made no bones about the fact that steering the state in the right direction under Trinamool wouldn't be a straightforward thing.'

I was interested in this portrayal. I'd met Trivedi several times at Manoj's parties, and our encounters were brief and unmemorable. We had to be reintroduced each time by Manoj, and behave as if there had never been a previous meeting.

'So is this for a piece, then?' I persisted.

'I thought I might have written something – but now . . .' Salim waved at himself in the bed, 'I've given up the idea. Anyway, I like being here, I like this city. I thought it would be good to spend some time here.'

I'm intrigued by this admission of admiration for Calcutta from friends visiting from Europe and America; they often tell me it's the Indian city they like best. Although I feel like an outsider to Calcutta myself, with hardly any close friends here, I must have become both inured to and invested enough in it to not be able to experience it as they do. I find today's Calcutta intriguing myself, but for altogether different reasons; and, as I've pointed out before, I'm haunted and impeded by my childhood vision of it in the sixties and seventies, when it was a great city. What must it look like today to the visitor? I try again and again to perform the imaginative feat, to put myself in his or her place, but can't quite succeed. Akhil Sharma's quizzical but considered, 'You feel something must have happened here,' is the only clue I have to what appears before the visitor's eye.

'Besides, I felt like my writing was closing up – I felt like I needed to get out,' he said. 'Do you feel like that sometimes? That actually going somewhere new, getting "out there", might get your writing flowing again?'

Despite being a very good writer, Salim is attractively ingenuous; you feel protective towards him and his queries, whether or not he has a stomach bug, or is in need of a doctor – there's a raw freshness to the persona.

I could see 'going out into the world' as a Hemingway-like ploy; the writer as explorer and operative, undertaking an excursion specifically in the interests of surviving, remaining alive, as a writer. I didn't see Salim as a Hemingway-type figure, though – there was an Indian softness about him which set him apart from Hemingway's hard, sentimental individualism; a softness that hinted at dependency – possibly a mother he was close to.

I myself had never consciously adopted 'going out into the world' as a programme for rejuvenation, and I said as much to Salim. 'In fact,' and I was thinking aloud for the first time about this in the room in Park Mansions, 'I can feel trapped in the whole business of writing, especially writing fiction, and have in the past. I find that what works best for me is a different kind of travel: between genres – into the essay, or story, or into music. I can't stay with one genre, especially with the novel, for very long. I feel restless, and must move in another direction – which is usually another form.'

Salim took this in with limpid receptivity; but I wasn't certain if it convinced him.

For about twenty years now, I'd heard one dramatic English word – 'bloodbath' – whenever that moment in the future was speculated upon, when power would change hands. Although this was now, for many, a certainty, the elections in Bengal were being completed without any major unrest, and when I went out on the morning of the 27th, the city was calm. There were theories explaining the tranquillity in a state whose villages and towns have been periodically agitated by political violence. The mercenaries who'd been the bottom-rung CPI(M) cadres were simply moving over to the other side, said one theory. The balance of power between the two parties was more equal than ever before, said another, and none would risk confrontation at this point. Most of all, everyone was quietly thanking the Election Commission which, with its no-nonsense 'presiding officers', was doing perfectly its job as impartial organiser and overseer and as conductor with multiple batons waving to an unthinkably intricate orchestra. The 27th had, strangely, been declared a public holiday. The roads, as a result, were sparsely peopled. Several times a year, Calcutta changes itself by suspending activity. It does this during *bandh* ('closure') days, when a political party will call for a general strike from work on a certain date in protest against some oppressive measure. The city empties and hardly anyone leaves home until 6 p.m. It does it during festive days, when the streets may be crowded, but both work and traffic are slowed down, calculatedly impeded, or stopped by spectatorial crowds. It happens during the monsoons, when the antique drainage, choked with new, discarded plastic bags, can't cope, and the roads are waterlogged, trousers rolled up, sandals lost. These off-days merge with each other in their epiphanic registers of withdrawal, celebration, and calamitousness. At some point, reading a book, you might think, 'But this isn't a holiday – the rest of the world is working,' and marvel at the way Bengal cultivates – and simultaneously mourns and celebrates – its disconnect with globalisation. That entire, useless day will have no function but to defamiliarise a city where little otherwise changes. April 27 had, deceptively, a similar air.

'There's nothing of interest in your area,' a friend, the political scientist Dwaipayan Bhattacharya, assured me. So, directed by him, I went to the faraway southern reaches of the city, which are still semi-rural, and to which development and real estate are threatening to come rapidly. A fairly recent highway, the Eastern Metropolitan Bypass, took me to Kamalgachi, where a man was selling watermelons from a cart on the side of the road, right next to a camp of casually congregated, but disciplined-looking, Trinamool Congress workers. 'How's voting been going?' I asked, and he grinned and confirmed it was going well. 'So I presume you're doing good business?' I said, glancing at the watermelons, to which he grinned again, enigmatic but not unmindful of the larger context I was drawing his attention to. I wanted to know if this was a regular spot for him; he shook his head, saying he had no fixed location. This strategic point on the curve of the bypass, not far from the narrow inlet of a lane that led to the polling booth, was, for the present, a useful place to be. He was dark, moustached, rakish-looking: I can't imagine he was more than thirty-five years old. Two older men, customers, had sniffed something anomalous about my presence and become curious. They too wanted to be questioned, and, in an unspoken pact, I obliged them. 'What do you do?' I asked. 'Hawkery,' said one a bit apologetically, making a Bengali noun of his profession. 'I used to work for Usha Fans, but there are no jobs in the fan business any more.' His friend was a mechanic for two-wheelers. 'Well, do you think paribartan will come?' I asked, deliberately throwing up the oft-repeated word. They laughed at the joke: 'Come it will!' said the hawker and former Usha Fans employee. 'Are you voting Trinamool?' 'We've finished voting,' he said, with the air of a man who's had his 'high' early in the day, and isn't entirely sure whether that's a good or bad thing. 'I used to vote CPI(M) once, but it's Trinamool this time.' 'Do you think they'll do any good?' 'I don't know, but it'll put an end to the *"aamar lok"* mindset.' *Aamar lok* means 'our lot': the hawker was referring to the rampant partisanship of which the Left in Bengal is accused.

'Is it true, what someone just told me about aamar lok?' I asked one of the CPI(M) men sitting at a table on the opposite side of the by-lane that went in at a right angle from the bypass, and which tactfully separated the small Trinamool and

Left Front contingents. He was a quiet, dark, portly man called Suleiman Sardar. He shook his head at the canard. 'Look at me. I've spent all my life as a driver, and I still don't have a government job.' 'Really?' 'Yes, and I've been working for the Party since 1980, when I was eighteen' – that made him my exact contemporary – 'and I got Party membership in 2000. My friend, who was a Party worker, was an auto-rickshaw driver, and died recently.' So the Party was their life, but it didn't follow it was their profession. 'What do you think the outcome will be?' – I gestured towards the invisible polling station. 'It'll be tight,' he replied, echoing Nirupam Sen, making me wonder if this was a last-minute Party line; but his settled equanimity suggested he'd come to this conclusion himself. 'Frankly,' he said, respectful but firm, 'there's no wind of paribartan blowing here.' It was as if this was a simple, physical fact of the weather – there was either a wind (*hawa*) or there wasn't. The young men of the Trinamool, to whom I'd spoken earlier, had a directly opposed view, however, and had volunteered: 'There's a wind of paribartan blowing here.' I tended to agree, but I was no longer sure if I could actually feel a wind or not. It was undoubtedly hot. I'd said to the Trinamool men, 'Will you reject the aamar lok ethos, or continue the politics of patronage? And will Bengal emerge from the rut of reactive politics it's been stuck in for two decades, where one party says to the other, "Whatever you do, I'll do the opposite"? If it doesn't, this state is doomed, notwithstanding the paribartan that may take place now.' Everyone I said this to on the 27th – because I repeated the questions at several places – nodded and shook their heads at the correct moments, with a sweet reasonableness peculiar to that day.

I went further south, past Narendrapur into Rajpur. The name invokes bygone grandeur, but, apparently even in the seventies, it was mainly rural, with fields predominant rather than houses. Boral, the village in which Satyajit Ray shot *Pather Panchali*, isn't that far from here. It was now defined by a main road with a small-town procession of shops and low houses on either side, with a maze of lanes emanating from it: a place to be passed through, its life wondered at through a car window. In a characteristic narrow alley off this road, wide enough for a single car, sat the Left and Trinamool 'camps', ignoring each other, at least two hundred metres away, according to the Election Commission's ruling, from the polling station. The Left greeted me jovially, among them my namesake, Amit Sarkar (known, he said, to friends as 'Babu'), and his ebullient wife, Rupali. She was particularly upbeat, showering my cupped palm with Chloromint chewing gum, which, according to laboriously funny TV commercials, has unique cooling qualities. She probably had abundant access to the gum since Mr Sarkar owns a medicine shop. No signs of down-heartedness were discernible – as if this group was either naturally playful and voluble or buoyed up by an oxygen they'd been breathing in for thirty-four years. The Trinamool man, hunched over a desk, was quieter; he was welcoming, but there was a shadow over him. He had the air of one who's been biding his time; in a sense, he was, even now, crouched in the wings, separate from the main drama. Serious and geeky, he turned out to be, sure enough, a computer graphic designer. He was doing this work from a sense of *apamaan* (of having been insulted) and *jaala*, he said – that is, a burning that may arise from resentment, envy, or a sense of injustice. 'You can't even get a tap installed in a new house unless you're a CPI(M) man,' he declared bitterly. He had two energetic, waif-like working-class men standing on either side (they'd occupied the small porch of a house), who were muttering their own stories and contributions, as if they might be otherwise heard by Mr and Mrs Sarkar in the distance, with whom relations were, naturally, polite but frigid. One, Shyamal Ray, was a fishmonger (but the word he used was 'hawker') at Gariahat, and the other, Mahadev Dey, also plied his trade at Gariahat (a twenty-minute walk from where I live), selling bags in front of City Mart. His old stall had been wrecked and his possessions looted by CPI(M) workers during Operation Sunshine in 1997, at one o'clock in the morning, he told me in his low, urgent undercurrent of words – Operation Sunshine being the government's attempt to rid Gariahat of hawkers and of the dreadful (now non-existent) stretch called, wishfully, the 'boulevard'. Some say it was a bankrupt government's response to the IMF's demand that it clean up the city before it received yet another loan – a demand at which Jyoti Basu had reportedly sniffed dismissively, *'Mamar badi!'* or 'Do you think Calcutta's your personal backyard?', which is what a *mamar badi* or maternal uncle's house is traditionally said to be for delinquent nephews. Mahadev Dey was a Left sympathiser but had grown disenchanted, until his vision of himself and his future had revived with his discovery of 'didi'.

People were voting at the primary school on the same lane, the Rajpur Harkali Vidyapith (established 1967). Despite being peopled and busy, it looked like a municipal husk of what it was, as if it had been built almost inadvertently, and with a minimum of fuss, to dispense the Bengali and English alphabets to the children of the less privileged. A BSF officer, a handsome, gracious South Indian, permitted me to interview the voters standing in the two queues: one for men, the other for women. The young men looked like they had no regular employment; they broke into a strange laughter on being questioned. They'd decided I was hilarious, sidling up to them, and had a hard time remaining serious or even civil – and I, once again after my schooldays (how appropriate, then, that this should be happening in a school compound), felt conspicuous and silly in the eyes of the hardened boys. When I asked them if their vote today was of particular importance, they appeared offended and vigorously denied it. The women were friendlier and more personable, and I had an easier time with them: I spoke to two board-thin working-class women who described their occupation with the English word 'housewife', though they could well have been domestic help. I tried to make conversation with a beautiful, stand-offish girl in a smart salwaar kameez, a student of art history at a little-known art college; further up the queue, a girl who, as it turned out, worked at a travel agency, kept turning back to look. 'Do you sometimes think you might need to leave Bengal for better opportunities?' I asked. 'No, I don't agree with that,' said the art history student, inching forward with the queue. But the girl at the travel agency, who was very close to the door to the classroom, swerved back again to look at me and said, 'There's no future here in my profession.' I moved towards her, like a salesman who has limited time to make a pitch. 'You think you'd have better prospects in Delhi and Bombay?' The art student, to whom I'd simultaneously flung this question through an instant of eye-contact, shook her head, sphinx-like and self-contained; but the girl at the travel agency conceded this with a helpless wisdom: '*I* think so. And that's what others in my profession say so too.' 'What do you think of Calcutta's present position? Do you know, for instance, that it was once, and for a long time, India's foremost city?' She confessed this was news to her. 'Perhaps. But the Calcutta I grew up in is all I know.'

I was beginning to feel hungry. I still wanted to go to Bantala, though – partly for its fairytale name ('under the tide'), partly because it had been put on my itinerary by Dwaipayan, the political scientist. All these – Kamalgachi, Rajpur, Bantala – were locations, he pointed out, that had undergone a trans-formation in the local panchayat elections in the last three or four years; they were all steadfast traditional Left bastions that had, only recently, gone the Trinamool way. When I gave him a report at the end of the day, telling him that, to my surprise, I'd encountered nothing but calm and tolerance at the polling booths, he sounded both intrigued and gratified. More than a month later, though, he issued a caveat: 'Amit, I think it would be wrong to arrive at any conclusions about these places on the basis of what you saw at the booths *at that moment.* That's what they may have been like on *that* particular day. Traditionally, these are places with a history of political violence. The entire South 24 Parganas area has been volatile for years.' This, despite those names out of which once nursery rhymes and stories must have arisen, when there was darkness after sunset and little of Calcutta as we've long known it. 'Rajpur', city of kings; and Bantala, making me think of the child's rhyme that had trans-fixed Tagore when he was a boy: *'brishti pare tapur tupur/nade elo ban'*; 'the rain falls tapur tupur/the flood comes to the river'.

Bantala was on the South's outer reaches, and a sly diversion off the bypass took me and the driver Biswajit into a clean, slightly desolate road going into the countryside, a canal on the left, in which, he informed me with insider knowledge, shrimps were cultivated; and bright green expanses with power grids and 'speed pumps' on the right. I can't drive; I'd had to bargain with Biswajit to come to work that day. He had to be back by half past two, eat, and then vote – or so he claimed. Then my parents' driver, Mahinder, who'd voted in the morning, would take me to my two other stops for the afternoon, on what otherwise should have been, for both of them, a day of gossip, discussion, and sleep – for such, for the working man, should be the day when power potentially changes hands. Instead, here was Biswajit at the wheel; and a few drops of *kal baishakhi* rain had begun to drop stealthily, threateningly, on the windshield. Where to go? For the first time, I felt far from home, because this road wasn't leading anywhere I knew: it was headed for the coast, and for the Sunderbans, where the tiger still lives. The bus stops made of concrete were sans commuters now – and, here and there, a few jean-clad men and women in salwaar kameez suits stood next to motorcycles, or sat atop the open cycle-drawn carts that are called 'vans'; these young people, absorbed in each other, and despite their casual sensual ease, seemed desperately impoverished and to have been plucked out of the wild. It was another world. It was mainly agricultural land that dwarfed these figures, who were neither of the metropolis nor out of it, neither of the land nor of the city – agricultural land that was predestined to be colonised one day, whatever the Trinamool or the Left had planned, by industrial projects. Amidst this paradox of desolation and bounty, we passed an optimistic sign that said MOOD 'N FOOD INDIAN AND CHINESE RESTAURANT – and, then, heralded by some fluttering paper Trinamool and CPI(M) flags threaded round one of the huge trees on the left, there it was on the right: a compound like a crevasse, well below the level of the 'highway', and, further on, near a colourless one-storey building, a long rickety line of voters.

I walked cautiously towards the primary school – that's what the low building was. It was more basic than the school at Rajpur; it had no more than two or three rooms. The big room, where the polling officers, the presiding officer, and the 'micro-observer' from the Election Commission were gathered, overseeing the mildly diffident but perpetual trickle of voters, was the main classroom: the wall on the right had painted on it large black Bengali vowels and a handful of consonants, as well as the face of the godlike educationist of the Bengal Renaissance, Iswar Chandra Vidyasagar.

I wasn't allowed to ask a single question: the Election Commission had ensured a mood that was sociable and regulatory, festive, but with a respect due to an occasion like, say, public examinations. Bantala clearly had a more notable record of unrest than the other stops on my tour. Feeling that I was impeding the smooth turnover of the queue, I went outside into the compound, where, again, women stretched in one line on the right, the men on the left. There was something resistant about these figures: they weren't peasantry, and neither were they wholly urban – poverty had made them small and wiry. They didn't belong to

Satyajit Ray's world, or Bibhutibhushan Banerjee's, but to a political dispensation under which even the vegetation looked stunted, and the greenery, once you took the 'highway' departing Calcutta, grew black with soot and dust. The village Bengal of books and films, a version of which I'd seen in my childhood on the road from the airport to the city, had been made sickly in the last twenty-five years – although its naturally bountiful colours still looked lush from the aeroplane window. These people were of, and like, that landscape, economically unviable but politically alive – they were what was left of that pastoral.

Were these people from Calcutta, though? Strictly speaking, I was still in the city. But throughout that day, during which I moved from the more far-flung southern reaches back to middle-class Ballygunge, voting in the afternoon with R, dropping her home at Sunny Park, and then being driven by Mahinder into the narrow lanes of Dum Dum-Rajarhat in the north, just as the elections were winding down after four o'clock, I felt the presence of a new city that had come up where the old had been. To be *in* it was not to be any closer to comprehending it than when I'd studied it from the aeroplane window a few days ago, with its once-magical clusters of plantain and palm trees and small terraced houses. Mamata Banerjee fits in well here, having emerged, like this tentative city itself, and the people I'd met on election day, without a past, and without that enervating legacy of humanism and high culture. As to whether she would give it a future we would discover on 13th May, when the results would be declared, and in the long-anticipated years to follow.

High Tea

In April 1999, almost as soon as my fellowship in Cambridge in England came to an end, I transferred what worldly possessions I couldn't ship back to India – mainly studenty things, plates from a Latin American shop, posters, a CD player – into the damp New Court cellars at St John's College. Panting at the end of the Herculean undertaking, I felt ready to surrender to the fantasy that had gripped me for almost two decades: of returning 'home', to India. But, for more than one reason, I didn't close my bank account on King Street. Fed up though I was with what Thatcher and Blair had done, between themselves, to Britain, I wasn't ready to give it up altogether. I also had some inkling that neither India nor Calcutta, my birthplace, was the sort of nation and city to receive their returning sons emotionally, with open arms.

In fact, I was welcomed, on my arrival, by a negative review of *Freedom Song* (which had been published seven or eight months earlier) in the *Statesman*, still, at the time, Calcutta's leading English-language daily. Reviewing is often a form of thuggery in Anglophone India, territorial, threatening, a way of roughing somebody up; and the Books pages are a bit like a lawless part of town, from which you have to be thankful to slip away with your writerly life – not to mention your dignity – intact. This review, which my father had kept from me, and which had shocked him slightly, had begun by quoting from Plato, and proceeded to claim that the 'novel is dead' after Angela Carter and Salman Rushdie. My poor novel – an example of the genre that had the temerity to persist after its demise – had been called an 'entomologist's notebook', and its characters compared to stick insects. To add to these insults was the insult of the review being quite poorly written by the Plato-reading reviewer, bristling with bad syntax and self-importance, and unaware of its missing articles. At thirty-seven, I was still young, but not entirely surprised. But some wishful part of me had longed for a warmer greeting.

Not everyone in Calcutta had viewed me with hostility, though a few people had. There were, for instance, readers who were effusive about my first novel, *A Strange and Sublime Address*, saying it had noticed the minutiae of their lives, details that lay perpetually before them, and which, as a result, they didn't look at. I was grateful for this generosity when it came my way, but I was also – for what reason I didn't know – suspicious, as if I couldn't accept the praise at face value. Among the people who sought me out was a couple called the Mukherjees. Their via media was a journalist who'd interviewed me for *Desh*, the leading Bengali-language weekly, who said, 'Would you mind if I passed on your address to this couple? The gentleman wants to write to you. They love literature, and entertain writers sometimes. Of course, they might be a bit insistent.' I reflected on this and enquired, 'Are they all right, though?', as if to preclude the possibility of their having a violent streak. The journalist (who, I'd soon find out, wasn't entirely 'all right' himself, and who'd take against me after my second novel, *Afternoon Raag*) thought about this briefly, and said, 'Yes, they're fine.'

So it was that Anita Mukherjee invited my wife and me to afternoon tea.

The Mukherjees lived on the ground floor of a two-storeyed building on Lower Circular Road. A narrow driveway led to the parking space by the entrance. A collapsible gate barred the doorway to the flat; behind it was the actual door, which was generally opened by the beaming Mrs Mukherjee.

Once we were inside this gently peeling, charming apartment, we'd turn left into the sitting room, where Mr Mukherjee would be seated on a chair in a newly ironed shirt and trousers, barely containing his excitement. He would then proffer his hand in a strange way, for us to hold and shake. He would be terribly apologetic, but mutedly euphoric.

Samir Mukherjee's reason for being apologetic was his inability to stand up to greet us, or come to receive us at the door. This was because he'd contracted polio long ago, in 1959. Polio, in Calcutta, was a disease that had disfigured the lives of the upper classes besides affecting the poor; I knew of at least two other people from Mr Mukherjee's generation who belonged to that same vanishing, near extinct corporate world in the city, who'd got polio at some point and dealt with it in their own manner.

The disease had reached a stage – when I first met the couple in 1992 or 1993 – where Mr Mukherjee stepped out of the house infrequently. The Mukherjees' tea time, as a result, was less about the guests than about Samirda (as we'd begun to call him), although Samirda himself didn't so much hold forth as urgently – but solicitously – question his guests, almost interviewing them, as if they were famous. He asked me, for instance, about books, about writing, about my parents, about Calcutta, and listened agog to my replies. I, on my part, felt I had to perform: felt that this self-deprecating man on the chair had the best seat in the house, that I was on a makeshift proscenium, that he was obscurely important and mustn't, at the end, be left unhappy. But I quickly began to feel at ease with this couple, not least because they laughed with what seemed like genuine delight at my jokes and occasionally rude observations about people – of which, obligingly, I delivered a constant stream over tea. There was something about the Mukherjees that invited this nonchalance; I'd take refuge in my careful, invented social persona when there were other guests around. This didn't mean that I had completely let go of the innate suspiciousness I felt in relation to people who claim to like my work. Samirda had made his thoughts known to me in a letter written on lined paper; it went on to a page and half, and informed me, eloquently, of how he'd been moved by my enshrining of the everyday objects of which a middle-class Bengali's life is composed. (Later, I'd find out that the polio had also affected Samirda's arm; that he'd dictate his letters – and the various missives he'd send to the editor of the *Statesman* at the time – directly to his wife, in whose neat handwriting Samirda's sometimes ornate sentences were transcribed. This explained, too, the odd, oblique, almost ambivalent way the hand was extended towards you for a handshake.) I was touched when I received this letter; then I began to wonder if there was more to it than met the eye. When Anita Mukherjee first called us to tea in her melodious, measured English, I had a – as it turned out, unnecessary – sense of foreboding.

After two or three visits, I noticed that the Mukherjees didn't join us for tea. A bowing and diffident servant in a short dhuti would bring in tea on an enormous tray about twenty minutes after we arrived, along with food on plates and, what seemed most important of all, spotless napkins. Then Anita would wait for seven minutes for the tea to brew, before pouring it, with an erect swan-like sureness, into our cups.

At some point, I asked them if they wouldn't join us. And this led, on Samirda's part, to a fumbling for words – an upper-class Bengali version of harrumphing. No, he explained, both he and his wife managing to become conspirators, they'd already had their tea. *This* was a sort of public ritual, at which they were purely spectators. For this reason – and not just because of the unexpectedly heavenly sandwiches Anitadi made – they appeared to their guests as transcendent, at a slight remove, belonging to a different sphere from the partakers of the tea, who had a more routine access to the world. I also began to realise that, having had their own tea at four, they'd begin to prepare for their guests' arrival; that, by six o'clock, they'd be in the sitting room, patiently waiting for the sound of the car coming up the driveway, which would be a signal – sometimes a false one – that the second teatime, the much-anticipated one, was under way. Possibly because there was such an undercurrent of excitement to this period of waiting, Anita Mukherjee, when she received us at the door, was warm, serene, even a little distant. True excitement is contained, and doesn't overstep its own measure.

There was another presence in the room, whom we encountered the moment we entered it, and then, as the tea unfolded, forgot. This was Samirda's mother, by then in her mid-eighties. She was seated right next to the door of the sitting room; at first, I found this odd – it was as if she was being kept apart from the inner circle of the tea: almost like a chowkidar whom no one notices. Then I realised she was positioned in a way that would facilitate an early exit, when she became tired. Her vantage point added a dimension to the room: just as Samirda and Anitadi spectated, with a sort of visible pleasure, upon their guests having tea and offering up opinions, Mrs Mukherjee looked upon this small spectacle – of her son and daughter-in-law entertaining their friends – with an enjoyment imprinted on her face as a small smile of contentment. She was a bit deaf; so her pleasure must have been largely visual and – though she sat separate from us – participatory. Her presence also clarified for me what I'd just had an intuition of during this elaborate ritual: that Samirda, like most Bengali men, myself included perhaps, had never entirely grown up – that there was a continuity, for much of his life (possibly enchanted, possibly oppressive at times) – with his childhood.

Mrs Mukherjee Senior was birdlike, but she was still beautiful, her straight hair parted in the middle and tied back severely, with a puritanical simplicity. She had a Roman nose. She also had a squint; what in Bengali is called 'lokkhi tera', or a squint that gives an auspicious femininity and softness to a woman's face. Quite a few years after her death, when I saw de Sica's film version of Giorgio Bassani's novel *The Garden of the Finzi-Continis*, the matriarch of the doomed Jewish family – who is only ever glimpsed in passing, in the drawing room, or taking a walk in the estates with her husband – reminded me fleetingly of Samirda's mother. Both women seemed – the real and the fictional one – to have been situated in a bygone aristocracy, and to know their precise place in it, while their children may have realised that the world they presided over had really disappeared.

On our first visits, my wife and I noticed that Mrs Mukherjee Senior said 'thet' for 'that', 'beck' for 'back'. It was a late Victorian pronunciation of English words, and should have survived, at most, to the forties. Samirda's mother must have picked it up in school, and she was quite unselfconscious about her distinctive approach to vowels. My wife, secretly, was startled into remembering her grandmother – her father's mother – whenever Mrs Mukherjee spoke; she was tickled (there's no other word for it) at this return, without warning, of what she thought was a bizarre and unique part of her ancestry. Her grandmother had died three years ago of cancer. R waited till the next meeting before asking Mrs Mukherjee (who always stooped forward slightly and clasped our hands when we said hello to her): 'Did you know my grandmother Anila Bose by any chance? You speak so much like her' – as if mere diction might open a doorway onto a once-known world. 'Bhona!' exclaimed Mrs Mukherjee – almost all Bengali pet names are supposed to be embarrassing, and my wife's grandmother's was no exception – 'Of course I know her! I was her junior by a few years at Loreto! Why, this is wonderful!' The Mukherjees, as a family, had a way of making emphatic, jubilant assertions; and it was now my turn to watch as they went into a huddle with R.

Samirda's lineage was what was once derisively called 'Ingabanga'. So was my wife's father's maternal line. Bhona played tennis, knew which knife and fork to use during the various stages of dinner, was aware that the knife and fork must meet in perpendicular unison on a plate to indicate a meal was finished, and called the coconut-flavoured, sugar-coated tea biscuit 'nees', where ordinary people said 'nice'.

The Ingabanga was a mutant produced by British rule and by aspiration – an obsessive desire to approximate and reproduce Englishness. This is not to say that the Ingabanga – or Anglo-Bengali; predecessor of the 'wog' and of the 'coconut' (brown outside, white within) – was Westernised, while the dhuti-panjabi-wearing bhadralok was pure and native. In fact, the latter was deeply cosmopolitan; even European, in some ways. He would have probably learnt English as a second language; but that didn't impede the bhadralok's intimacy with the West. While the bhadralok might know Milton and Marx as well as he knew the novels of Bankimchandra Chatterjee, he might not – unlike the Ingabanga – pronounce English words perfectly, or be conscious of the difference between Camembert and Stilton, or have tasted asparagus. One of the joys of Anitadi's teas was listening to the conversation, mainly because of how beautifully the Mukherjees spoke English: it lost its Anglo-Saxon consonantal hardness, and became a liquid murmur in their mouths. Tagore wasn't Ingabanga: he lamented, often histrionically, his lack of command over the language, exaggerating, deliberately, his deficiency – a calculated and inverse showing off. He was actually very well-read in English literature. But he did confess, as I said earlier, to not being able to distinguish between the pronunciation of 'warm' and 'worm': a common Bengali conundrum. An Ingabanga wouldn't have that problem. Still, simply being an Anglophile didn't ensure you were Ingabanga. For instance, Nirad C. Chaudhuri, who dedicated his first book to the memory of the British Empire, was an East Bengali provincial raised in a small town; he had an extraordinary breadth of reading and was a master of English prose style, but had learnt English as a second language. That he took to wearing a bowler hat and a suit after moving late in life to Oxford, or interrogated his often famous guests about wine and Mozart, couldn't change him from being an eccentric Bengali Anglophile into an Ingabanga: nor would he have wanted to be one. For the Ingabanga was a person of privilege, yes, but also caricatured as a slightly fatuous servant of the British: the member of a disliked minority in Bengal that had surrendered to the English way, of which the observance of table manners was just a symptom.

By the time we met the Mukherjees, the exacerbations caused by Empire and the British were distant enough for us not to mind too much whatever remained of that age, in whatever form – even anecdote, or tea and sandwiches. In fact, in the 1990s, privileged pasts, with a sort of fin-de-siècle energy, were making a comeback. This energy coincided with the advent of globalisation and economic liberalisation, and with the end of the Nehruvian era, with its various self-imposed austerities and hypocrisies. People – some of whom even claimed to have socialist leanings – said they were descended from maharajahs, although titles and their hereditary privileges had been emphatically rescinded by Indira Gandhi: one of her few near-autocratic gestures that had a moral rightness to it.

In the nineties, though, almost every upper-class person boasted of having a familial connection with either a maharajah or a governor, or a legendary name in the freedom struggle; in Bengal, people disclosed how they were distantly related to some iconic figure in the Bengal Renaissance, or to a colonial aristocracy that counted Sir and Lady So-and-so among its members. India, under the new free-market dispensation, was having to manufacture a new elite, and shamelessly plunder, recoup, and excavate the old elite while doing so. So, not only was the maharajah, with his turban and tiger skin on the floor before him, returning from the dead, but, in Calcutta, the Ingabanga too.

The irony, of course, was that Samirda was genuinely the progeny of an old elite that was petering out.

Having grown up in Bombay, with the sort of parents I had, I knew almost nothing of the importance of family connections. I couldn't say I was related to a celebrated figure or household, and didn't spend too much time wondering about these things; maybe, in the seventies, this was still not a way of conceiving of your place in the world.

Besides, I am an only child, and so is my father; I lived with my parents in a luxurious island of self-sufficiency. 'Family' – especially my mother's family – was synonymous to me with the faraway (since many of my uncles had settled in small towns after Partition), with whatever was different from ourselves, and with being a seedbed for human foible. I knew my uncles, my mother, my aunt, were gifted, and that I might have inherited a bit of whatever little talent I had from them; but those uncles were great time-wasters too, and could spend an entire morning expending a great deal of emotion and even reasoning deciding which was the better fruit, the mango or the custard apple, the more melodious singer, K.L. Saigal or Sachin Deb Burman. So I came to believe, perhaps mistakenly, that families were not distinguished by their connection to history, but that they were a counterpoint to it; that history paled into dullness in comparison with the strangeness of family.

'Aristocracy – tell us another!' says Bassani's narrator of the last patriarch of the Finzi-Continis, Professor Ermanno, and his wife Signora Olga. 'Instead of giving themselves such airs, they'd have done much better, the both of them, not to forget who they were, and where they came from, if we're to believe that the Jews – Sephardic and Ashkenazi, Western and Levantine, Tunisian, Berber, Yemenite and even Ethiopian – in whatever part of the world, under whatever skies history has scattered them, are and will always be Jews, which is to say close relatives.' The narrator, who's in love with the young daughter of the family, is reminding us, with bitter irony, that, at a certain point in history, no Jew, whatever their hubris about pedigree and wealth, could escape the disgrace of who they were. Rich Jew and poor, dark and fair, were part of a single unhappy family.

The Calcutta upper class was also all related to each other: I realised this after I moved here. More exclusive than the Jews, less endangered, they seemed to know each other by name, and, if they didn't, had the knack – or helpless habit – of unearthing connections. They might have once married outside their immediate circle: into a bhadralok or educated middle-class family, for instance. (The word bhadralok is admittedly slightly slippery; since it's synonymous with 'gentleman', it could well be claimed by any member of the landed gentry or even the suited Ingabanga clan who wished to be part of the new dispensation that came into being by the end of the nineteenth century, of secular individuals identified by their sophistication and learning, rather than the extent of their property and land.) Whatever the nature of these marriages, it's true that my family (East Bengali landlords on my father's side, who lost their properties with Partition; colonial engineers on my mother's side, who lost face and status after her father's early death) could hardly claim to be part of this web of relations in Calcutta.

◆

My wife herself is a product of a series of marriages that travelled, confusingly, in several directions. Her mother was a daughter of a manager of a Tata factory in Jamshedpur, outside Calcutta. Naturally, the family had bhadralok ambitions, and my mother-in-law had talent – which is why she went to Santiniketan to study Tagorean dance. Not long after, my father-in-law, an engineer, fell in love with this undeniably beautiful woman. In proposing to her, he was departing his small, charmed, stifling circle; but he was too besotted to bother – besides, he was in secret rebellion against his parents: the distinguished father and the high-nosed mother. His father, Satish Ranjan Khastgir, was of a Brahmo bhadralok family, a noted physicist, a colleague of the great Satyen Bose, and a D.Sc. from Edinburgh. The painter Sudhir Khastgir was Satish Ranjan's younger brother.

My father-in-law's mother, Anila, came from one of the most accomplished Ingabanga families in Bengal; her grandfather was P.K. Ray, the first Indian principal of what was then surely India's premier institution of higher education, Presidency College; her grandmother, Sarala Ray, founded the Gokhale School. Anila's great-grandfather, Durgamohan Das, had founded the intimidatingly renowned Doon School.

When I met R, this personal lineage – not that she was overly aware of it – had all but dissolved into the everyday. It was now available in anecdote, transitorily. By the time I married R, her father had retired from a public sector job in Hindustan Copper. Still, she couldn't entirely escape her past: this was apparent from the way she thought she heard her grandmother speaking the first time she heard Samirda's mother, and was startled by her narrow, anachronistic vowels.

R's grandmother Anila – echoed belatedly, and unwittingly, by Mrs Mukherjee – hadn't been wholly happy marrying a dhuti-wearing physicist. Her sights had been set on, and imagination fired by, the celebrated Bengali physicist Prasanta Mahalanobis.

But the shy man in the dhuti, bespectacled, serious, had been invited to the house to meet the middle sister, herself a studious, reticent type. While leaving the house, he noticed a young woman seated on the staircase behind the banister, giggling. He asked her parents for her hand, leaving, in effect, the older sister forever single – or, as they called such women at the time, a spinster. My wife was close, I think, to her grandfather, and to the sister who was spurned by him in favour of Anila. When I was getting to know R, I discovered she still dreamed of her Mejo thakuma and her dadu.

What Anila Khastgir née Bose really felt about her marriage to the physics professor in lieu of the legendary Prasanta Mahalanobis is difficult to tell from the stories she told my wife – and no one else. Certainly, Satish Ranjan Khastgir earned the devotion of his students, and his granddaughter's affection, but not the sort of national eminence that Mahalanobis or Satyen Bose did. After retiring from his post as Khaira Professor of Physics at Calcutta University, he and his wife withdrew to the pastoral of Santiniketan, which was, by then, in the late sixties, just beginning to go to seed. Anila survived her husband, who, despite being a teetotaller, died of a mysterious liver disease; and R remembers an incident from a weekend when her grandmother came to visit them in their flat in Mandeville Gardens in South Calcutta. A man who lived in a neighbouring street, Suren Thakore Road, unexpectedly called on the family, asking if he could talk to her. He had spotted her on her arrival, he said; he used to live near the big house in Dhaka where her father, a barrister, was once posted, and he and his brothers would climb up a wall and watch, unobserved, as the two sisters played tennis with their English friends. Anila Khastgir was amused, but, after the man's departure, she confessed to being a bit down-hearted – that so little remained of that girlhood, and also of the barrier defining it, which had, all those years ago, made that act of spying necessary.

❖

It was difficult for me, at first, to understand the significance of these special Calcutta families, with their past careers, and their often unexceptional present-day representatives. I began to realise that there were a fair number of them around. Many of the worthy people in Calcutta's upper-class history had never quite reached my consciousness when I was growing up, and if they did – say, the founder of this or that school – they remained at a great distance which I didn't feel any impulse to cover. Similarly, the Mukherjees: I had no curiosity about their forbears, but kept going back, primarily, for Anitadi's incomparable sandwiches.

These were made of an ordinary but soft sandwich bread which Anitadi bought from the 'market'; she never used the posh Calcutta Club loaf which was evidently good for morning toast but not for the teatime sandwich. They had canonical fillings – chicken and mayo, egg, cheese, and tomato – but, on occasion, Anitadi would give us the idiosyncratic, very personal yoghurt and chives, or add spring onion to the cheese. Even when it was just egg, the sandwich had the capacity to surprise us. It was as if it possessed some of the irreducible ingredient that made the Mukherjees what they were. I could never bear to eat the sandwiches – except in interrupted stretches – because, otherwise, they were gone as soon as they'd arrived. They were perfect to look at, spotless rectangles, but – a fact hidden till you tasted them – quite unresistant; a mouthful announced itself to your palate and then immediately melted to a residue. There were other attractions on the plate, usually expensive high-calorie tarts or a mousse from the nearby Kookie Jar, all meant to convey a surplus of a very unBengali well-being. Never, for example, were we served the traditional Bengali teatime meal: the deceptively light, puffy, deep-fried luchis with aubergine or potatoes. *That* sort of tea would have engendered its own over-familiar universe, its protagonists and rooms, the home of the bhadralok – but not Samirda's and Anitadi's world, with its silently paired sandwiches and the still life of the Kookie Jar cakes.

Mrs Mukherjee sat upon her chair in the ground-floor flat in Lower Circular Road, almost meditating, except for the wicked, abstracted look the squint gave her, and the inward smile. She ruled the tea from the margins, like a person who wields an obscure power but holds no office. Going in and out of the room, Anitadi would bend to take a query, clarify something, laugh at what the older woman had said.

It had not always been so harmonious. When Samir Mukherjee got polio in 1959, Mrs Mukherjee had been certain that her son should never marry. No woman would look after him properly, or be patient enough: the marriage would be a disappointment for her son.

Then, in 1965, Samirda met his wife-to-be on her twenty-first birthday: 17th July. It was at a rooftop party at the plastic surgeon Jaya Roy's house on Landsdowne Road: as in the perennial moment of noticing that precedes love and sometimes marriage, Samirda saw that she was 'sitting quietly', not talking to anybody. The heroine must always be reticent and unsociable until the protagonist arrives. He asked to be introduced, and informs me they 'clicked' at once. Samirda had probably a great deal to give of himself to the right person. He gives a bit of himself to his guests at tea, and what he offers at some point struck me – once my natural distrust began to wear off – as true and simple, almost too simple (this might have been a cause of the distrust), undiminished by circumstances and even the delusions of his class. So it wasn't surprising that Anita Roy, as she then was, liked him: for being 'well-turned out' and for his 'impeccable manners'. He, in turn, liked her 'charm and reserve', her 'baby's face' and her 'tall, willowy figure': what he calls, touchingly, her '*mojar chehara*'. '*Mojar chehara*' could be translated, variously, as 'funny looking' or 'interesting looking' or even 'charming to look at'. Today, Anitadi still has that mojar chehara; tall for an Indian woman of her generation, her hair is steely grey, but, otherwise, she is attractive, partly because of her contained demeanour and the emotion and laughter she holds in check – she's perhaps more attractive now than she was at twenty-one, with a retrospective allure that's rare and not to be discounted. She almost always wears pale tangail saris, and her complexion is what racist Indians, when they're being polite, call 'dusky'. Spotting her and then winning her over hints at what Samirda's chosen function and project in life would be – not to be a man of great ambition or corporate vision, as his immediate ancestors had been, but a self-deprecating connoisseur of comeliness. In his wife-to-be, he'd found someone who didn't regard this project (she couldn't have known, and nor could he, that it was going to be a lifetime's work) as mere indulgence.

When Anita Roy and Samir Mukherjee finally married in February 1968, the tumult and far-reaching Naxalite disturbances around them – about to permanently transform this city – were echoed by a different kind of exigency. Samirda's mother disowned him. She asked him to leave the majestic house, his maternal grandfather's, in which he'd grown up, largely happily, and which, by the time I met him in 1993, was Viswa Bharati University Press's Calcutta office. So he and Anitadi moved hastily to what Samirda calls, casually, a 'pied-à-terre', but what must have been quite a smart apartment, in swish Tivoli Park (finally razed to the ground in 2010) on Lower Circular Road, probably a fifteen minutes' walk from the mansion from which he'd been ejected by his mother. Her objection to the marriage didn't have to do with the bride's lineage, or, for instance, the fact that Anitadi's mother was an 'Anglo-Indian' (Anitadi's father was a well-known general surgeon). She simply couldn't bear Samirda getting married.

Mrs Mukherjee was much too fond of her son, though, for the estrangement to last long. After three months, returning from Ranchi, where she'd fled to escape what Samirda calls the entirely 'imaginary' scandal of the marriage, she met the newly-weds and 'forgave' Samirda. The couple continued to live in Tivoli Park, though, in the magic of what can only be called a 'service apartment'. Strictly speaking, what they lived in was a 'cottage', being provided with lobster thermidor and fish Portuguese and gateaux by a cook called Daniel, who catered to some of the building's fortunate tenants and homeowners. One of the legacies of the Bengali Ingabanga community is its fanciful obsession with 'continental', what in these plebeian times is briefly, and with proprietary nonchalance, referred to as 'conti': not French cuisine, or Italian, or Spanish, or even English, but a sui generis colonial variant, much of which, like Indian food in England, is unavailable anywhere else in the world; you must come to Calcutta to procure and taste it, and you must leave Calcutta to understand it is a fiction. Some of these dishes (like chicken Tetrazzini, which I first heard of from Samirda, immediately deciding it sounded like a hoax) remain as stubbornly unchanged since they first appeared on the menu as the old government buildings facing Chowringhee. When Samirda wishes to convey to me that the ten years he spent with Anitadi at the pied-à-terre were happy ones, it's not his own life or hers but the lunches and dinners he describes. In 1978, there was a rumour that Tivoli Park might be purchased by a contractor and torn down; the Mukherjees thought it was time to depart the pied-à-terre. By now, the mansion in which Samirda had grown up had been sold to Viswa Bharati; a wall had been erected in the middle of what had been his late maternal grandfather's garden, and, on the other side, a two-storeyed house had come up. To the ground-floor flat of this building moved Mrs Mukherjee Senior and her long-forgiven son and daughter-in-law; here, roughly fifteen years later, after going up the narrow driveway, we encountered the small family of three gathered discreetly to receive us.

The professional antecedents of Samir Mukherjee's immediate forefathers, and his own, belonged to a company called Martin Burn Ltd. Created originally in 1890 by Sir Thomas Acquinas Martin and Rajen Mookerjee (later Sir Rajen), it went on to become Calcutta's foremost construction company, and build landmarks like the Esplanade Mansion. This building, if you make eye contact with it during a traffic jam, still, in that brief, lethargic duration, has the power to arrest you with its art nouveau take on the Tower of Babel, to be both of and not of the billboards, the swarms of hawkers, the buses that take off without warning at terrifying speed, and the pedestrians constantly rushing about the Esplanade. It is one of those many things that make Calcutta at once a European city and a Bengali one.

Burn and Co. also built the monument that serves as a metonym for the city on magazine and book covers, and in documentaries on television – when, that is, the destitute and Mother Teresa aren't standing in. The work of William Emerson, the architect of Bombay's magnificent Crawford Market, Calcutta's Victoria Memorial is a monstrosity, the curiously private and laborious vision of a person who either didn't know Calcutta or deeply disliked Queen Victoria. A leaden idea, it weighs down resignedly on the generous expanse it occupies not far from the Race Course, given an intractable presence by Burn and Co., inspected and ignored today by tourists from obscure Bengali towns.

Sir Rajen Mookerjee's son was Sir Biren – I don't think knighthoods are hereditary, so to produce two Knights of the Empire was no mean feat for a single Bengali family – and Samirda recalls him being in charge of Martin Burn (which was created in 1946 after a merger) when he was working there. Sir Biren was, among other things, Samirda's maternal granduncle. His wife was Lady Ranu, who excites few fond thoughts in Samirda, and whom he tersely calls a 'skinflint'. Growing up in Bombay, I was completely unaware of Sir Biren, and later only tangentially. In the seventies, in the nation-building calm of what remained of the Nehruvian age, the idea of an Indian Sir Someone was no more or less than embarrassing: but, then, many things embarrassed us at the time which don't any more. Later, when I was told that there existed, in Calcutta, someone called Lady Ranu, I was mildly scandalised and sceptical, and a little concerned too, as you would be if you caught some-one you knew leading, stealthily, a life of make-believe. The make-believe, surely, was not only on Lady Ranu's part, but the person who'd mentioned her as if she were not a figment of the imagination. Yet, she – despite my initial refusal to take her existence at face value, and despite Samirda's glum assess-ment – was a minor celebrity in her time, beautiful, a socialite who socialised with Tagore, but, in the end, famous, simply, for being Lady Ranu. Names like 'Sir Biren' and 'Lady Ranu' con-tinued, for a while, to be oxymorons; until I saw them finally as someone's uncle or aunt, or husband or wife, or, importantly, someone's boss.

Samirda joined Martin Burn in 1956, soon after returning from Cambridge. Many of the male members of his father's generation, and his grandfather's, presided over this company in positions of power. Samirda, however, was content not to leave his mark; he was merely, as he puts it, 'visible' in the office. In Cambridge, he'd had an astonishingly good three years. Still not entirely comfortable with the opposite sex, he'd gone merrymaking and drinking with his upper-class English friends. He'd come back to Calcutta from Trinity with a Third in History ('Wasted an opportunity to learn anything'). Then he settled tentatively into employment, into becoming strategically, and merely, 'visible'. But he continued, nevertheless, the business of enjoying himself: of flirting with the pretty *taansh* or Anglo-Indian secretaries, of listening to Pam Crane singing at Trinca's at Park Street, of eating out at Firpo's and the Skyroom. In other words, instead of pursuing his ambitions (he tells me he had none), he set out to take pleasure in the bits of the city he delighted in. He couldn't have known, then, that the city – eventually a certain stretch on Lower Circular Road, leading from the Mouchak sweetshop towards Exide Batteries and Calcutta Club – would become, over the next five decades, his permanent abode; that he'd go away from it less and less, even for holidays. He was a bit like the traveller in the de Chirico painting that V.S. Naipaul invokes, 'The Enigma of Arrival', where, according to Naipaul, the visitor to the city in the picture, with a ship in the background, gradually forgets he's supposed ever to go back – except that Naipaul's visitor is a migrant, while Calcutta, to Samirda, is home, and it was home he wouldn't be leaving. For isn't the idea of home premised upon departure, and travel upon the possibility of return, and the foreclosing of that possibility? Although he'd often enlighten our teas with his heavy, dramatic nostalgia for England, Samirda had forgotten, in some basic way, that it isn't necessary to live and die at home. In that sense, and other ones, the Calcutta he inhabited when we first met him in 1993 wasn't a real one.

By all accounts, he'd begun to lead a secret life at Martin Burn. He'd become a regular reader of *Encounter*. He also became an executive in the purchase department of Indian Iron and Steel, an important subsidiary of Martin Burn, but spent much of his time making conversation with the clerks, some of whom, deceptively unprepossessing, were startlingly well read and genuine enthusiasts. He himself had embraced Evelyn Waugh – *A Handful of Dust*, et cetera. From the crowded shelves of the Calcutta Club library he'd pick up writers in vogue who are no longer read today – as is the fate of most authors stocked in clubs – writers like Elspeth Huxley, for instance. Then he contracted polio and experienced pain and, almost for the first time, hours of palpable boredom; this must have been easily alleviated by human company, however, no matter if the company comprised doctors, because he recalls them noting he was cheerful and jovial even in his discomfort. I can't imagine Samirda not being polite, despite being in the presence of doctors, because politeness is a sort of oxygen for him, and he derives from it both happiness and a reason for being. He's better at it than most people I know. And the matter of happiness: it's true – I've sometimes wondered if he's incapable of being unhappy. It's not the contentment of a man who's achieved something, or the natural well-being of an altruist, or the joy of a mystic whose source of pleasure is elsewhere, or in the divine: it's something else. Perhaps it's a deficiency. It's the strange contentment of one who's largely happy to be alive, to be helped by his wife on and off the bed (after polio, he acquired callipers for his legs, and, for many years, walked for short stretches with a stick), to offer a vicarious sort of hospitality to his guests, to be, in the best sense, even when his powers were diminishing, perpetually on the mend.

When we first met the Mukherjees, Samirda was largely homebound, but still making the occasional excursion – twice a month to the Calcutta Club, for instance. Samirda and I had brief discussions about the club, because we had a minor difference of opinion about the sort of recreation and relaxation it offered. Having then just become a member myself, I had no real moral leg to stand upon; but I still hadn't forgiven the club for throwing me off its premises repeatedly in the seventies when I would come visiting from Bombay in the obligatory costume of the teenager: kurta, jeans, and chappals. What put me in a perverse militant mood each time I approached Calcutta Club in that decade was not just the obfuscatory regulation concerning attire that inevitably denied me entry – clearly I already knew the regulation and what was awaiting me from each previous experience I'd had, and was deliberately, with the bit of Quixote in me that every person has, going clubward looking for a joust – it was the high-handed way I was disposed of I had most trouble with. I've been twice to the Athenaeum in London on a lunch invitation and lent a jacket and tie both times at the entrance by staff who had an air of brisk understanding and commiseration. At the Calcutta Club, I was treated as millions are daily in India: as one intrinsically below par. Then, in a final act of subterfuge, I became a member, before membership became unaffordable. Even so, I felt staff recognised me, with their unerring instinct, as one who'd taken up membership not for the usual reasons, but suspect ones. This staff is mostly new, and ignorant of my history; but I believe they have found me out, and the first thing they do when I step into the club is gaze steadily at my feet, to check, presumably, if I'm wearing shoes, strapped sandals, or the inadmissible strapless sandals. I'm clearly capable of anything. Now and then I will have a complaint whispered to me by a steward, that what I'm trying to pass off as my trousers are actually jeans. Both the staff and the club's members are great connoisseurs of people who are pretending to wear one thing but are actually wearing another, of those who look, to the untrained eye, rule abiding, but are not.

Samirda, though, was well loved at the club – with good reason: he was still 'impeccably turned out', as Anitadi had noticed on their first meeting; he was charming; he hailed from a distinguished Calcutta family – and the receptionists and khansamas who studied me with icy contempt wouldn't have dared greet him with anything but a smile.

But it was becoming increasingly difficult for Samirda to climb up the steps to the foyer without help or without drawing excessive attention to himself. Steps, now, were a ubiquitous impediment to his enjoyment of society. He refused dinner invitations, including mine – God knows I wanted to reciprocate in kind what had by now become substantial cups of tea and a limited but delectable array of sandwiches – but he turned down these invitations whenever he had a premonition that steps were involved. And since he didn't like the fuss made over him at the Calcutta Club – 'spectacle' was the word he used of himself – he stopped going there by the end of the nineties.

More and more, over the years, when we went to visit the Mukherjees – perhaps three or four times annually, perhaps more, perhaps less – I had the sense of a man in a very particular kind of space: living in Calcutta, but a Calcutta he saw relatively little of, a city reported on by a stream of visitors and read about in the morning newspaper. The city I'd moved to in 1999 – Kolkata – he hadn't experienced much of firsthand. Yet he couldn't help being of it – despite the fact that the Cambridge of the fifties, with its 'old chaps' and 'backs' and cycling students, was still very – almost ludicrously – real and immediate to him. I'd just moved back from Cambridge, in fact: a wet, miserable, redneck town as far as I was concerned, which became inert and ear-splittingly silent after six in the evening. But the way Samirda questioned me about it made me realise that he presumed I'd returned from the Cambridge of the fifties, with the same people going about their business, without hiatus or interruption, today as they had then. Similarly, when I mentioned my ongoing trips to Europe, he couldn't understand why I so hated travelling. He'd gone to Europe once, at the end of his Cambridge stint, with his father and brother, passing through Austria and being astonished by the glamorous Alps, catching a glimpse of snow, a great valedictory passage, without him necessarily thinking of the tour in those terms at the time. Now he wanted to know, rapt, whether it was that Europe I was flying to. He had trouble believing it was anything else. Did the pâté de foie gras and the strawberries not have the same flavour?

What of Calcutta? It was that troubled and tragic time between 1968 and 1972 that he and Anitadi seemed to find most vivid. This was the period when the Naxalite revolution exploded, and then, in a few years, was brutally suppressed. 'It was a fun time,' says Anitadi, with an odd, subversive excitement as I sip tea late into the evening; and it's intriguing to hear those years, known mainly for their violence, invoked for their charm. But never before had the Mukherjees experienced the closeness and the thrill of danger – ideology breathed new life into their drawing room in Tivoli Park, and into the incipient adventure of their married life. Naxalite artists and film-makers like Utpalendu Chakrabarty became interlopers during teatime. Samirda began to subscribe to and read the Naxalite journal *Deshabratyi*, and its English version, *Liberation*. Chaperoned and guided by the swanlike Anita, he saw his first Bengali play, *Tiner Talowar* (*The Tin Sword*), written by the great, vociferous Marxist playwright Utpal Dutta.

This mood – of cultural ferment and economic and social unrest – had been building up for years. It would, with its animosity to the oppressor, put an end to companies like Martin Burn and others. But it produced an incongruous gaiety. Utpal Basu tells me there was a 'new Renaissance' then – by which he means a sort of efflorescence that rivals and parodies the famous

Olympian Renaissance of the late nineteenth century, which produced Bankimchandra Chatterjee, Iswar Chandra Vidyasagar, Swami Vivekananda, the Tagore family, and many other mythic actors. Utpalda's list of figures from *his* Renaissance in the sixties is provocatively wide-ranging: the filmmakers Satyajit Ray and Ritwik Ghatak, the sitar maestro Ravi Shankar, the football player Sailen Manna. To this must be added Utpalda himself, and his fellow poets, friends, and contemporaries who, like him, are associated with the journal *Krittibas*: the poets Sunil Ganguly (sober but epic), Shakti Chattopadhyay (perpetually drunk, often missing, quickly dead, and frequently worshipped), Sarat Mukherjee (famous for his first book of verse, *Rimbaud, Verlaine evam nijaswa*), and the sly prose writer Sandipan Chatterjee. And, of course, there was the 'Hungry Generation' group of poets of which Shakti Chattopadhyay was also a part, and with whom Utpalda hung out: he reminds me that the rubric 'Hungry Generation' came from Keats's passionate remonstrance to the nightingale: 'Thou wast not born for death, immortal Bird!/No hungry generations tread thee down . . .' Indeed, the portrayal of humanity – and perhaps England – in Keats's ode is not too far from the circumstances in which many young people found themselves in Bengal at the time, conditions that would eventually galvanise Naxalbari: 'The weariness, the fever and the fret /Here, where men sit and hear each other groan:/. . . Where youth grows pale, and spectre-thin, and dies.'

My first remembered impressions of Calcutta are of that troubled, pulsating time. I would come to my uncle's house in Pratapaditya Road for a month and a half during my summer vacations, and sometimes three weeks in the winter – and the volatile atmosphere, the hammer and sickle painted on walls, the home-made bombs being detonated in the distance (Pratapaditya Road was an area of disturbance), the refulgent Puja annuals that my cousins got as gifts, the *adhunik* songs on the radio, with their peculiar but characteristic melodic leaps, would be mixed up for me with the enchantment of the holidays, and with their melancholy, their inevitable coming-to-an-end. I didn't want Calcutta – *that* Calcutta – to come to a close. Like Samirda and Anitadi, for whom the Naxal years are inextricable from the romance of their early married life, that period for me is inseparable from vacations and a sudden, infinite surplus of time. The Naxals were liberating Bengal from the bourgeoisie; Samirda, thrown out of his house by his mother, was liberating himself from Martin Burn and his own high bourgeois ancestry; and I was liberating myself from studies, discipline, knowledge, and my home in Bombay.

I pointed out earlier that Samirda and his wife like to listen to their guests at tea, to – and this is especially true of Samirda – throw them a question, draw them out, and then to quietly watch. But it's clear from what I've written that Samirda must also tell, that he is a raconteur. Some of what he revealed I fleshed out and filled in later, but much of it – anecdote, reverie, throwaway observation – emerged over teatime.

Samirda has met a long procession of people during these teas, and many more before his sedentary style of existence began; behind his shield of politeness, of one who has nothing significant to offer, he's studied them and their delivery closely. Now and then he'll mimic somebody: become, for instance, one of the privileged, possibly dead, 'duffers' in his family ('duffer' is an epithet he uses of his more benign Ingabanga relations), and, at another moment, assume the shrewd, narrow-eyed air of an East Bengali politician, letting loose a *bangal* snippet from the corner of his mouth.

Samirda knows that it's not just what you say but how you say it that makes you intrinsically interesting. His mimic's knack is evidence that he doesn't view his invitees without amusement; that he isn't entirely at their mercy. He annihilates himself while attending to them as they finish their éclair from Kookie

Jar; then, at some point, he annihilates them by *becoming* them in a little spontaneous display before another set of guests.

Someone I know, also a well-to-do victim of polio and frequenter of the Bengal Club, but one who continues to walk with crutches with a staccato, oppositional ferocity, once told me that Samirda hadn't tried hard enough; that he could have been more mobile if he had. I'm not qualified to judge this statement. But with Samirda I've felt that he saw movement as he did his place in history – metaphorically: as something which he didn't wish to struggle to attain, and which he was content to let slip and go its own way while he quietly went his. For this reason, his drawing room was where everything happened for him.

Mrs Mukherjee Senior was becoming more frail; by the end of the nineties, she couldn't observe the teas in their entirety. At a certain point in the evening, she'd go inside. She'd also grown more hard of hearing; but her curiosity was strong. She might want to know what had suddenly caused excitement or laughter; then Samirda would interrupt the flow of things in a loud dignified voice, shouting at her patiently in his perfect English – 'NO MA, WHAT AMIT SAID IS . . .' because, invariably, the assumption was she'd misunderstood. And she would look startled and chastened, and remind her son with a pained, Victorian firmness, 'There's no need to shout, baba, I was only asking . . .' ('Baba' was a term this family of three used of each other – in fact, of anyone in their company – to express affection. They made it particularly forgiving and emollient.) Once these exchanges were done, conversation was resumed.

Samirda once told me that his mother's finances had run out when she'd been forced to sell the one hundred thousand shares – 'a decent number, giving her decent dividends' – in Martin Burn in the eighties. He'd left the company in 1986, ten years after its future had been sealed by nationalisation, and as the new Calcutta under the Left became a location inimical to private enterprise; since then, he'd had no reliable, regular income, except the 'measly', ever-decreasing (in real terms) Rs 600 he got as a pension.

Towards the end of the millennium, Samirda also sounded more anxious than I'd known him to be. The property he lived in, the two-storeyed building, was tangled in some obscure but fatiguing litigation with a charitable and spiritual organisation. The organisation was behaving in this matter with less empathy and greater aggressiveness than it likes to be known for. Of course, Ramakrishna, sage and idiosyncratic figurehead of the organisation, had once astutely advised his fellow seekers: 'You can't be shy and retiring all the time. You need to know when to bare your fangs.' Those words had a powerful subterranean message in an age of colonialism. But the mystic may not have wanted his followers to bare their fangs at this Cambridge-educated bhadralok with polio. The problem had arisen from some reckless action by a loopy relative and his wife, who had involved the organisation in a transaction that had been interrupted upon their deaths. The organisation, as a result, had turned its attention to these surviving Mukherjees. In a state of panic, Samirda had begun disguising his voice when taking telephone calls, croaking 'Hello' in an anomalous, dislocating manner to ward off bogus litigants. His relief was audible when he realised it was a harmless acquaintance at the other end; 'Sorry, baba!' he'd say, sometimes adding 'Dash it all!' before explaining the situation, and then finally let the conversation embrace the usual constellation of subjects – Sandipan Samajpati, the young classical vocalist; beautiful society ladies (Samirda, with his wife's blessings and abetment, was a passive aesthete of feminine beauty); the present Marxist government (he and Anitadi had, at some point, resolved that they were fellow travellers).

✦ ✦ ✦

Samirda was all praise for a certain Mayank Shah, whose virtues he began to enumerate to me in the mid-nineties. Shah was a Gujarati financial advisor through whom Samirda had discovered the infinite promise of equity. He'd put Samirda's savings into the market; 'He's doing wonders with my money, baba,' I was told in a tone of grateful disbelief. 'I hope he's being careful with it,' I said at one point, sounding elderly, fussy, and superstitious about unforeseen material gain, and feeling a little envious of Samirda's triumphant entry into the new financial order of risk and growth.

Then, in a few years, he was groaning and complaining bitterly. 'Awful fellow – he doesn't pick up the phone any more.' Mayank Shah, who'd come every week in the mornings bearing good tidings, had vanished temporarily. 'I've lost lakhs, baba.' The reason for Shah's new elusiveness was that he'd played with his clients' money; he had, lately, become his clients' debtor. '"Give me one month Mr Mukherjee. I will return every paisa," he's saying now,' said Samirda, unable to resist derisively replicating Mr Shah's Gujarati inflections. All this happened well before the crash of 2008, at a time when the market, like the unfathomable gods of Hindu mythology, was appearing fully incarnate to its devotees, and offering them boons and wishes of their choosing. People were reaping the most absurd and undeserved rewards: new cars, new houses, new lives that the market had the power to create, for its followers, out of a little bit of capital. As a result, a new faith in fate and destiny – *bhagya* – was in the air: I heard the word mentioned deferentially, with wonder, by speculators, Bollywood singers, even book distributors – anyone who had anything to do with success. I recall a conversation I overheard when my second novel, *Afternoon Raag*, was about to be published in 1993. I was visiting my distributor, the savvy and expansively affectionate Lal Hiranandani of India Book House, at his well-lit office in a dingy building on Lyndsay Street. I'd groped my way up the dark staircase, and spotted Lal: he was speaking to a man (to whom he smartly introduced me) who looked like he'd never read a book in his life – probably a link in what was then a still fairly untested chain of Anglophone book distribution. They were staring, with a shared consternation and air of surrender, at the cover of the British trade magazine, the *Bookseller*, which announced news of Vikram Seth's imminent *A Suitable Boy*. Lal's interlocutor mentioned (in a dreamlike, rehearsed way, as if they'd had this exchange many times before, and would be compelled to have it again) the size of the near-imaginary advance the book had got – and, in a tic that Indian traders have, quickly translated the sum from pounds to rupees: 'One and a half crores.' There was no more than a moment's silence; then he touched his forehead and said, *'Bhagya.'* I'd never heard that word – immemorial, belonging to an arcane, resilient universe – used in such a context before, though I've heard it employed with that meaning since. It was as if the author, and his book's merits, were irrelevant to the money it had earned: some ineffable element, which he called bhagya, but which was a bhagya that played upon, and through, the market, had produced this result – and confirmed the significance of his profession and calling, where he was an anonymous link.

Destiny, assuming Mayank Shah's misleading persona, had, however, badly let down Samirda, and he was understandably bitter. About the matter of money, he was possibly a bit of a 'duffer'; as we've all been proved to be.

The late nineties was a bad time for Samirda and Anitadi, coping with the charitable organisation and Mayank Shah. Apparently Anitadi would go to the court in the morning because of the litigation to do with the property, and come back dispirited and bewildered, not having followed a word of the legal gibberish.

And yet, at teatime, she was contained as ever; you relaxed as you were taken out of the uncertain realm of your own decisions, your own volition, into a place where she was the one in control. She knew just how long she had to wait before she poured the tea; you didn't have to get anxious about it, because she was obeying an invisible metronome. Even Samirda, despite his mild agitation, was calming and reassuring. They represented the continuance of a wishful gentility; we, their guests, needed to see them in that way for about an hour, or an hour and a half. We had an idea that their lives were falling apart, but the tea was a rebuttal, for all concerned, of this melodramatic piece of knowledge – we wouldn't be here if things were really bad.

Some sort of quick remedy was needed, though, for the mess Mr Shah had made.

One afternoon, Anitadi, midway through the tea, said cheerfully that she wanted to sell two Chinese vases. Would we keep that in mind in case we knew any buyers? We were taken aback and shocked, but, at the same time, felt almost privileged we'd been asked. Anitadi's eyes had a mischievous and confidential gleam – as if this, too, were somehow a 'fun time', like the Naxal period had been. There was a quiet effervescence about her.

A few months later, they told us they were thinking they'd sell the painting in the drawing room. Did we know anyone who'd be interested? The painting, as you entered the room, occupied the wall on the right; it was fairly large, dark, and, to my eye, unremarkable. I presumed it had no importance except as a half-hearted piece of family history, bought more to decently cover a space than to be looked at. I either sat with my back to it, or opposite it, depending on which side of the centre table I was seated. Now that Samirda mentioned they might want to sell it, he turned his head, as if to check if it was still the same painting, and I saw Anitadi regard it steadily with her calm, democratic gaze – a gaze that's never either superior or obsequious – as if she were reassessing it, judging it in the light of something; as a result, I too felt encouraged – and obliged – to study it. I saw nothing in it that didn't seem vague and phantasmagoric – the silvery glint of water, a solitary boat on a ghostly journey, and a kind of faint miasma at the back, which may have been foliage, rocks, or even cloud.

I didn't care much for this kind of twilit pre-Raphaelite or Orientalist scene – I hadn't decided which it was; whether the river was a tributary of the Ganges or a stream in Scotland or England – which is why I'd avoided looking at it carefully. It might have been done by a relative, or even a friend. But Samirda recently told me that the painting was a picture in the manner of van Ruisdaal, except that the signature was missing – which is why a benefactor called Amber Patra bought it for only 40,000 rupees. Who is van Ruisdaal? A seventeenth-century Dutch painter, he was well known for his wooded landscapes and his clouds. As I look at his paintings, while they appear, one by one, on the Net, restored to a strange newness and clarity, I think I like his work; it isn't romantic, but worldly and precise – the clouds and woods and details are very real and still. A patina must have darkened the picture in Samirda's drawing room, obscuring its colours and bringing to it that twilit, Orientalist mood – which eventually dampens my spirits, and which is maybe why I'd never acknowledged it.

There were other things the Mukherjees sold at the time that I had no idea of. For instance, a golden fob watch that he recounts to me suddenly in a conversation, when I'm asking him about the painting. 'And, oh yes, there was a fob watch,' he says; and this is the last item in the inventory he's made for me, before I hastily ask him to stop – I don't want to know more.

They'd also sold a marble table to a lady I know slightly, a vivacious socialite. Samirda, inexplicably, begins to chortle; he can't help finding the ups and downs of existence entertaining. I'd heard once that the socialite herself was now in straitened circumstances, but this may be no more than the pointless gossip that circulates among a very small set of people in the city.

However, I do know that Anitadi wanted to rid herself of a necklace. She brought it out into the drawing room, and showed it to R and me: I recall the moment, and seeing the ornament, but have absolutely no recollection of what it looks like. Anitadi describes it as a 'Victorian necklace'; R thinks of it, for some reason, as an 'Edwardian knot', as a piece of jewellery belonging to and devised in the twenties or thirties. It was a long, long thing, strung with pearls, says R, ending in a knot, from which two short tassels hung. It wasn't the sort of jewellery that she would wear – strange and impractical, despite being beautiful. Besides, it was probably too expensive. What sort of social gatherings would she have worn it to?

Whether Anitadi inherited this from her mother-in-law or from the Anglo-Indian side of her family I haven't asked. It doesn't require pointing out that it wasn't a piece of traditional Indian jewellery. Firstly, the Indian woman prefers gold to any other precious metal or stone, except possibly the diamond. However, the Ingabanga had internalised, and paid homage to, the English ethos in a number of ways, including their taste in certain strains of jewellery. In the history of Indian jewellery – a history of longevity and continuity – the English ethos is a fleeting, almost momentary, interruption, and as good as a secret, since so few adhered to it. The Ingabanga, in that interim, went off the colour of high-carat gold, and even had it mixed with alloy for their ornaments, to dull their yellow gleam. What R calls 'blue-blooded Bengalis' would find this dilution outrageous, and another symptom of the ridiculousness of the Ingabanga world.

Among the ornaments my wife was gifted by her family upon our wedding was a gold bangle inherited from her tennis-playing maternal grandmother, Anila. My mother offered to have the bangle 'broken' and redesigned by a jeweller: a common enough practice, where the Bengali will take an old piece to their jeweller and, instead of selling or exchanging it, will have it rejuvenated or updated to another form. R was, naturally, sentimental about the bangle; but, newly married, she was too polite to say no to this helpful suggestion. The bangle itself was a curious mixture of East and West, of the Bengali and the English, and was a perfect material example of the notion of the Ingabanga. Its circular body was made according to the traditional style of the 'lichu-kata bala', the 'litchi-cut bangle', so that tiny bristles like the ones on a litchi peel appeared on the gold. At one place on the bangle there was an embossed carving – the head of a dog. It was a Labrador with drooping ears. Beneath my mother's helpful offer perhaps lay a disguised animosity towards the Labrador. And it was the dog, which R found absurd, which she in retrospect grew attached to – as a symbol of a history that may have been embarrassing, but was precious because of its short-lived uniqueness. 'Should I ask him to remove the dog?' asked my mother. 'You'll never wear a bangle with a dog's face, will you?' R appeared to agree. The agreement was only an instance of confusion and letting go. The Labrador disintegrated, and was replaced by a peacock, but the rest of the bangle returned intact.

The Mukherjees sold the Victorian necklace or Edwardian knot or whatever it was for one lakh rupees. Anitadi, at the time, was detached and rational about it – as she is about many things. 'What'll I do with it? I'll never wear it,' she'd said reasonably. 'One lakh is a good price, baba,' says Samirda to me today. A moment later, he's not so sure: 'Or who knows? Maybe it's not a good price. I never knew that much about money' – chortling again with pleasure. Ah, but he had his perfect spoken English, after all, his elocution. Where would he and his family have been without it? The conversation veers towards a subject seldom broached – his younger brother Prabir, who's been living in Spain for decades. 'He was much cleverer than me. Did better than I did at Cambridge.' As in? 'He got a 2:2 in economics.' A 2:2 – so not so much better, then. 'I got a third – a matter of shame. It was because I never liked economics and never understood it.'

The apartment on the upper storey was Prabir's. Yet Mrs Mukherjee, in the late seventies, had asked her younger son to give her the flat so she could rent it out for a supplementary income. (The house, of course, was hers.) This had caused bad blood between her and the – if not estranged, then distant and distanced – younger son.

A Marwari family lived upstairs and paid a static, meagre rent. When I'd said to Samirda that selling the house would be a panacea to his problems – of all things that come to the rescue of the Bengali middle and upper classes, inherited property is the most commonly invoked, and the most effective solution – he'd said, 'But there's a garden at the back, baba. I go for walks in the morning with Anita. There's a mango tree there, and wonderful birdcall. I don't know what I'd do without it.' Samirda's letters to the editor and to his friends were always fulsome and often lyrical, and so was his endorsement of this back garden. He also cited, as an obstacle to the sale of the house, the litigation with the charitable organisation; and, of course, the troublesome Marwaris upstairs.

Nevertheless, the house was sold in 2006 to a property developer for a sizeable sum. This wasn't surprising, given that property prices were going up and up in Calcutta in the new millennium, and given the house's location on Lower Circular Road.

The Mukherjees – Anita and Samir – now live in a posh apartment building called Balaka on Ballygunge Circular Road. Mrs Mukherjee Senior died only a few months after the move. She was ninety-five.

I've always liked these apartments. The building came up in the mid-seventies, almost opposite the erstwhile Tivoli Park (still, then, extant, with the Mukherjees occupying a 'cottage'), a belated, elegant gesture towards corporate living in a city, by then, largely without corporations. One of my father's colleagues lived in the building for a while; I remember visiting his son there in the early eighties, and taking in the magnificent view from the ninth-floor balcony – magnificent not because it was scenic, but marvelling at the city's intricacy and difficulty, its distant humming and beeping, its various shades of brown and grey, its sudden stretches of green, its splendid, still, leaden sky, all revealed from left to right before darkness came. I loved Balaka for the smartness of its apartments and for its view; but I had no premonition that I'd one day enter it again.

Samirda's drawing room has lovely wooden floorboards; but the teas have moved to the bedroom, so that he doesn't have to take the trouble to emerge. We find him on his bed (a high hospital bed it is), seated and leaning backward, still proffering his hand oddly, and with that disarming gentility; part yogi in his posture (he has, in fact, started doing one of Baba Ramdev's breathing exercises to keep his nasal passages clear), and part public schoolboy, as his feet are always in socks, whatever the weather, to protect him from the threat of a cold. Besides, as Tagore once pointed out, no person of Ingabanga descent would be caught in human society without their socks on. The Mukherjees, you feel, live at last in the present – a shrinking of space and time into this apartment which has almost accidentally, but properly, become their home. And the present is always built upon the decimation of the past, its erasure, the drawing room with the new floorboards acquired only once the skeleton of the past has been taken out and laid to rest.

Italians Abroad

Italian food was *not* always a worldwide phenomenon. Pizzas may feel timeless, of course; it's hard to recall when they didn't exist. Even when they were physically absent in India (in the early seventies), you encountered them time and again in comic books. An insouciant boy named Jughead, eyes shut, was repeatedly interring the long triangle into his open mouth. It would have been impossible to guess then that in two decades the pizza – no toppings, just a lot of tomato purée smeared on a cardboard-flat circle of bread, covered by a supplement of cheese – would become an indispensable component in the diet of gregarious Gujarati and North Indian families (people without pretensions, but with an appetite), and even turn up not far away from *uttapam* and *rava dosa* on South Indian menus.

In the seventies, I remember from my visits to London, Italian restaurants did very modest business. Italian waiters in spotless white clothes were always seated in an abstracted way within, waiting, without a great deal of conviction, the customer's arrival. When they did arrive, the waiter showed no great excitement, but an ironical air of vindication that some people had nothing better to do than eat at Italian restaurants. For the London customer, Italian restaurants were then principally famous – in an unarticulated way – for their red and white chequered tablecloths. Their unmistakable pattern, imprinted on the mind's eye, suggested the secluded world of Italian gastronomy. A strict and limited gastronomy it was: minestrone soup, comprising a lot of diced carrots, potatoes, and celery swilling about in reddish tomato-shot water (the tomato is the Italian chef's default condiment, something to reach for absently before any thoughts or recipes have germinated in his head); spaghetti bolognaise, as well known as Pompeii and the leaning tower of Pisa; spaghetti napolitana, where the chef had little more to do than empty a muck of tomato purée on a bed of worm-like pasta; spaghetti and meatballs, really more of a comic diversion for children or a prop on film sets than a real dish; and the layered and steaming lasagne, with its bright red tomato borders and its exorbitance of cheese. In that lonely world, visited once in three years, this was plenitude. In those days it didn't matter that business was scarce; like a flag from a different country, restaurants could survive emblematically and indefinitely on foreign soil.

Spaghetti was, by silent consensus, the one respected pasta. Sometimes its blunt, midget-like, pug-nosed cousin macaroni would make an appearance in colleges and hospitals, even in India: food to amuse the convalescent. It was not just the increased activity of the European Union (morphed anew from the European Community) but the fall of the Berlin Wall and the rush of globalisation that would release into the world the bewildering variations on spaghetti – the flat, tapeworm-like tagliatelle; the slim linguini and anorexically slight tagliarini; spinach pasta and wholemeal pasta – as crazy and multiracially colourful as the Carnaby Street hairstyles of the sixties;

and something called 'fresh pasta' in English supermarkets, bunched-up, fluffy bundles.

This cataclysm approached India in a manner of speaking, without any seriousness of detail. All foreign food is doomed to be consumed in India not so much by Indians as by a voracious Indian sensibility, which demands infinite versions of Indian food, and is unmoved by difference. However, come Italian food did, given momentum by its new world-conquering pedigree. And it first nudged Calcutta in its new avatar in 2003, in the form of an Italian chef, Alex Bignotti, who looked about sixteen years old, and who, one day, appeared in the Taj Bengal hotel in order to bring real Italian flavours to the menu. A frail, small, and perky young man, he did this successfully, introducing cappuccino of wild mushroom and cherry tomato bisque to the coffee shop. A few years after moving to Calcutta myself, I tasted this cappuccino and thought it was unusual: I asked to see the chef to check out his features and demeanour personally, and to compliment him. This was when Bignotti was brought to our table, like a tentative and slightly suspicious schoolboy. I was taken aback – not just by his pale youthfulness, his air of being an underage Gujarati bridegroom lost at his wedding, but the fact that he was here at all. He must have been Calcutta's first skilled import in decades – at least from Europe. Although his name was blazoned on the new menu booklet, I don't know if anyone properly registered his presence. Anyway, there would be a feeling, mordant and inevitable, and one that often attends visiting chefs in the city, that Bignotti's presence in Calcutta meant that he couldn't be good enough. Of course, his culinary skills belied this local prejudice. He'd come from Milan – actually, from a town a few miles outside it. Given his unassuming boyish looks, you thought of him less as a global chef than as someone you might glimpse on an afternoon, cycling up that town's narrow alleys. Then, one day, just as we were beginning, patronisingly, to take him for granted, he had gone – to Bombay, we later heard, the latest stop on his mysterious journey outward from that Milanese suburb.

Not long ago, I met the head chef of the Taj Bengal, Mr Sujan Mukherjee. We sat in the Hub, the very place that had been reinvented in the early 2000s from a previous incarnation of the coffee shop, the Esplanade, and among whose first smart initiatives was the acquisition of Bignotti. Mr Mukherjee had heard of Bignotti, but narrowly missed running into him. He himself reached Taj Bengal from Delhi in 2005.

At this time, he says, the Taj appointed Bignotti's successor – Anteleno Medda.

'Can you spell that?' I ask him, my pen raised.

However, googling him, I find no trace of him – unlike Alex Bignotti, who readily springs up on a couple of sites. He seems to have aged, and departed his late teens. He's also left behind a favourable impression before moving on to wherever he is now (chefs are like the double agents of yore, playing on all sides of the international divide); I say 'left behind' because among the results comes up a plaintive message: 'Where is Alex Bignotti? I used to know him in Mumbai . . .'

There's no denying that Anteleno Medda, or whatever his name was, did exist – because I saw him myself at the Hub, a short, stocky man in a chef's pristine white uniform, moving about the tables with an easy familiarity, stopping to chat with a bunch of foreigners (foreigners to us Indians; they may, of course, have been his countrymen). I thought, Now who is this?, intrigued by the European men in chef's attire filing into this city.

Today, Signor Medda is not to be found – not just on Google, but also in the Taj Bengal.

'What did these chefs think of Calcutta?' I ask Mr Mukherjee.

This seems to me a paramount question – I believe that, given the unique extremities of the profession, its frayed tempers and tears, its hunting after the aroma of perfection, a chef's view of a city is different from anyone else's. Which is why I returned to it twice.

Mr Mukherjee gives me, inadvertently, three different responses in the conversation.

'The weather,' he says. 'They cannot stand the weather. Of course, David Canazi' – noticing my blankness, he adds, 'You know David Canazi, who started the Italian restaurant at the Hyatt, and is now running the one at HHI' – that is, Hotel Hindustan International (Indians adore abbreviations); noticing I'm nodding vigorously, if implausibly, Mr Mukherjee continues – 'for him it is different, he loves the place, he fell in love with a Bengali woman and married her – oh, he loves it here!'

The matter of love and the intercultural Cupid (the Orientalist William Jones had anyway pointed out that Cupid and the Hindu god Kama, with their aerial vantage point and amore-inducing bows and arrows, belong to the same teeming family of divinities) – this matter of love distracts me momentarily with the thought of Shaun Kenworthy. He's someone who, thirty years ago, would have been an oxymoron or a contradiction in terms: an English chef. Well before the idea of the expatriate British chef (not to mention the rude, hyperventilating British chef) was turned into a commodifiable oddity by Gordon Ramsay, Shaun Kenworthy had come to Calcutta, to work at the Park Hotel. Given our residual fascination with our former colonial masters, Kenworthy was given a warm, overweening welcome; given our disenchantment with ourselves and the city we live in, the welcome was accompanied by a suspicion that he wasn't good enough. Nevertheless, Kenworthy had a life in Calcutta outside the kitchen, and Kama took aim, ensuring he made this place his home. Calcutta's Page 3 readers – followers of tabloid trivia – were, a few years ago, made privy to Mr Kenworthy's wedding pictures.

✦

The second explanation Mr Mukherjee gives me for the restiveness of the Italian chefs is that they 'fail to understand totally
vegetarian food'. Why is this so? Vegetarianism in Europe is
hardly the outré fad it used to be in George Bernard Shaw's
era: in fact, many morally irreproachable people in the West are
now vegetarians, as we well know.

No, it emerges that Mr Mukherjee means a community that
constitutes his regular clientele: he is too civilised to single them
out by name, but it's clear he's referring to the Marwaris. This
community has, as a rule, and for centuries, adhered to 'total
vegetarianism'. It's logical that the economic demography in a
city will be reflected in the demography of the restaurant in a
five-star hotel; that, eventually, whoever it is that pays for the food
will determine what shape and form the menu takes. Anteleno
Medda may not have had time to grasp this; but Mr Mukherjee,
the head chef, knows it very well, as do other Bengalis, seething
with envy at their lapsed suzerainty in their city.

I guide him gently towards this area of resentment.

'There are people who say,' I put to him, 'that menus in
Calcutta cater excessively to vegetarians.'

'No, that's not true,' he says. 'Of course, the largest group of
customers which keeps coming back is Marwari.' This, in contrast
to Bombay, say, where no one community necessarily possesses
greater spending power than another and all kinds of people and
tastes are encompassed by that ambiguous, uncomfortable category, 'the rich'. 'But Bengalis come as well – mainly during the
Pujas and the Bengali New Year and of course during Christmas
and New Year.' At other times they are presumably simmering
resentfully about Marwari eating habits or migrating to America
– there's no use denying the undercurrent of contained disdain
that the Bengalis and Marwaris feel for each other, a tacit staking
of territory in which the latter now has the upper hand; nor that,
without them, there would be relatively few partakers of night life
and eating out – indeed, of the recent, celebrated, tinselly glimmer

of the 'new India' – in Calcutta. Not that the Bengalis in any way represent the values of the old bhadralok Calcutta, though they might like to think they do; their values are no different from the Marwari's or anyone else's today, except they appear to be more at sea about how they relate to them, and to their own singular history. But Mr Mukherjee, the head chef, is undoubtedly a bhadralok, or at least astute; he makes no tasteless remarks about the vegetarians. 'It's easy to have a non-vegetarian menu. One pork dish, one seafood dish, one chicken, one beef, one lamb, and you're done! But it's harder to think up a vegetarian menu with flair and variety. That's why people keep saying things like, there's very little interesting vegetarian fare in this restaurant.'

Of all human types, the Bengali experiences the most acute deprivation I've noticed anywhere on being denied his or her quota of animal protein at mealtime. It could be goat's meat, chicken, fish, or even the common egg; but one of these needs to make an appearance before lunch and dinner draw to an absolute close. A vegetarian meal is not a meal; it's a preamble, a preface. And animal protein isn't a main course for the Bengali; it's what wine is for the Frenchman – something integral to the meaning of mealtime, something to unconsciously savour.

This preference, of course, could be explained away by looking at the past, but exactly which past it's difficult to decide. For instance, Bengali Hindus are traditionally, and roughly, divided into two sects: the Shaktya (or the followers of Kali) and the Vaishnavas (the devotees of Krishna). These are no longer living categories, but the yearning, in the Bengali, for something more interesting than vegetables in his or her diet could be a remnant of the influence of Shaktya sacrifice, involving the bloody and passionate slaughter of the goat during the Pujas, portrayed with a mixture of horror and amusement by Nirad C. Chaudhuri in *The Autobiography of an Unknown Indian*. My father's family belonged to the Vaishnava sect, known more for its ecstasies and devotional pieties and its figurehead Chaitanya's message of love. My mother used to once tease him for his family's symbolic slaughter, in Sylhet, of a white pumpkin during the Pujas, in lieu of a goat. Indeed, vegetarian food used to be reserved as a punishment, an austerity, for Bengali widows, who had to wear white, shave their heads, and even forgo garlic, onions, and root vegetables in order to repent at leisure the deaths of their husbands. Though that world is largely vanished, you see that unmistakable widow's air of lack – a strange, irremediable melancholy – among Bengalis at parties where no meat or fish is being served. On the other hand, goat's meat at a buffet or wedding immediately attracts a queue, and brings back that sacrificial mood of revelry, the upbeat, impatient hunger for the recently killed animal.

The other event that comes to mind in this context is the birth, out of nowhere in the early nineteenth century, of the modern Bengali – a person (unlike, say, the Marwari) without much of a history, as Bankimchandra had lamented. From the very beginning, this arriviste and upstart anointed himself with the blood of the animal – in fact, of the so-called sacred cow. Members of the radical boys' club, Young Bengal, began in the 1820s to scandalously, and pointedly, eat beef – in order to subvert outdated and hollow mores, to outrage their contemporaries, to transgress taboos. Beef-eating was at once the precursor and the opposite of the Gandhian hunger strike; not a moment of self-denial, but an unthinkable self-indulgence – a political, anti-religious action undertaken (as these things are) with religious fervour. It earned the perpetrators much scorn and laughter.

Perhaps only wine, in the Western world, possesses these several, contradictory associations: orgiastic, excessive, religious, transubstantiating. And possibly this is why the Frenchman sips his red so slowly and thoughtfully. And also why many educated Bengalis, even now, attack their steak with a peculiar satisfaction.

✦

'Also, the Italians couldn't stand the way Indian diners are always interfering with the menu,' continued chef Sujan Mukherjee, heading for the crux of the matter. 'It drove them mad.'

'Interfering? In what way?'

'The Indians want things prepared in their own way. It was too much for the Italians to take.'

Again and again, I'd confront the same story in relation to this subject – of chefs who'd fled the city and what little of the 'new India' they had to cater to within it because of the latter's careless ignorance and contempt of some of the sacrosanct protocols of Italian food.

'Like – al dente,' said the head chef. 'Indians don't understand al dente. They say the pasta hasn't been cooked properly, that it needs to be boiled for longer.' He shook his head. 'They couldn't take it.'

The hazards and travails of a foreign climate! In the nineteenth century, entire colonial families used to be wiped out in these parts over summer and the monsoons by humidity, cholera and malaria; the headstones and plaques in the Park Circus cemetery bear testimony to the variety of the dead, from the dribbling infant to the newly-wed, the hopeful English bride to the senile Anglo-Indian. More than a hundred years later, it was the new India that had both inveigled and assaulted these chefs, Bignotti and Medda and others, paying them no less than $5000 monthly and then threatening them with a kind of annihilation.

'You know, the Italians like to use fresh tomatoes as a base and not do too much to them,' said Mr Mukherjee. 'Just sauté the tomatoes lightly, sprinkle basil on them. While Indians use tomato ketchup in their pasta sauces. They don't understand the concept of fresh tomatoes.'

Outrage after outrage . . . It was clear that there were many things that this new India, as it resided and thrived in Calcutta, wanted to eat or own, but essentially didn't comprehend or care for. Many memories and spots of time to do with my encounters with the new India – mostly here, in out-of-the-way Calcutta, but not exclusively here – coalesce for me as Mr Mukherjee and I talk over cups of black coffee.

For instance, cheesecake. It was not until early 2011 that I tasted an authentic version of this dessert in India, in – and why not? – a recently opened American coffee-shop chain. Oddly, colonialism hadn't introduced the cheesecake to the Indian middle class, but globalisation did – triangular pretenders that were dead ringers for the original, but tasted exactly like mousse. The new India was consuming this happily, paying more for the doppelganger than many can afford for the real item. I once interrogated a chef about our national inability to produce real cheesecake. It seemed to me that a country that was replicating and inventing software but couldn't make cheesecake simply wasn't interested in doing so. Naipaul, in 1970, had observed mischievously in his excoriating *An Area of Darkness* that Indians still hadn't learned to make cheese and bleach newspaper. I recall Khushwant Singh scolding Naipaul – who was in absentia – on television for the remark about paper, pointing out that he was clearly ignorant of local problems and conditions. I didn't want to get into this sort of debate about something as trivial and rarefied – though in Europe it's a pretty humble object – as cheesecake. Nevertheless, the chef I'd put the question to – the chef, as it happens, of a new-fangled luxury hotel then recently opened in Calcutta – said the local problem in this case was lack of recourse to Philadelphia cheese: an essential element in cheesecake, he said apologetically. I was struck by the fact that a high-fat cream cheese marketed by Kraft held the key to a dessert that had reportedly been eaten in ancient Greece; and that its absence should be responsible, in some way, for cheesecake arriving in India as a sort of creamy soufflé. Of course, these were agonised but private preoccupations: too embarrassing to share with and disclose to friends. Yet they were related to the conundrum of the 'new India'. In the meanwhile, people in Calcutta were, and still are, eating this soufflé/mousse at regular intervals, blissfully calling it cheesecake. 'A rose by any other name would smell as sweet,' someone said; and sweetness may have been the issue here – that, as long as it was sufficiently sugary (the great requisite of Indian, especially Bengali, sweetmeats is they be true to their name), it didn't matter what it was called.

A newly created landscape engenders new names: this must be as true of India post-globalisation as it once was of earth. The Bible tells us how Adam, after his entry into Eden, went about naming the animals. But it doesn't tell us if he named them correctly – if what he called a 'horse', for instance, was really a horse. Perhaps the Bible doesn't remark upon this because it didn't really matter. And something very similar is happening in the 'new India'.

My wife and I once slipped into an expensive restaurant in the Taj Hotel in Bombay during a visit. The experience I had there isn't unrelated to what I've just described above, and possesses some of the characteristic resonances of life in the 'new India' (most of these post-globalisation epiphanies arise from eating out).

I found ginger pudding on the menu: one of my favourites, a fragrant piece of colonial stodge, available once in some schools and now in a club or two but hardly on a restaurant menu. Though it was teatime, I ordered one with alacrity.

The waiter brought me a pudding encircled by thin white single cream. I scooped a section up greedily, already made nervous by the numerous raisins in it, and snapped it up. I called the waiter.

'This isn't ginger pudding,' I said to him. 'It's Christmas pudding.' It was early January; no hint of ginger on my palate. The waiter stood before me with an old stoic calm; then, as if he'd understood, he nodded. If I, a customer of the 'new India', had named the pudding 'Christmas pudding', he, a mere attendant in Eden, wasn't going to argue it was something else. With an apathetic dignity, making no comment on my wastefulness, he lifted up the plate and left.

He returned with another plate of pudding that looked identical to the previous one.

'Ginger pudding, sir,' he said, smiling.

I looked at it with apprehension. It could be, I said to my wife before transferring a spoonful mouthward, that the Bombay Taj ensures that both Christmas and ginger puddings look exactly like each other.

I called the waiter. He approached me as he would a violent lunatic, warily but deferentially.

'It's still Christmas pudding,' I said. I made a supercilious remark of which, in retrospect, I'm ashamed – but maybe the context justifies, or at least exculpates, it: 'Do you know there's a difference between Christmas and ginger pudding?' My trouble is that my weakness for ginger pudding is matched by my distaste for Christmas pudding. Anyway, the Taj charges its customers a high price for what it puts on its menu. Was there a secret falling out, in India, between chefs and customers? Had the former realised that the 'new Indian' was incapable of tasting what he or she ate? And had Indian chefs, consequently, embarked quietly on a deliberate plan of mystification – quite distinct, for instance, from the low-cholesterol crusades that many Western chefs are busy with?

A portly gentleman with a conciliatory air came to my table and said he was the chef. He leaned forward and whispered, as you would when warning a reckless friend: 'Sorry sir, there's no ginger pudding left today. We only have Christmas pudding.'

By this time, I'd almost forgotten what ginger pudding tastes like. My foundations had moved slightly; I was ready to accept anything offered to me by that name. I was willing to be naturalised into the 'new India', when the chef's explanatory words brought back to me a flood of memory.

'I'm sorry, I don't like Christmas pudding,' I said.

'Indians are not very experimental,' says chef Mukherjee. He gestures towards a handsome, giant jar of black olives in the buffet. 'Nobody eats those.' Then adds: 'Even cheese. They have no interest in cheese.'

'I see. What kind of cheese do they know then?' For a largely vegetarian middle class, relatively newly empowered, the tepid enthusiasm for cheese is striking. For decades after Independence, Indians made do, happily, with Amul, a tough, feisty, all-purpose government-processed cheese, more an unanswerable piece of legislation than a dairy product, with which it seemed you could do almost anything. Its great virtue was that it took an unthinkably long time to go stale.

'Cheddar,' he replies. 'They've also heard of the usual stuff – Gouda and Emmental, but not much else.'

'What about olives?' I ask. 'Those olives you pointed out are bottled olives. We hardly get fresh olives in India.'

'Indians don't *like* fresh olives,' says chef Mukherjee, making it pretty clear he doesn't like them himself. 'They're extremely salty.' Briefly at a loss, he breaks into Bengali – '*Ki rokom ekta kash achhe na?*' ('Don't you think they have an acidic aftertaste?') It's an aside: as if we are sharing a little-conceded but incontrovertibly plain fact.

Fresh olives are among the main upper-class travellers of globalisation; they're also one of its chief acquired tastes. Their saltiness, to the initiate, seems excessive; they then swiftly become addictive.

India has traditionally ignored the olive; and, it seems, the 'new India' will continue to do so. Even chef Mukherjee's bottled black olives, which are duller and less tart than fresh ones, are destined to be looked askance at and avoided by the diner. One lazily presumes the Middle East is closer – spiritually, culturally, geographically – to India than it is to countries like Greece, Italy, and Spain. But the olive's absence from our lives tells us otherwise. The well-to-do Indian's view of the olive is still predominantly, and narrowly, Victorian: it's the putative source of an oil which is occasionally applied to the bodies of infants and the aged.

No wonder Bignotti and Medda wondered, at times, where they were.

Sujan Mukherjee brings a paradox to my attention. 'Most chefs worldwide use local, fresh produce and local ingredients.' This is true; the use of local produce in cuisine is a fetish in the capitalist West.

'People here don't *want* local produce when they come to a five-star hotel,' he tells me. 'They want something from far away.'

That's odd: because what he'd said so far (confirmed by my own experience of liberalised India) is that the well-off, when they eat out, don't particularly like engaging with the unfamiliar. Or could it be that they believe they do?

'For example, they're unimpressed when they see a *begoon* on the menu,' he says, spontaneously, acerbically, using the Bengali word for 'aubergine'. He then approximates the supposedly cursory speaking style of a Bengali customer: '"Why have *begoon*," they say, "when I can get it in the bazaar?"'

I'm now beginning to wonder if the Taj Bengal has acquired any foreign chefs after Medda and Bignotti. 'In fact we have a foreign chef at the moment,' confesses Sujan Mukherjee brightly. 'Really?' 'Yes, the head chef at the Chinoiserie, the Chinese restaurant – chef Lian Yu Li of Nanjing.'

'That's wonderful!' I say. The Chinoiserie is too expensive for even a dedicated and foolhardy eater-out such as myself; I haven't dared go near it in years. 'How does he feel about being here?'

'Oh he's very happy!'

'He's happy to be here?' I'm making comparisons, thinking to myself whether unhappiness and an unrealistic streak of perfectionism (which inevitably leads to unhappiness) are congenital to Europeans like Bignotti and Medda; whether some Asian reserve of contentment and compromise allows Lian Yu Li to feel at home here, and maybe in the world.

'Oh yes!'

'What does he think of Calcutta?'

'He doesn't have much to do with Calcutta,' says chef Mukherjee, moving in his chair and making a clarificatory gesture. 'No, no – he comes to the Taj, goes to the kitchen, then leaves with me for the Taj apartments. We come back together the next day, and it's the same thing again. He hasn't seen much of Calcutta at all.' So it's a cycle of sleep and waking, then, of making dim sum and hot soup; then returning to an apartment and going to sleep.

It's an intriguing arrangement. Even Calcutta, in the 'new India', can be turned into a kind of non-place: a lounge or lobby which you need never exit, except to finally go to the airport to get on to the flight to Kunming.

'He's very pleased about the direct flight to Kunming,' reveals chef Mukherjee.

Chinese food has long been Calcutta's favoured foreign cuisine: it belongs to the eternal, and now paradoxically lost, childhood of the Bengali middle class. Its bottles of soya sauce and Han's chilli sauce, its minutely chopped green chillies swimming in vinegar, its chicken sweet corn soup, chilli chicken, sweet and sour prawn, spring rolls, and American chop suey are all part of a delectation free of guilt about fried food and unburdened by connoisseurship: a simple, elemental pleasure. It goes back, this cuisine, to the time when Calcutta was a Bengali city, and never dreamed it would be otherwise. To the old guard belonged restaurants such as Waldorf (on Park Street), Jimmy's Kitchen (which my maternal uncle, always emphatic in his loyalties, swore and even threatened by), Mandarin (which was born in the post-Naxal era as a downmarket imitation of the older restaurants), Hatari (a meeting place for middle-class couples, its shabbiness the perfect milieu for its spring rolls), Peiping on Park Street (always preternaturally crowded, I recall from childhood, with every kind of bhadralok, of which little remained when I visited it in the late seventies but its inflated reputation). There are others, except their names elude me. But, even as I formulate that sentence, two return: one is near Statesman House, on Central Avenue on the way to North Calcutta, a mysterious, disreputable place, such as Chinese restaurants – at least the good ones – were classically designed to be; and another one is located on the 'arcade' on Chowringhee near the Grand Hotel, on the vestibule thronging with tourists, locals, magazine vendors, blind beggars, and sellers of little plastic toys, to which my father came once weekly (so he'd told me in his lucid days), when he was a student, for the pure, solitary joy of a plate of American chop suey. I know the first one no longer exists; the second, even if it does, as good as doesn't. I've seen them both at some point in my life, but can't summon up their names. I go to R, a truer Calcuttan than I, and describe the first one; 'I know the place you mean – wasn't it it Nanking?' I dismiss the suggestion outright. I go to my father and ask him, very loudly, if he can recall the Chinese restaurant he used to visit on Chowringhee. At first, alarmed by the volume at which I'm speaking, he's anxious, and worried that something's wrong; then he's got it, his face is lit by a smile of comprehension, he nods vigorously. He still has the ability to remember many things, my father, but can't any longer express himself coherently. 'Is it the Hong Kong?' I ask loudly but, I hope, tenderly; he shakes his head, the

Hong Kong rings no bell. It's my maternal uncle, finally, who supplies the names over the phone; at eighty-five, he's clear-headed and still a great advocate of those restaurants. 'That was Nanking near Statesman House!' he exclaims, proving my disagreement with R, a bona fide Calcuttan, was ill-advised. 'What an amazing place it was! I took my in-laws to eat there soon after I was married. It wasn't much to look at from the outside, so they weren't sure about it – but they loved the food!' He's puzzled by the second one; there was never a Hong Kong restaurant in Calcutta, he says. Then he knows the one I mean: 'New Cathay – of course, New Cathay! Fantastic place!' That's it. When I tell my father, he nods, his eyes bright, and mumbles the name. He's relieved I have my answer. When my uncle says 'New Cathay', and I repeat the name to him, then to my father, a sensation passes through me, an imperceptible lifting of the diaphragm, as if the excitement might, who knows, make me weep – not for my father, not for New Cathay, but for something gone, which I can no longer make present.

The new international Chinese food came to Calcutta well before chef Lian Yu Li arrived at Taj Bengal – with the advent, in the nineties, of a new luxury hotel, ITC Sonar Bangla, on the featureless EM Bypass. Word began to spread, via Anglophone dailies and among the affluent, that Pan Asia had the most chic Chinese food in town. No sooner was news circulating than I was invited by a well-worn society magazine called uncannily, *Society*, to have lunch with my wife at the Pan Asia for a feature. I wanted to be snobbish and turn down what was surely an improper request to a serious writer (as I'd begun to see myself), but gave in, as I sometimes do, at the prospect of what promised to be a terrific free meal.

I didn't quite know what to expect, but the name itself – Pan Asia – carried the clipped accent of globalisation, and had little to do with the smoky Orient of colonisation, which had given

birth, everywhere, to restaurants with names like Nanking and
Golden Dragon. The interior was dark, but not dark in the way
that Chinese restaurants used to be – atmospherically dark, so
that you had to peer hard in the barely lit gloom before you
spotted the chillies submerged in the vinegar, and only ever
saw your soup in half light and half shadow; and its few colours
came from the suspended Chinese-lantern lampshades and the
red dragons on soup spoons. No, Pan Asia was dark in a business
lounge way, the dark and quiet of a space in which you don't
expect to be threatened by crowds of people, its decor angular
and minimal, without undue references to the Orient. Speaking
of crowds, not far from the ITC Sonar Bangla was where the
post-middle-class bastion of Chinese cuisine – post-Waldorf; post-
Nanking; pre-Pan Asia – had sprung up in the last two decades, in
the tannery district, Tangra, catering to the vernacular clientele
of this city that was now without a definite name – Calcutta,
Kolkata – serving all kinds, from real estate promoters and their
families to academics and theirs, all who'd been levelled out
into one harmonious congregation by Left rule, serving anyone
who'd brave that intricate maze of lanes and plunge headlong
into the stink of the tanneries. Tangra was, thus, at once famous
and infamous. The Chinese had traditionally been in the tannery
business; and, at some point, as the respectable Chinese eateries
of yore became a spent force, the Tangra families must have
decided it was an opportune time to set up restaurants. In
the early eighties, as Calcutta imploded and the middle-class
migration outward soared and eating out dipped, Tangra began
to gather a reputation for providing 'real' Chinese food cooked by
'real' Chinese families, this 'realness' authenticated and properly
endorsed by the smell of the tanneries and drains surrounding
places like Golden Joy and Beijing.

Now, here was the crystalline, refracted Pan Asia, offering
not only real, upmarket, international Chinese cuisine, but
international Mongolian and Japanese food too. Chinese food

once belonged to the domain of the neighbourhood – not just Chinatown; any neighbourhood – an ethos of loiterers killing time on workaday porches and signs with a particular kind of English lettering denoting the Chinese were nearby. Pan Asia implied there were no neighbourhoods; there were lounges, constituting brief, tranquil arrests on overnight journeys. At least that's what we felt it was telling us as we slipped from the early afternoon sun into its interior. Its already celebrated, blade-thin, rectangular grill was on the left, with bar stools on every side. There was almost no one in the restaurant but us; it's an experience I've only had in the static sadness of Indian small towns, of eating out without the general – and, really, indispensable – accompaniment of other customers, enrhythmed in the semi-animal bliss of now noticing, now ignoring, now being noticed, now being ignored; no, in the small town, you are alone, being lavished attention by three waiters who've been galvanised by your sullen otherness, and item after item which you'd abstractedly ordered now stubbornly makes its way towards your table. At Pan Asia, the three of us, the journalist from *Society*, my wife, and I, sat side by side on the bar stools like partners at a séance, and watched the short, agile young chef's hypnotic dicing of vegetables, his playful shoving and retrieval of cuttlefish from different directions, as if they'd never once been alive and were no more than a kind of ornament, like pasta shells. His spatula was at once a magician's wand, bringing forth an illusion, and a conductor's baton, making music. Everything he touched – vegetables, cuttlefish, prawns – were somehow reduced: he knew the art of transforming the plentiful into the economical. When we asked this performer respectfully if he was from China, he said no, he came from Nepal. 'Chinese chef come and give me training,' he explained.

The food had been made with finesse. It had what we now think of as the strengths of good Chinese food: delicacy, simplicity, a fastidious avoidance of overcooking, a resultant crunchiness, a hushed regard for the taste of fresh ingredients. All this was new to Calcutta: an alien and as yet untested idea. We were later – though we were uncomfortably full – forced to try Japanese ice cream, in green tea and litchi flavours. We succumbed completely to Pan Asia. We set aside our vestigial dignity. We even took in our stride the cheesy photographs of ourselves that appeared later in *Society* magazine.

For a week later, our mood alternated between a marvelling at the green tea ice cream and a corroding guilt about the Mephistophelean pact we'd entered with *Society* and Pan Asia, in a country in which farmers frequently subsist on mango leaves and every other day kill themselves. Then, a year later, we set aside our scruples and revisited Pan Asia. We perched on almost the same bar stools. We stared, agog, at the performance. But something had changed. It was the food. The prawns were covered in a giant melt of thick, rich, creamy sauce. The green tea ice cream had become, mainly, home-made vanilla; you had to strain with fanatical, blind faith to believe you could taste green tea in it. I had one of those schizoid moments I'd had with cheesecake and ginger pudding: had I simply imagined, or invented, the earlier experience?

'No,' said the chef, confirming I was still moderately sane, 'Indians not liking those subtle flavours so much. They're saying what is this ice cream, it's not sweet. When American or Chinese visitor come, I making food more Chinese way.'

'Then you should have made it more Chinese way for us,' I said, barely able to contain my frustration.

'I'm not knowing, sir,' he responded wistfully. 'Next time . . .'

If, indeed, there is a next time. 'Kormaisation' is what this process, integral to Indian cuisine, might well be termed: a suffocation of individual ingredients in the interests of the sauce poured over it, the result of a dozen impossibly unlike condiments brought to a simmer and then turned into this all-purpose national deluge. It's what had happened to the prawns.

That chic, suggestive, but eventually vulnerable taste had perished only a year after it had arrived here.

There's indeed a 'new India' in Calcutta, although we place it generally in Bombay and New Delhi. It has risen stubbornly on the remains of the city as it was, and has even been extending it outward since the mid-nineties. The Taj Bengal, where I'm interviewing the restive chef (he must go to a staff birthday party), arose in a serene, historic location in Alipore a little before the 'new India' came into being; the hotel was almost an afterthought on the ubiquitous Taj franchise's part. You could view it as an early sign of investors' faith in Jyoti Basu's West Bengal; Basu, who, by 1989, when the Taj Bengal came up, had noted the changes sweeping the Eastern bloc and the world, and begun making terse noises about attracting 'multinationals' to Bengal. A historic spot it occupies, the Taj, the half a square mile around it more or less as the British left it: early pastoral Calcutta, defined by a sort of rural calm, on the right, with a rivulet running through it towards Kidderpore; and, to the left, a five minutes' walk away, the grand mansions and estates once occupied by the literature-loving Warren Hastings, governor general of India, who was tried and impeached when he finally left this city for his native country in 1784. Important intellectual work was achieved here, just outside the Taj, or within a two-mile radius from it; work we either take for granted or have forgotten. For instance, the fact that the *Bhagavad Gita* has long been a book known worldwide owes much to Hastings' advocacy of that text, which he noticed when it was translated into English by Charles Wilkins of the East India Company. Hastings' one-time mansions have, fittingly, been converted since Independence into the National Library. Even closer to the Taj Bengal than the National Library is Alipore Zoo, a mere two minutes' stroll across the road, another great, and fatally damaged, colonial heirloom. Its vivaciousness, comprising caged animals and middle-class children, survived to the late sixties, from when I recall not only the Bengal tiger, but loping white albino tigers, a gruesome, vile-tempered, and evidently miserable hybrid of a tiger and lion called the 'tigon', a patient, reptile-long queue waiting to entire the House of Reptiles, and a cafe in which we ate sliced egg pakoras with ketchup – although an aunt tells me her son and I spent our excursion urgently keeping track of crows. The zoo, today, hardly has a middle-class visitor; what you see, instead, is an array of humanity, tourists from small towns, villages, and suburbs, casually strewing plastic bags in their wake, lower middle class, working class, or plain poor, come to admire and wonder at and heckle the animals, whose responses range from indifferent to bewildered to contemptuous. These visitors are themselves hardly better looked after by the nation than the inarticulate inmates of the zoo, but are full of energy and noise, exotic in their colours and behaviour, a reminder that, often, it seems in Calcutta that the bhadralok never existed, and we're back in the extraordinary world of the early Kalighat paintings. Having 'done' the zoo, this lot will then proceed desultorily to other significant colonial landmarks in and around here, throng the Victoria Memorial, laxly explore the maidan opposite the Race Course, and sit beneath the statues of British Tommies, Indian freedom fighters and great Bengali visionaries and writers munching *jhaalmuri* and sucking ice lollies bought from the men positioned with carts. They may not muster up the courage, though, to invade the Horticultural Gardens, which is in the other direction, further up from the National Library, because it's still the domain – with its prim, carefully nurtured plant life – of the shorts-wearing affluent. The other parts of colonial Calcutta in the immediate environs, however, they've annexed, and are at ease in. Inside the Taj, with chef Mukherjee, it's hard to be aware of this ebb and flow; but, even if you're ignorant of the existence of the zoo opposite, you'll hear the tigers roaring, or surely the elephants trumpeting, at night – the cool nightfall of Bengal. The Taj is Janus-faced; one face looks towards, and is blind to, the historical city; the other face gazes welcomingly at the imminent (since 1989 at least) arrival of that 'new India'.

Globalisation first made its presence palpable in Calcutta in the nineties with gated clusters of buildings which had peculiar names like Hiland Park and South City and Merlin. Some of them rose rapidly; others, caught in some legal tangle or other, took years to complete. These gated buildings had, or were meant to have, their own gymnasiums, swimming pools, and recreational clubs – sometimes even their own schools, Jacuzzis, shops, and cinema multiplexes. In contrast to their near-nonsensical names, names at which you could neither laugh nor rage, but register as a mark of a puzzling shift of mood – in contrast to these names, their messages to the potential buyer were solemn and ingratiating. For example, Hiland Sapphire, an ongoing part of the Hiland Park project on Ballygunge Park Road, almost next door to where I live, gravely informs (mostly expatriate) customers: 'A symbol of sophistication, a mark of dignity, Hiland Sapphire certainly is the residence of choice for the manor born.' By becoming a microcosm, by being self-sufficient, they fulfil a fantasy that many Calcuttans have secretly had for years: to live in the city without in any way depending on it, or being beholden to it, or subject to its vagaries.

In the meanwhile, two new hotels came up near Salt Lake, a suburban development that, by now, was beginning to feel derelict – came up without too much explanation, the ITC Sonar Bangla and the Hyatt, on stretches of wilderness that had no past, overlooking the EM Bypass. Who would stay in them? Surely business was going to be disappointing? The answer was – they were coming up as part of a larger wave. Calcutta was changing, was going to change, and the hotels would be there, prepared to participate and contribute when the change came.

On some such foresight was built New Town in Rajarhat, about twenty minutes away from the Hyatt, emerging on flat expanses of horizon and land on which the sun had been setting and rising without anyone taking note, except for straggly peasant families who could now be pushed aside with impunity, or appropriated as labour for the planned offices and residential tower blocks. The new IBM office compound was demarcated here. It appeared, for a while, that Rajarhat might spawn a Bangalore, a city geared towards the future. Then, one day, it felt like Rajarhat's plans – like Calcutta-Kolkata's – had been arrested midway, abandoned in a moment of despair and indecision. There's a long highway cutting, in a series of right turns, through Rajarhat to the airport, and people take it as an alternative to the old route via VIP Road, to avoid the slow-motion bazaar-like stoppages on the way, at outposts like Ultadanga and Baguihati. (I should add that this 'old route' is itself a 'new route', and I remember well the older route to the airport through Manecktala in the early seventies, when, in the aftermath of the Naxal agitation, to be spotted in an Ambassador car was still a sign of bourgeois hubris, and a dangerous provocation to the crowd.) I probably first took the Rajarhat detour to the airport one dawn five years ago, and felt oppressed: because I'm always intimidated by silence and emptiness, and hadn't realised there was so much of them to be found on this journey. That year, the buildings and offices began to rise in a spurt of brashness and colour, and with the swagger of liberalisation – a swagger that, like a card sharp's bravado, promises it can pull off any trick, and does. It's the swagger that produced the township of Gurgaon on the outskirts of Delhi. But from 2008 onward, I began to feel on my airport journeys that the project had been hastily set aside: that new buildings were coming up, but the card sharp had made an exit. Rajarhat was now a frozen city, nascent, like one of those unfortunate kingdoms in children's stories where everything is pretty and spotless, but has a dread spell cast over it.

I encountered this weird enchantment – the fairy-tale stillness of a globalisation that has no real resources – when my wife and I visited Pan Asia a third time, surreptitiously. It was afternoon; the glass doors were locked.

Was it a public holiday? (Within, the shadowy outlines of waiters lurked aimlessly. We stood like Hansel and Gretel, with nothing to fear really, only having to cope with a vague bourgeois deflation, a feeling of thwarted entitlement, at the end of our trek.) From Pan Asia – still, then, maybe the city's most discussed Oriental restaurant – we retreated in consternation, as from an illusion or a mirage, and were informed apologetically that all but two of the ITC Sonar Bangla's dining places remained shut for lunch except on Saturdays and Sundays. There just weren't enough customers to justify a daytime opening; so Pan Asia remained out of bounds, secret and semi-dark. Tellingly, the Sonar Bangla's customers didn't notice; they made robustly for the buffet at the coffee shop.

This inactivity at Pan Asia wasn't emblematic; it felt accidental. No matter that industry and investment were failing to arrive in the city as they'd once, in the early 2000s, been expected to; new luxury hotels were planned regardless (as I write this, a new Marriott and a second Taj, to be erected near the Ruby General Hospital, are rumoured), like a transformation compelled to march into existence to a faraway drumbeat. So it was with residential buildings in general, even well after the crash of 2008, a setback which signified neither one thing or the other to Calcutta – the gated enclaves kept coming up and multiplying, as did tall clusters of apartment blocks, fancifully renamed condominiums or 'condos' for the Bengali buyer from

New Jersey. On the ragged highway of the EM Bypass, and sometimes in the centre of the city, hovering over, say, a resistant traffic snarl on Camac Street, billboards promising the bucolic spaciousness, birdcall, and organic delights of new property rivalled the ubiquitous and conventional advertisements for gold jewellery and fairness creams. Among the stellar faces addressing the crowd- and traffic-entangled sojourner from those hoardings was the gifted actress Konkona Sen Sharma, looking unlike her usual self, and the tabla maestro Bickram Ghosh, as adept at playing complex time-signatures on his cheeks as upon his instrument, and his wife, the beautiful Tollywood star Jaya Seal. Bickram Ghosh, in particular, bearded, with the alchemic air of a wizard (he is, not to forget, a genuine tabla wizard), proliferates everywhere, presiding over the city's contradictions, its slightly inebriated, expanding property prices, and its ambiguous prospects, and, with his wife, smiles inclusively, without noticeable condescension, from a huge billboard near the Sonar Bangla, seeming to hold the key to the hope, the obduracy, and the curious fantasy of living in Calcutta.

To be asked to promote a new building is a peculiar accolade. Soon after I'd moved to this city in 1999, I was approached by someone representing a builder who asked me if I'd act as a presenter for a video meant for prospective buyers of flats in an already well-publicised development. To help me overcome my resistance, this man told me that the last presenter for one of their new and coveted apartment blocks had been Victor Banerjee, familiar to international Anglophone audiences for playing Dr Aziz in David Lean's fervid interpretation of *A Passage to India*. Victor (who is a friend) was, by now, a Bengali icon and a mascot and badge of honour for anyone who had anything to do with him in Calcutta. Once I'd disguised my embarrassment (after receiving the vituperative review in the *Statesman* on arriving here, I was steeled for any kind of interaction), I didn't have the gumption to say 'Yes' to the man on the telephone. Instead of an outright 'No', I quoted a fee more appropriate to Shah Rukh Khan than one who writes my kind of fiction. 'I'll get back to you,' said the man; but didn't.

Globalisation may have come to Calcutta in relatively small doses, but it has nevertheless entered people's bloodstreams; it makes them behave in certain ways. There was a time when bandh days – days of (usually) twelve-hour-long closure enforced by a political party or even the state government to protest one grievance or another – were total write-offs, neither working days nor holidays (since no one risked going out till 6 p.m.), but, instead, longueurs of monastic contemplation. In today's Calcutta, this doesn't hold. I noticed this more than a year ago on going to the Forum – wondering if our tickets for the 6.30 p.m. show of a movie were any good after a bandh (introduced whimsically, without much prior warning) whose cut-off hour, as usual, was six o'clock. Instead, I found the Forum as stiflingly crowded with shoppers, film-goers, idlers, and the curious – generally, people at once importunate and at a loose end – as a rave is full of, and pulses with, revellers. They'd clearly rushed out of their abodes in the last thirty minutes (as had we), as soon as the clock struck six, to congregate here. This is what globalisation, more potent than a booster injection, more tenable than an infection, is capable of doing; of being, even before it's a reality, a symptom.

Sunday, now, is the busiest day of the week. In the India I grew up in, Sunday reached its peak around midday with Ameen Sayani's sonorities on the *Bournvita Quiz Contest* (which only had a following among proven devotees of radio), then declined into the ennui of afternoon and the Sunday Hindi film, all that happened later falling headlong towards the pointless human struggle that was Monday. In England (though things improved in the nineties), I was aware of Sunday being an abyss to the soul, a precipice that stealthily opened after Friday's and Saturday's crowded frenzy. Today, the fact that the Protestant work ethic (of which Monday is the prophet and beacon) has lost its reproachful edge in Calcutta is clear from how unbearably busy Sunday evenings are – with long traffic jams in front of South City Mall, and not a table free in restaurants on Park Street. All this – in a city without any demonstrable reasons for consumerist hope or activity. Shaped by student life in England, my wife and I are aghast at this frenetic sociability before the new week begins, this almost philistine uncaringness for the idea of Monday morning. 'Indians have no thought for tomorrow,' she says with Olympian finality, as if commenting on a race she's recently discovered.

Malls, these days, are where you go in good times and bad, however variable or uncertain the future. When they first began to come up, they were looked upon by the last progeny of the bhadralok with a mix of suspicion, regret, and grudging pride, as standard bearers and omens of the city to come. Regret, because they often came up in what were, to the bhadralok, historic locations – as in the genteel calm (a calm that indicated, by the eighties, a condition close to extinction) of Elgin Road, from where the aristocracy had either departed, or closed ranks on the world. Here rose the Forum, a dazzling two hundred thousand square foot space on six levels, inclusive of a cinema multiplex and, later, a many-tiered car park. Almost next to it, on its right (if you're facing the Forum from the Elgin Road entrance), is the art deco house which has always puzzled me, now in near-desuetude, wittily recalling a ship, complete with portholes, alluding to some maritime fancy, its driveway and porch obscured by foliage. How can it, with its air of being afloat, not bring to mind the de Chirico painting Naipaul describes? Opposite, the Forum overlooks the Netaji Bhavan, the house where Subhas Chandra Bose lived, and then fled the

British, and India, in disguise, finally resurfacing in Japan as the Commander in Chief of the Indian National Army, never after to be glimpsed again. Next to this mysterious building, which is still pervaded by a misplaced undercurrent of loss for the youthful, bespectacled Bose, is Brajen Seal's mansion – not the philosopher Brajen Seal, but another – which resembles a book open at several pages, a house in which no one could possibly live, so quiet it is, its gate fronted by an improvised tea stall under a tree, and a phalanx of drivers biding their time while their employers shop in the Forum. I once trespassed into this place during the monsoons on the pretext of looking for someone, just after it had stopped raining at dusk, brazenly climbing up the stairs to the first floor, intuiting the presence of others, entering the hall that went past the closed doors of rooms, noting there was some medicine and a glass of water on a small table, and an easy chair, then shouting, 'Hello! Anyone there? *Keu achhe?'* No one answered, but I now knew the house was inhabited. I was transfixed – both by my own transgression and by the potted plants on the terrace beyond the blurred window, quietly dripping water.

On the left of the Forum are the Roy Mansions, half of which is now demolished, and half occupied by Simaaya, a resplendent retail outlet for kitschy, expensive saris. Soon after we were married, and before Roy Mansions was forever altered in this way, I went with R and my in-laws to have dinner with her grand-aunt, the late Potty Mami, who lived in slightly shabby many-roomed grandeur in the immense flat on the ground floor, which is today's Simaaya. There, I was served cold consommé as the first course for dinner, but, before that, instructed in helpful terms of the distinguished maternal lineage of my father-in-law's extended family, Potty Mami's recently deceased husband being the grandson of P.K. Ray, the first Indian principal of Presidency College, and she herself the unlikely but friendly granddaughter of the historian R.C. Dutt, author of the *Economic History of India* among other landmark works. I was only a few months married, and was just being made aware, in this well-meant, intrusive way, of a Calcutta I'd never known, missed, or mourned.

In the Forum, you could forget all about Calcutta, and spectate – the main occupation of the visitors, surpassing even shopping – on the new breed of people walking past. This new breed (to which you yourself belong) may or may not be the citizens of a contemporary India, or even of a new Calcutta, but it's here you see it in its full, surprising sweep and heterogeneity, ranging from members of the upper class, to the odd European, to college students, middle- and working-class people, and provincial families of different religions, some women fully enclosed in burqas, others flaunting bright saris, these families – especially the women and children – frequently creating an obstreperous distraction before the escalator, akin to inexperienced swimmers by a poolside, wanting, but hesitant, to take the plunge, pleased and shy at once at making an exhibition of themselves, cheered and scolded by the more daring members of the family, averted with an inured sigh by the veteran escalator-users, who dart past them straight into the moving staircase. Years have gone by since the Forum, and then the City Centre at Salt Lake, and then South City Mall near Jodhpur Park (at a million square feet, once the largest mall in Asia; then India; then East India – malls shrink constantly) were opened to the public, but this brief disruption and sundering – the awkward woman and child gazing with an air of judgement at the escalator, the husband and infant in his arms rapidly moving upwards and away from them – continues to recur. This is the new breed, and nowhere does it feel more at home than in the mall.

And it's always possibly to get a sighting of the famous. In the slightly quieter, halcyon days of the Forum, I often spotted June Maliah, reputed for her roles in Bengali cinema and especially soap operas, as she suddenly appeared from the edge of an escalator, or floated easefully a level below with her children. More than once, I've noticed the ebullient Bickram Ghosh somewhere in the distance, *mast* or happily preoccupied like the rest of us. Recently, I saw Srikanto Acharya, the dapper singer of Tagore songs, waiting expectantly before the lift with his family.

What takes place in the malls seems unconnected to what's happening in Calcutta, or West Bengal, or even to markets globally – I say this as one who's visited them when things looked optimistic for the Left Front; when the future became murky for them; after they were jettisoned; before the recession; after the Indian markets limped back to life. The new breed has found its own rhythm here, a rhythm that might be hard to decipher, but difficult to deny. This is also where – besides exploring their options and assessing each other – they appear to find themselves. Never have I seen, in malls in other countries, the number of people I've noticed at South City or the Forum leaning against balconies, studying the lower levels, or the people ascending, apparition-like, on the escalator. It might be a mood that's an offshoot of our weather (with its warmth and torpor) which gives us, childhood onward, a lonely, godlike vantage point on life. I know that to spectate thus on the movements of other people is a deep comfort to the purposeless and the homesick. I had a friend in Bombay, a classmate from school who couldn't kick his drug habit, who, every twenty minutes into our conversation, would go out into the balcony, to involuntarily lean upon the banister and regain his inner calm. I've also noticed, often by chance, the silhouettes of maids who've worked and lived in our apartment, leaning and looking out into the compound while the world grows dark. What do they see?

In the South City Mall, especially, with its bewildering turnover, I've almost felt emboldened to stop passers-by and ask them where they're going – what they're doing here; what they want to buy; where they come from. I haven't done so. The only time I approached someone out of the blue within the mall's special shell, unintroduced, was when, ascending to level two, I was startled to see five or six large African men ranged gracefully across the balcony. They turned out to be Nigerian soccer players in the employ of Mohammedan Sporting Club; celebrities with a tentative air, desiring, impossibly, not to be noticed, and somehow achieving this desire. From maybe the beginning of the twentieth century, football had been the prime passion in sport in Bengal, and, in the late seventies, the game was commercialised unbelievably, with star players departing for rival teams for the lure of a big reward, in the manner of their better-known European counterparts. Team coaches emerged as indefatigable personalities in their own right – the balding P.K. Banerjee, referred to as 'Peekay', once a star footballer himself, became the immensely successful brain behind East Bengal and, later, its rival, Mohun Bagan. Of course, Bengali football (synonymous, then, with Indian football) was played on a planet distinct from the one international football thrived in; football persisted in Calcutta as many obsessions did, as a miniaturist's art, undertaken ferociously but microscopically, for its own delight.

In the eighties, the three main clubs – East Bengal, Mohun Bagan, and Mohammedan – began to acquire foreign – mainly African – players, who were admired by crowds for their skills, and for being strange trophies in a culture that possessed few of these. The most famous of them remains the striker Chima Okorie, who played for all the big teams. In the meanwhile, cricket was in the ascendancy, and, although Bengal produced no cricketer of charisma until Sourav Ganguly's debut in 1996, football was gradually removed from the sphere of middle-class enthusiasm, and became – along with *gutka* and betel leaves – largely a proletarian addiction.

So it was an education to run into the Nigerians in the mall, and to be reminded of just how out of place they were – not because of their race, but their casual urbaneness. They let down their guard a bit when I said I was a writer; we even talked about Nigerian writing (who knows when national literatures will come in useful?), and Achebe came up immediately, and then, to my surprise, even his near namesake, Adichie – Chimamanda Adichie – whom one of them had heard of ('She's a young writer,' the tall man said to the other, for whom Achebe encompassed all Nigerian writing) and whom I claimed to know slightly. I then asked them the unavoidable banality – *What do you think of Calcutta?* – and though they weren't forthcoming or eloquent, they admitted, in a non-committal way, to loving the mall, and said they returned a few times weekly.

The Italian problem was suddenly brought home to me again, in the monsoons of 2011, when a team from the *New York Times* style magazine came down to Calcutta to produce a feature. The core of the team was a father and son – Max Vadukul, the photographer, whom I'd met fourteen years earlier in London for an infamous *New Yorker* photo shoot of Indian writers, and fresh-faced young Alex, who'd just begun his career as a journalist. The two had been thrown together by the editor, and concluded that, so far, in the last twenty-four hours, working with each other had been fine. The editor, who apparently had an unerring instinct in such matters, had told them she had a powerful feeling that Calcutta was the new 'happening city'. 'It's where you have to go,' she'd advised Max and Alex. They'd come armed with the knowledge that this was the place that had given birth to 'all the writers, intellectuals, artists, and film-makers', that it was a city of culture, and they radiated outward in various directions from the Grand Hotel, where they were located, looking at the city before them in this pre-ordained light. It was a bit like visiting modern Athens and believing you were in ancient Greece; and, certainly, there are enough surviving ruins and monuments in Athens to sustain, if you so choose to, that make-believe. In Calcutta, though the time lag, in comparison, is much smaller, it's more difficult to confuse *this* city with that other one, from whence came 'all the writers, intellectuals, artists, and film-makers'. But maybe it seems that way to me because I'm both an outsider, out of sympathy, and not as much one as Alex and Max are.

On their last evening here, Max generously offered to take R and me out to dinner. 'No, not Bengali food,' he said. 'We've eaten enough Bengali food.' R, opportunely, suggested a place we'd only lately heard of – an Italian restaurant with an Italian chef that had sprung up near Menaka Cinema and the lakes: for me, the domain of childhood, a short walk from Bhowanipore and my uncle's house – the short stretch of world I'd reimagined for the purposes of *A Strange and Sublime Address*. How could there possibly be a new Italian restaurant here, in a place that stood, for me, in the interstices of the literature of neighbourhood, my own writing, and my first intimation of what a city was? 'Casa Toscana,' said my wife; it had been preying on her mind. 'Casa Toscana it is!' said Max; and Alex, who was still taking things at face value, and is half-Italian, added, 'I like Tuscan food.'

The restaurant was crowded; there was no table to be had. Often, a restaurant – especially if it's an old one, or a European eatery, or akin to a cafe – will transport you to a foreign city; it'll fill you with a fleeting conviction that the street outside the glass window is strange. In Casa Toscana, I experienced another kind of déjà vu and confusion; that I was in Bombay – not in the city in which I'd grown up, but today's lit-up Bombay, where people of all kinds, rich and poor, Indian and Western, arrive to fulfil some need. Casa Toscana was bathed in that pink light. For the first time, I sensed that globalisation was *here*, in Calcutta. Two tall, anorexic European women, one blonde, the other's hair dyed jet black, were coldly receiving customers and checking if they had bookings. I tried my charm on them, and even mentioned the *New York Times*; Alex was disarming, leaning past me to say, 'Italiano?' What better topping could this new eating place come with than to have Italian hostesses escort Calcuttans to an Italian supper? 'No, I'm Croatian,' she said, in a precise accent I've frequently overheard in London, and with the preliminary iciness that East European women have before they become loquacious. Both Alex and I felt humbled, provincial, as people from Calcutta or London or New York often do in Bombay. There's something about the unprecedented, blasé mix of globalised India that's nervous-making, and threatens to make you forget your education, and feel diminished and small.

Nevertheless, we were given a table, largely because of the slightly inscrutable but obliging proprietor, Saket, who, Pilate-like, sized us up in a glance and, for whatever reason, thought we were a worthwhile investment. We were guided past the clink of the cutlery and the din of customers by the dark-haired woman, who informed me cheerfully she was Russian. (I had a premonition, then, of some story involving restiveness and deprivation, accentuated to me by her thinness, and knew that moment that I wanted to interview her and the blonde woman, but was tardy on the draw; when I phoned the restaurant two months later, their contracts had ended and they'd left Calcutta, for either fresh pastures or old.)

I spent most of that evening in Casa Toscana recovering from the impact of Casa Toscana. The main subject – maybe the only subject – of conversation, comparison, and analysis at our table was the restaurant itself. Both from the point of view of Alex and Max, visitors, and my wife and myself, natives, it represented an evolution impossible to anticipate. Archaeologists might discuss and describe the site they're visiting, but that kind of behaviour isn't common to diners. Writers, yes, will sometimes feel they've found a subject, and begin to talk about it nonchalantly in its very presence. Alex scribbled notes about the music ('well-known over-the-top dramatic opera track'); Max pointed out the light bulbs overhead had been displayed to echo MOMA – all our knowledge and half-baked memories were summoned to consciousness and brought to bear upon our observations. Of course, we commented on the food the moment we ate it – not as food critics would, but as those who, with a faraway look, were condemned to deciphering a national and local mood. 'Yes, the spicy arrabiata is good' – conceded Alex. In fact – disappointingly, on one level; thankfully, on another – the food was mostly good. The famous, reclusive Italian chef – where was he? It was a melodramatic, sordid story. The chef – a genuine Michelin-star cook – was well departed; he'd lasted four days. I knew marriages, in a strange bid for immortality, could be perilously terminated in this way; but employment? Saket found a few minutes in his hurried, breathless round to tell us a story that was becoming trite – that this chef's patience had been worn thin by customers. A source later told me that Saket's financial terms had caused the breakdown in relations and the sudden exit from Casa Toscana; but why not have those terms clearly agreed to before arriving in Calcutta? It sounded mysterious, but exemplary. Alex and I turned subtly to observe the other diners – not critically, but gripped by the spirit of discovery. 'Look,' we nudged one another, glancing unobtrusively but comprehensively, 'they're sharing the pasta.' I saw a waiter portion out a plate of pasta to a small family. There was an unshakeable and overriding Indianness to the operation; I thought again of the Italian chef who'd waited, and waited, and, on the fourth day, made his escape.

East European women may well have been introduced to Calcutta by Shah Rukh Khan and the Indian Premiere League. For those who are still unaware of the Indian Premiere League or IPL, it was the 'brainchild' (the Indian media's favoured word) of the youthful, dubious, but until then unproven and little-known tycoon Lalit Modi: a cricketing extravaganza in twenty-over cricket in which celebrated and up-and-coming and even unheard-of players were auctioned to newly created cricketing enterprises. These enterprises – or 'teams', as they're popularly known – are each named after an Indian city or state, but not yet – as with the Harlem Globetrotters – a neighbourhood. Modi has now lost the franchise he created, equally for his shady dealings and his brashness; but he did persuade some of India's most ubiquitous and well-worn industrialists and film stars to invest in the teams.

Calcutta's team – which, at the moment, has no one from Calcutta in it – is called, in the allusive, comic-book style of most of the team names, Kolkata Knight Riders. Its chief owner is the solitary figure atop Bollywood's pinnacle, the actor Shah Rukh Khan, who has no history of involvement with Calcutta. One of Modi's many innovations was creating teams that would give voice to the voluble partisanship of a place without necessarily having anything to do with the place itself; another was to import cheerleaders, shaking their hips, fluttering, peacock-like, their pom-poms, fitfully electrified, and electrifying others, each time a run was scored. The cheerleaders were met with grave reproach by both cricket purists and common-or-garden puritans, and then – as is the case with so much in Indian public life – lazily accepted and secretly looked forward to. This was how East European women began to reach, in small contingents, the cities – and Calcutta, in the wake of the Kolkata Knight Riders. There was a time when fans lurked in hotel lobbies in wait of players; now there was a strange transcontinental entourage to stare at.

Shah Rukh Khan became famous for the post-match parties he threw at the ITC Sonar Bangla for the team, cheerleaders, and a handful of unspecified others: models, businessmen, actors, motley KKR well-wishers. These parties, it was told, went on into the morning's small hours; reportedly, Khan was at them himself. By the accounts of astonished hotel staff, he bounced back early the next day, or went off to catch a flight to Bombay, without any perceived need or desire for sleep. It soon became clear to me that Khan's mysterious staying powers in Hindi cinema had less to do with his talents than with his youthfulness and inability to become fatigued. On the Eden Gardens ground, during a match, he was almost always on edge, like a coiled spring, pumping the air to cheer his team, deflated very briefly when the innings reached a bad end, then running down and spryly annexing the field. Hearing of the Sonar Bangla parties, I thought for some reason of Gatsby, and the questions that character raised. Not that Khan's origins – unlike Fitzgerald's character's – were an invention; although he'd once issued a Fitzgeraldian caveat, implying that he was, in some sense, unknown to himself: 'I am an agent for an actor called Shah Rukh Khan.' No, what brought Gatsby to mind were Khan's parties, and his freedom from ordinary bodily demands before he took the early morning flight out. This is exactly what startles Nick Carraway when, exhausted, he thanks his host before leaving his party at dawn: '"Don't give it another thought, old sport." The familiar expression held no more familiarity than the hand which reassuringly brushed my shoulder. "And don't forget we're going up in the hydroplane tomorrow morning, at nine o'clock."' Where the terrific energy of the free market and its players comes from has long troubled those who've viewed it from the sidelines.

Two months after Casa Toscana, I sought out David Canazi, whom I'd never entirely forgotten since chef Sujan Mukherjee mentioned him as the man who'd set up the Italian restaurant in the Hyatt, then married and settled in Calcutta. It was years since the Hyatt had come up on the EM Bypass; and Canazi was now, after the decade closed, evidently introducing Italian food to diners at the coffee shop in Hotel Hindustan International – once, long ago, Calcutta's best-known hotel after the Grand (albeit a very distant number two), and today well known for having once been Calcutta's best-known hotel after the Grand. The bourgeoisie and the rich in Calcutta – unlike their counterparts in, say, New Delhi – don't socialise in five-star hotels; which might be why it was after three decades that I stepped into HHI, asking for directions to the coffee shop.

Mukherjee had informed me that Canazi was a pioneer, one of the first to propagate 'authentic' Italian food in these parts; but he'd escaped my attention. I wanted to confront this pioneer face to face; I was also interested in his metamorphosis into a bona fide resident. The others had moved, vanished, or fled; Canazi had not only married, set up shop, but, as it turned out, engendered a family. Meeting him was probably the closest I'd come to interacting with a 'white Mughal', eighteenth-century Europeans who arrived on these shores and were eventually assimilated – 'assimilated but unconverted', perhaps, as Isabel Archer was in her brief, adoptive English life in *Portrait of a Lady*, but nevertheless taking on family, manners, customs, language, and dress. What would it have been like to make their acquaintance, before the whole business of being Indian, or European, or Bengali, or English, became watertight? Even the Orientalist William Jones, hardly a white Mughal, was known to wear local clothes made of muslin in the heat. Canazi, however, when he emerged from the kitchen after fifteen minutes, was shielded by his apron.

◆

I was promised black coffee while waiting at Mythh, the coffee shop. Canazi was a small, slight, focused man (his squint intensifying his look of concentration), who hadn't lost his accent, and was quite masterful as he instructed the deferential suited manager to supply my coffee, which had not appeared. He took me to a table in the corner of what was like a gallery or balcony at the edge of the coffee shop, which looked large and lit from where we were, like the stalls or orchestra in a theatre, and our location and observation point adventitious, remote, à la the theatre box in *La Loge*. This balcony was Canazi's privileged Italian promontory inside Mythh, an extension of the coffee shop, but gently separated from the hoi polloi milling towards the buffet by an elegant railing, a change of floor tiling, and a *lakshman rekha* or invisible boundary. The diners in the balcony (which was a balcony partly of the imagination, since it was on the same level as the coffee shop) may as well have been invisible to those in the stalls.

One of the first things I learnt from Mr Canazi was that his name was actually Davide Cananzi – he handed me his calling card – and that he'd joined the Hyatt in 2004 and worked there for one and a half years. 'Canazi' was chef Mukherjee's well-intentioned misnomer; Cananzi was the man before me. 'I would have left in three months,' he admitted, with the air of one reminiscing about an episode whose immediacy diminishes as the days pass, 'but I met Suparna and I got married.' 'Where did you meet her?' 'In the Hyatt,' he said. 'She was in customer relations.' They'd married in 2004 – an almost instantaneous development, then, which points to an auspicious momentum in Cananzi's beginnings here.

He was Sardinia-born, bred in Toscana. When he left Italy for Berlin and Paris he was only sixteen, but already, precociously, had a diploma in hotel management. He worked in Dubai and Barbados before he found himself, in 2004, at the Calcutta Hyatt.

'I would have left in three months,' he said again. 'Calcutta wasn't ready for innovation.'

He spoke, in his long, retrospective assessment, of 2004 as if it were another age – by 'innovation' he meant the uncompromising taste of Italian food, and a deep resolve to ignore local demands and tantrums.

'In the first two months, I had fifteen to twenty covers,' he said, still scarred by that experience of adversity. By 'covers' he meant daily customers at the restaurant. Then, self-belief – and the hotel's willingness to go out on a limb and back him – led to triumph. 'By the third month, we had fifty covers.' He had not diluted his menu. 'It was a challenge to educate people to eat as I eat.'

William Jones's late-eighteenth-century mission, in the end, was to educate Western scholarship about Indian antiquity and the Sanskritic inheritance; he pieced these together painstakingly through his researches here, in between appearances at the court and fulfilling his duties as a judge. His precursor, Nathaniel Halhed, a 'writer' for the East India Company, and a translator, had, besides composing English poetry, clarified to the local populace the rules of their own language, compiling, with the collaboration of Brahmins, the first Bengali grammar in 1774. Cananzi, two hundred years later, was neither intent on giving Bengal to Bengalis, or India to the world; he was engaged in a more resistant task, in an environment that was, in this regard, oddly unprepared – the unnoticed business of bringing Italy to Bengal.

'Local basil is fantastic,' he said, with a characteristic generosity towards conditions on the ground. 'But it has an aftertaste of mint.' The taste of 'real' basil was unknown to the people around us. Such hurdles were conquered and made irrelevant; and there was his already-stated adherence to the principles of Italian food, his inability to relax the rules, unlike, say, Alex Bignotti – a chef he adored and whose culinary skills he admired. 'For instance, if you make penne arrabiata with mushrooms, do not call it penne arrabiata. By all means make it, but call it something else.' This was only a hypothetical recipe; but it symbolised the fact that the Italian character and its quiddity tended to disintegrate and vaporise in the Bengali context.

What was it, after all, to be Italian – especially here? Cananzi confessed that the 'name tag' of 'Italian chef' had 'become a burden'. Other chefs of his rank were simply called 'executive chefs'; but the moment people heard he was Italian, he became, inescapably, 'Italian chef', as if he couldn't possibly rustle up tandoori or Japanese – which he said he enjoyed doing. This was a surprising turn: that Cananzi, at least on some level, felt pinned down to Italian cuisine. 'What kind of food do you have at home?' I asked. 'Mostly *Indian* food,' he shrugged, 'Bengali food.' I had a vague, provisional vision of him with his family, in home clothes, busily partaking of daal and rice. 'Do you speak Bengali?' I asked him. Half my mind, as I put the question to him, was already ferreting away, unearthing similarities between Bengali and Italian. This habit of mine, belonged, of course, to a line opened by William Jones, who, late in the eighteenth century in this city, had hit upon his theory of 'Indo-European languages', a family of tongues including Bengali, Hindi, English, French, Persian, Italian, Greek, Latin, whose words derived their roots, he claimed, from Sanskrit. I knew very little Italian, except what I'd memorised from the menu, words such as carbonara and penne, but had noted, once, that certain everyday words spoken in Spanish and French, like, say, '*que*' or '*pourquoi*' for 'what' or 'why' were near identical to '*ki*' or '*kya*' and '*kyon*' in Bengali and Hindi respectively. Also '*basta*', or 'enough!', frequently heard in Almodóvar films, seemed like a close neighbour to the North Indian '*bas*', meaning the same thing. But these exclamations or imperatives were the language of daily parlance, of the community, and I didn't know whether '*basta*' or '*bas*' had a Latinate or Sanskritic pedigree – but there were any number of grander words where that lineage seemed

irrefutable, and rang out repeatedly and gravely like a bell toll-
ing, as in the Latin *'morte'* for death (the ugly Anglo-Saxon
'murder' in all likelihood a descendant of the same family)
and the Sanskrit *'mrityu'*. Where would all my amateur speculations have been if not for that Welshman, who, with other
British people, and the great Bengalis to follow, had turned
Calcutta into a crucible of world history? 'Yes, I know Bengali'
said Cananzi. 'I know it quite well.' I didn't care to test him.
'It was tough learning Bengali,' he confessed. 'Also, I had little
English at the time – I had to leap straight into Bengali.' Then
he added something at which I pricked up my ears. 'There are
lots of words in common between Italian and Bengali – also
between Italian and Arabic, you know?' This latter insight must
have come to him during his stint in Dubai – and, anyway, the
Ottoman Empire's reach had been immense since the fifteenth
century onward – but I was more interested in the overlaps with
Bengal, with which Italy had had no significant historic inter-
change since Tagore's visit there at the beginning of the Duce's
reign. 'For instance?' I asked him. 'Like *forno*, for instance – it is
the word for oven in Italian. It is also the same word in Bengali.'
'Excuse me?' Cananzi had been misled; the Bengali word for
'oven' is surely *unun*. 'I haven't heard that word,' I said, puzzled. 'But you know – the English "furnace" is very close to
it.' I pointed this out in a conciliatory way. 'Are you sure?' said
Cananzi. 'I was told by a Bangladeshi that you have *forno* in
Bengali.' We placed the debate in abeyance. I began to gossip
with him about other Italian chefs in the city, a part of me still
wondering if he'd noticed the proximity of al dente – the ideal
chewiness of slightly undercooked pasta – to the Bengali *daant*,
whose ancestor is the Sanskrit *danta*. *'Danta'*, 'dental', *'dente'*: all
variations of 'teeth'. At some point down millennia, the coordinates that governed and linked certain languages to others
were lost. Then along came Jones, who, in his imperious way,
suggested that once there used to be a bit of the European in

the Oriental, and vice versa. This notion was embraced with alacrity by the new Indian, especially the Bengali, eager to join the freemasonry of the modern, and eventually forgotten by all but a handful of Europeans. For Cananzi, whatever his recent affections, Calcutta certainly was no Rome.

This much I deduced from my little gossip about the chef who'd made a run for it from Casa Toscana. It had taken half an hour for me to notice that Cananzi was well informed about, and a fair judge of, his Italian rivals in Calcutta. 'Is it true that the man wasn't Italian at all, but an Italian-American from New York City?' 'No, no,' said Cananzi. 'He was from Ravenna. He had spent many years in America.' According to Cananzi, the absconder's name was Rimini. 'He was a Michelin-star chef,' nodded Cananzi, as if there were no getting around this intractable fact. 'But Calcutta is not a Michelin-star city,' noted Cananzi. I felt chastened. Yes, seen from that perspective, the match was indeed ill-fitting. 'Calcutta doesn't have a conception of fine dining,' he continued. 'What I give to diners here is "Calcutta fine dining."' I could clearly see the scare quotes around the term. Instead of interrogating him on the meaning of 'Calcutta fine dining', I got to the basics and asked him what 'fine dining' was. 'Firstly, the time you give to eating. In Italy and France, a "fine dining" experience can take up to three or four hours. But Indians are not willing to spend so much time on food.' He added, opening himself up to a broader sweep of truth-telling and stocktaking: 'Delhi has no fine dining. Is an old-fashioned city. Bangalore' – his eyes lit up peremptorily – 'is a fine dining city. There, they know how to invest. To make money you have to know how to lose money,' he concluded – a little aphoristically.

There was nothing supercilious about Cananzi; but, despite his readiness to talk, there was a resistance about him – not to me; it was more an inward physical tension, as if his responsiveness and intelligence had been translated into bodily alertness. He was not a busy or fussy person, but I didn't have the impression that he was ever quite still. He was a low bristly shrub that had been transplanted; he was getting used to his environment, which, every few years, was a variation on the previous one, and for the moment was this coffee shop.

It was three months after the elections, and I was interested in whether he'd reacted to them in any way.

'I'm not a lot into politics,' he said, unsurprisingly: reportedly, aesthetes seldom are. 'But good that change has happened,' he confessed, echoing the Trinamool's much-advertised mantra of paribartan. 'Calcutta was growing slowly because previous party didn't want investment from foreigner companies,' he observed, as others before him have. Now he had a sense that the state would be more swift on the uptake.

'Calcutta has changed a lot,' he told me, pursuing the theme of paribartan but widening it from its Trinamool-specific definition, speaking again in the reflective tone in which he'd described his first ambiguous months at the Hyatt, purveying genuine Italian food. 'India is changing. India is the new China. And Calcutta is opening its eyes.' He assured me, 'It's more cosmopolitan. Less "racist" than it was.' He'd chosen the word deliberately, and I was on tenterhooks as to his possible meaning. 'Earlier, when foreigner walked down New Market, people would stare as if the person was an alien, and the boys would cheat him. Of course,' he conceded, 'it's a little bit like that in every city in the world.'

Then, quickly reviewing his seven years here, his thoughts converged upon a deeply felt analogy: 'Bengalis are amazing people of the heart – like Italians.' There was a time – the early twentieth century, in fact, when Bengalis had just come into their own – when Italians were not quite embraced by the new genteel arbiters of culture in Europe and America, but were seen as untrustworthy and different, if the stories of Henry

James or Mann are anything to go by; or, from the point of view of the restless, working-class Lawrence's letters, were thought to be strangely, comfortingly elemental. 'But when it comes to language, Bengalis are like Germans. That's why I quickly learned the language. Bengalis, like Germans, won't talk to you unless you speak their language.' East Germans, perhaps; almost all the educated West German people I know make a fetish of speaking perfect English.

There was traction, for him, between his former home and his present one. His brother had visited him; last Christmas, his parents came to Calcutta. 'I had heard of Calcutta many years ago because of Mother Teresa, but I had no interest in it. But I always wanted to visit India.' Still adorning his Italian-Bengali comparison, he told me that the two were 'eighty per cent the same': a remarkably high proportion of any national or social character. 'Family oriented, cost oriented – they are not into spending too much.' Giving the lie to Elizabeth Bishop's speculation, 'Is it lack of imagination that makes us come/to imagined places, not just stay at home?', he seemed to feel, at certain moments, that the memory and presence of home were never that far away: 'There are places in the south of Italy that are even dirtier than Calcutta.'

Europeans who visited Calcutta on the eve and in the wake of the British Empire each handled the experience differently. In *Hartly House*, the first English-language novel about the city, it's as if we've been placed in a time machine and transported to a hazy future, and not back to the Calcutta of the late eighteenth century when the book is actually set – to a place where there are no Indians, Bengalis, or Hindus, only an odd Morlock-like tribe known as the 'Gentoos'. In this city, the English had their weird recreational parties late into the night, until dawn approached, because it was too hot to move during the day. Summer, and the heat, in particular, had to be survived;

Thomas Babington Macaulay grumbled with abrasive dignity in a letter to a friend, 'We are annually baked for four months, boiled four more, and allowed the remaining four to become cool if we can.' The Bengali historian R.K. Dasgupta tells us with relish that Macaulay confided in his correspondent that the 'local fruits were "wretched"'.

> 'The best of them is inferior to our apricot or gooseberry . . . A plantain is very like a rotten pear . . . A yam is better. It is like an indifferent potato.' He must have been all the more thankful for his expert cook, whom Lord Dalhousie pronounced 'decidedly the first artist in Bengal.' . . . In brief, Macaulay could not find 'words to tell you how I pine for England, or how intensely bitter exile has been to me'.

All this had to be overcome and outlasted, not to mention the diseases brought on by humidity. The obscure author of *Hartly House*, Phebe Gibbes, writes in the opening of her novel that 'the Eastern world is, as you pronounce it, the grave of thousands'. William Jones himself died at the end of April, with the onset of another summer, in 1794, of, according to his friend Lord Teignmouth, 'a complaint common in Bengal, an inflammation of the liver . . . He was lying on his bed in *a posture of meditation . . .*'

To these deaths and others must be added the millions who perished in the man-made famine of 1943, when local traders were hoarding grain while supplies were being diverted to British Tommies, a reminder that colonialism didn't necessarily make life in Bengal any easier, or longer.

In comparison – and unrelated to the fact that Calcutta is hardly the historic centre it then was – Cananzi has weathered well. He points out to me the glass-paned, conservatory-like space at the end of the faux balcony we're sitting on, where you can dine in greater, deeper isolation if you wish. Or, of course, you could remain in these imaginary outdoors. Before I leave, he introduces me to his latest contribution to 'Calcutta fine dining': an elegant, economically stated menu, as well as a charming 'interactive' one, something between an iPad and one of those books of fairy tales with 3D illuminations shimmering as in a pool, that one got sometimes as a birthday present; you may not only choose from the menu, but design your own if you wish, by touching the icons, the small bright signifiers of pasta and risotto and antipasti. Immediately, predictably, I feel the lure of the seafood risotto. 'You must come and dine here,' he says, this being the most logical and civilized progression from our peculiar acquaintanceship. 'And you should surely let me know when you're coming.' I already see there are advantages to knowing him.

Study Leave

I didn't go to Norwich this autumn. I invoked 'study leave'. And so it was that I got to be here during the season of *sharath*, which begins in mid-September. It occurs to me that, in other years too, I'm in Calcutta when sharath is barely beginning because I don't fly to England before the end of September; but I must be too full of foreboding – at the thought of the flight – to heed it. By now, the rains are as good as ended – the showers are begrudged when they happen – and there's a new stillness to be sensed, even in a city as busy as Calcutta. This ebbing of one season into another is near unnoticeable (and, as I said, hardly registered by me on the eve of departure), but must have been quite an event in small towns and villages. Tagore, in one of his songs, alludes to it as a time of valediction – but then, every month and a half brings on the mood of valediction to the Bengalis, a hiatus, in which the last intimacies of saying goodbye are performed: for, by mid-October, they'll be bidding farewell to the mother-goddess.

Now, when I return to the song I was thinking of, introduced to me by my uncle in London when I was studying there, I see it's about the end of a thundershower in the month of *bhaadra*, which just precedes the onset of sharath: 'The rain-shower ends, I hear a tune of valediction/bring your songs to a close/ you're going far away'. In the beginning of September, as I think of Norwich, the lines sound as if they're directly addressed to me. '*Chharbe kheya opar hotey/bhaadra diner bhora srotey re*', it continues – 'The canoe starts out for the other bank/In the powerful current of a bhaadra day'; then 'It rocks midway in the swirling water'. There are inner rhymes (*hotey, srotey*) in the Bangla lines I've transcribed. I can't translate the finely judged words or the lines' perfect symmetry, but they mainly achieve their beauty because Tagore adds nothing: he's making a statement of fact, just as the remembered lines from a child's primer (*jal pare/pata nare*; 'rain falls/the leaf trembles') that first drew Tagore to poetry state a fact. Here, Tagore seems to be telling us that no afflatus or elaboration is necessary, because the world is at its most compelling as it is.

When I think of that song, I hear my uncle singing in his low, unsteady, pleasant voice. It's a voice that sounded as if it needed warming up before it got going, or wanted kick-starting – but it never did get going. 'The pollen from the *kadamba* has covered the forest floor,/The bees have forgotten their way among the *keya* flowers,' he sang softly, with a mad intensity. He told me that there was nothing poetic about these lines – all was fact, evidently; the bees did get confused after rainfall; they lost their sense of scent and their way to the flowers. For a quarter of a century, he'd lived uninterrupted in north-west London; these songs approximated photos or home movies of where he'd come from. What made these photo-substitutes talismanic is that no one else nearby could understand them or knew very much of the place they'd recorded. In Belsize Park, in a bedsit that overflowed with carrier bags, Bengal didn't exist except in those songs – and Tagore songs were both cheap and many, a dime a dozen. 'The wind's stopped in the forest today,/Dew pervades the air,/Memory's aftermath in this light becomes shining drops of rain'. The last untranslatable image – *'alo tey aaj smritir abhash brishtir bindur'* – would bring him close to tears; for the Indian is genetically programmed to feel an acute intimation of parting on any mention of the rain.

Sharath, I realised for the first time during this 'study leave', was spring's mirror image. It had that gentleness and equanimity of light; June and July's mulching, rotting humidity had almost vanished. There was a hint of a second flowering; illusory, but convincing. Whoever devised the six Indian seasons took into account this nuance and play; they knew the year, like a day, is not only a progression, a movement from one phase to another, but a passage through echoes, reminiscences, and expectation, through intermediary periods that recall one another, as dusk and twilight do in the day's twelve hours. To these reminiscent moments – as when, after the monsoons, you were suddenly in the midst of spring – these devisers had given names, making them seasons, rather than tactfully ignoring them. In fact, part of the great unacknowledged joy of sharath was to know that it *wasn't*, actually, spring. Spring, or *basanta*, is arguably the more famous season, given its bright flowers and sexual birdcall; but you're always aware of – and are trying to ignore – the prospect of another withering summer. With sharath, there's an intake and release of breath as you stand in the stillness; *there is no summer to come*; the temperature will rise for two weeks in October, then fall again; and the inevitable temperate calm of *hemanta* will continue into winter. All this I began to learn in the first few weeks into 'study leave'.

Though one wouldn't suspect it, there are concordances between Norwich and Calcutta. Both are geographically to the east of the nation. The east – except perhaps at the beginning of the day, or in the golden age – historically constitutes the margins. People still 'go West', not eastward. Norwich confirms this by its isolation, especially from London – London might be an international financial hub, but Norwich has limited access to it. There's no dual-carriage motorway connecting it to the capital; you enter Norwich by a road that's slightly wider than a country lane. The railway track is ancient, and it makes some of the other obsolete railway lines around England look efficient and smart. Also, the towns just south of Norwich – from Diss and Manningtree to Ipswich – are where the most suicidal and unhopeful people in England live, and there are repeated 'fatalities' on the tracks, whereby some poor, terminally life-hating soul becomes a reason for an abortive or delayed journey. These conditions make many self-proclaimedly normal people suicidal, meaning that the prospects of increasing fatalities in the environs of Norwich will continue to be high. Every weekend, 'engineering works' have been taking place on the Norwich railway lines (to either modernise or salvage them) with an infinitely patient, scholarly regularity, so that commuters returning from a Saturday in London must be offloaded at Diss and transferred to a bus, arriving after four hours instead of the usual two into the familiar cathedral town.

Calcutta, until exactly one hundred years ago from when I write this the Empire's 'second city', is today comparably cut off from London – from the rest of the world, even. (It was in 1911 that, alarmed by the swelling Swadeshi movement in the state, and forced to reunite the Bengal they'd partitioned in 1905, the British transferred the capital to Delhi; and it strikes me as odd that there were no centenary events in Calcutta to mark the advantages and disadvantages of not being a capital city.) Today, you may fly uninterrupted from Calcutta to Dhaka or Bangkok or Singapore; anywhere else, and you must be offloaded at Dubai, or Delhi, or Frankfurt, like the returning commuters to Norwich, and put on another flight – and not just on Sundays. Still, Norwich's isolation feels more ancient. Partly it's because it's so much older than Calcutta. In fact, in the eleventh century, Norwich was apparently a city of immense importance, second only to London; this, you'll agree, has a disturbingly familiar ring. Perhaps to speculate upon what Calcutta will be centuries hence, one must study the Norwich of the twenty-first century: a place that has as good as forgotten its past. To me, travelling to it in the autumn is a bit like going to Africa in the colonial era, or at least what it was like for Marlow, in *Heart of Darkness*, to sit in England, back from the Congo, and feel the one inexorably flow into the other. So it is that I've stared out from the heavy glass-paned windows of my sixties-designed visitor's flat into the broads, from which gulls rise periodically, and sensed the presence of the primordial; Marlow's famous words come back – 'I was thinking of very old times, when the Romans first came here, nineteen hundred years ago – the other day . . . Light came out of this river since . . . We live in the flicker – may it last as long as the old earth keeps rolling! . . . Sandbanks, marshes, forests, savages – precious little to eat fit for civilised men, nothing but Thames water to drink. No Falernian wine here, no going ashore.' Easy to feel, at certain moments, like that Roman when I'm in Norwich, especially as I stare out of the window from Suffolk Walk; and forget Calcutta, a much younger, more recent, city.

Hardly into my 'study leave', I notice the frail bamboo outlines for the Puja *pandals* begin to appear in street corners. Their context, in the intersection, is so urban; regulations permit these apparitions to hold up or divert traffic during the Pujas. But, in this phase of their construction, when they're intricate husks, their fragility visible to the public eye, they're reminders of an ancient Bengal – which may not exist anywhere at all today except in these fleeting cameos.

There's little doubt Durga Puja began as a harvest festival. One story has it that the first time it became an urban event was when Raja Nabakrishna Deb of the Shobhabazar Rajbari (or the princely family of Shobhabazar) in North Calcutta organised a Puja for Lord Clive in 1757, to celebrate the British victory at Plassey – to mark, as it were, the passage of power from Siraj-ud-daula to the East India Company. The Rajbari has recently issued an official rebuttal of this account. Anyway, as Kaliprasanna Sinha's anarchic verbal record from 1860, *Hutom Pyanchaar Naksha* (The Night-Owl's Sketches), shows, most of the powerful Calcutta families had appropriated the Pujas by the middle of the nineteenth century, making them an occasion for boisterous, often competitive, celebration. At some point, the Pujas passed from the domain of the families to the *paras*, or neighbourhoods – often, stifling, cloistered, ten-foot-wide lanes lasting no more than a quarter of a mile. It was at this time that the Pujas – despite their name, which means 'worship' – must have become secular, roughly four or five days of pretending to pay obeisance to the goddess, of wearing one's most uncomfortably new clothes, of commingling, communal eating, flirting with cousins, followed by more communal eating. For the middle class, there's no withdrawal from the Pujas – it permeates the interior and the exterior, the apartment and the street, equally. It must have been in the late seventies and early eighties, after the Left Front had come to power to begin what surely no one thought would be a near-interminable tenure, and Bengal began to grow increasingly isolated, culturally and economically, that the Pujas started truly to prosper. By the early eighties, without anyone quite noticing or certain of what had happened, they'd become the world's most extraordinary festival, holding absolute, even tyrannical, sway over the city for as long as they lasted. By the early nineties, the noise and crowds were forcing what remained of the middle class in Calcutta to leave their homes, and check into a guest house or hotel in Ooty or Puri – in other words, to spend the Pujas elsewhere. Some of the elements of today's Pujas must be immemorial – the sound of the *dhak* or drums in the morning approaching the apartment block; the actual worship performed (I use that word literally) by the priest, and his exhilarated *dhunuchi* dance later. Others may have emerged in the fifties or the sixties – the spectacular pandals in different parts of the city; the excursions undertaken to admire the goddess, whose likeness may be made on traditional lines, or to resemble a contemporary movie actress. (This year, I believe I spotted a Durga modelled on one of the blue people of *Avatar*.) But it's in the early eighties, probably, that the attention shifted from the mother goddess and her family in the pandal – which is a marquee of variable size made of bamboo, papier mâché, cloth, and other material – to the pandal itself. The pandals have, in the last twenty-five years, been made to look like the Titanic; the General Post Office; the Fountain of Trevi at Rome; the Winter Palace in St Petersburg; the Tagore house in Jorasanko; the Egyptian pyramids; old, disused theatres, houses, or temples – in fact, anything that catches the pandal-maker's fancy that year. The intention is not so much to entertain as to disorient and astonish; to tap into the Bengali's appetite for the bizarre, the uncanny.

The lighting, done by 'the men from Chandannagar', a town about thirty miles away from Calcutta, also contributes to this realm of astonishment. They follow no convention of 'beautiful lighting'; the counterpart of the Puja lights are not the Christmas lights hung on Regent Street, but the patterns created by the plastic spiral stencils sold on streets, going round and round with your pen in different ellipses; the shards of colour that rearrange themselves within a kaleidoscope; covers of exercise books; pictures blazoned in the local tabloid; 'breaking news' messages and TV bulletins. Sometimes they swirl and form patterns; sometimes they depict the treasures contained in a child's textbook, even something like the secrets of the inner ear, with the eardrum, the anvil, and the cochlea; often, they will represent – in repeated, moving sequences – an event that's recently captured the imagination: rumours, in 1990, of a plague in Calcutta; Satyajit Ray receiving an Oscar for lifetime achievement; Princess Diana's sudden death in a car crash; Amitabh Bachchan hosting the Indian version of *Who Wants to Be a Millionaire?*; the two aircraft flying straight into the doomed Twin Towers. They flash; they swiftly enact an episode; they begin again immediately. They're meant to tell those stories until dawn, even when there's no one in their proximity; just as, in some secret reflex, you'll think of them after that year is over.

The myth of the Pujas is a simple one – full of rural sweetness. Durga, the mother, comes to our world from her world in the Himalayas, usually in early October, to slay the moustached asura who's sprung out of the body of a buffalo and is now oppressing us all. Some such episode involving a bully must have occurred in our childhood, and we'd called upon our mother then to set it right. The Pujas are, in part, an ever-returning homage to that magical sense of being rescued, so indispensable to children. But we're mostly grown up now, as we mill around the pandals, and we know that asuras aren't easily disposed of, that mothers aren't all-powerful; and it has to be admitted that it's this sense of irony about the mother, and our stubborn denial of reality, that gives the Pujas their tenderness, and makes Durga, paradoxically, so strong. For she's infinitely empowered by our need.

She arrives on a lion. Her ten arms are as familiar as some other physical deformity might be in someone you've long known. She's also called *mahishasuramardini*, 'she-slayer of the buffalo-asura'. Arrayed on both sides are her children, Saraswati, Lakshmi, Kartik, Ganesh. According to the ordaining of the almanac, Durga may use a canoe or an elephant for transport. But she's always depicted upon a lion. By the end of the Pujas, the myth moves into its second phase – of valediction, reminiscent, once more, of the sweet, powerful yearnings of rural life. By now, Durga has become our daughter; it's time for her to go back to her husband, Shiva, in the Himalayas; *her* holidays – not just ours – are done. We've become her father; and, like every father, we know it's futile to want to keep back a married daughter – she's not ours to keep. In the Pujas' ten days, we've somehow aged and spanned a lifetime, from being child to parent, as characters often do in the course of a novel.

Usually, I'm in Norwich before the goddess arrives, let alone before she's departed for the Himalayas. At least, that's been the case since 2006. But, in 2010, I asked for 'study leave'. And though I stayed in Calcutta in 2011, the Pujas, before I knew it, were gone, with that faint, bittersweet surprise that overtakes you when things long anticipated are suddenly over. A day later, the pandals looked prematurely empty, the idols had been transferred to trucks and taken to the Hooghly river to be immersed; and, in two days, those pandals were being shorn patiently of their phantasmagoric and duplicitous outer covering, whatever it was that made them look, in the past week, like mock-landmarks or mock-monuments. I went past them in a car that week, as they became naked, overarching outlines of bamboo, tied together by rope – an extraordinary experience of illusory joy, to see them thus, almost exactly as they'd begun to appear three weeks ago. It's as if some lost part of your life had returned to you, in a second lease of life, in a way it can't from a photograph or recording – it's that moment when the Pujas will soon begin, it's late September and the pandals are being hurriedly completed, and you haven't gone to Norwich. It's a twin season, just as sharath is to spring, dusk to twilight. This interval hasn't been named yet, but it does come up before the week reaches proper closure.

Those frail bamboo husks are, for the time being, the last evidence in the year of the great craftsmanship of rural Bengal – the old ingenuity that's channelled, yet again, into an event such as the Pujas. Something like the shapeliness of those husks, so finely put together despite their angularities, with none of the ricketiness that bamboo scaffolding has when buildings are being painted, is what the traveller Al-Biruni must have run into when he was here, in Bengal, in the tenth century, and found, he claims, not an agricultural but an artisanal society – people everywhere, not growing things, but making things with their hands and implements. I too feel as if I'm witnessing the products of some gift, or talent, special to these parts for centuries as I watch the bamboo structures being dismantled.

By craftsmanship I mean a quality of tactility, of 'madeness'. It comes from the instinct to shape and touch things, to impart an intimacy to materials. By the 1860s, that urge seemed, super-ficially, to have been superseded; Bengalis had ceased becoming artisans and had begun to become artists – poets, sculptors, composers, and, later, filmmakers. As if keeping pace with this change, certain words developed new and startling meanings. For instance, *sahitya*, which had meant 'text' or 'textual content' or even 'literary content', came, by the end of the nineteenth century, to mean, specifically, 'literature', or the literary canon. Similarly, *kabi*, which was the word for an author of a scholarly or orthodox kind, now referred to a 'poet', in the modern sense of the word. The Bengalis had become moderns; no, they *were* moderns. Speaking of Ishwarchandra Gupta, the great idiosyncratic poet of the nineteenth century, and the major poet of Bengali literature before it became a proper literature, Bankimchandra Chatterjee pointed out in 1885: 'Ishwar Gupta is a kabi. But what kind of kabi?' He proceeded to clarify that Gupta might be a kabi, but that he was not a 'poet' – deliberately using the English word. But the desire to be an artisan – such as, in a sense, Gupta was – would never quite die in the modern Bengali. The major Bengali painter of the twentieth century, Jamini Roy, a well-to-do bourgeois who studied the conventions of European painting at Calcutta's Government College of Art, achieved his stylistic breakthrough by turning to the *pats*, or paintings, by the anonymous patuas of the nineteenth century who plied their works on a variety of sacred and profane subjects in the vicinity of the Kalighat temple. 'I am a patua,' said Roy, firmly distancing himself from the term 'painter', in an unwitting but obverse mirror image of Bankimchandra's remark about Ishwar Gupta.

Tagore, *the* great Bengali poet, in Bankimchandra's sense of the term, with his beard, long hair, piercing gaze, and loose robes, the very image of the Romantic, also had deep artisanal impulses that overtook him spasmodically. Witness to these is his interest in bookmaking, in block prints and in engravings; his wonder, as a boy, at discovering the typeface from a printing press; but, most of all, his absorption in not just the style or content of writing, but its primary medium – handwriting or, in Bengali, *lipi*. For Tagore, handwriting is a craft, upon which he lavishes a subtle affection and which also becomes a means of exploration – it's no accident that Tagore's paintings, embarked upon in old age, arise from his manuscript corrections and deletions. It's also probably logical that one of the products that Tagore endorsed in an advertisement was Sulekha ink. No other modern writer, or culture, has given to handwriting the curious place of privilege that Tagore and bhadralok Bengal have. It's where labour and design converge.

✦ ✦ ✦

Just before the elections, a man called Sandip Roy and I met in a coffee shop near my house. Sandip had asked to interview me for a new web magazine set up by a television channel; he wanted my thoughts on the elections.

We discussed the Trinamool Congress, Mamata Banerjee, the Left Front – and Calcutta, of course. We'd both just returned to the city – I, from a short trip to England; he, from a few years of working in San Francisco. His mother was old; he'd made the move with this in mind, and was barely beginning a new life here – where he'd grown up, unlike me. We began comparing Indian cities – a common pastime when you're talking about one of them.

'Well, Bombay's main preoccupation is money, and Delhi's is power,' I said, unconsciously parroting received wisdom. 'Maybe Delhi these days is about *both* power and money. And Calcutta . . .'

'Calcutta's preoccupation is, "Will you be eating at home tonight?"'

He had echoed, verbatim, what my mother says to me, or to me and my wife, whenever we go out in the evening. It's a question asked uninsistently, but with measured desperation – meant to exert a silent pressure on the person going out of the door. Sandip Roy's words made me realise that neither I nor my mother are alone or unique. Very few people return to Calcutta today except to be with parents.

When we moved to Calcutta, my father was nearing seventy-eight; he'd accomplished his three-score-and-ten without any major hitches; and, as I write this, he's less than two months away from being ninety. At seventy-eight, he was still more active and agile than I am now, though, with hindsight, I can see the stealthy signs of dementia – mainly a slight loping oddness of gait – were already present.

Our plan, from 1999 onward, if the world didn't end on the stroke of midnight at the millennium's end, as many had hinted it would, was to 'divide time' between Calcutta and England. This was what we'd been doing anyway; but the intention was now to invert the previous allocations of the year – to spend fewer months in England, more in India. Part of the reason for this was I didn't want to discover one day that I was old, not far from death, and still living in England; for some reason, it didn't seem like the right ending for the story my imagination had constructed of my life. I'd seen it happen to others – couples who'd lived much of their adult life in Bicester, or Rochdale, or in Newbury Park; always deferring the day of departure, always behaving as if they were temporary residents who'd been in England for only the last few months; then, when the time of departure came at last, it was a further deferral of their plans – it was a departure to the afterlife, no doubt another limited stint before they made their way back to Bengal. They were the banal counterparts of the figure in the de Chirico painting which V.S. Naipaul invokes in order to reflect on what he's still doing in Wiltshire after so many years. We do what we do only with part volition – that much is a truism. I was determined to be neither like Naipaul nor that figure – and to exercise a choice while I was still conscious of the need for it.

My daughter's coming to the world in 1998 gave me a reason to speed up that decision. And being an only child made necessary that anomalous arrangement – of living with my parents – upon our move. I say 'anomalous' not only because such modes of coexistence are long out of date, and an embarrassment, but because they were adhered to not out of any sense of convention – both R and I grew up in nuclear families. So we did what we did as an experiment – the mirror image of what those Bengalis in Bicester do, testing a way of life until it becomes their own without having to acknowledge it. To participate in it, I needed my wife's tacit agreement. This wasn't the way she, or I, had conceived the future; for her, living with ageing in-laws in the city she'd grown up in, and with her *own* parents a five minutes' drive away.

But we were both fairly sure we were happy to give our daughter the childhood I'd never had, a Calcutta childhood; I'd intuited that, for the middle-class child at least, a Calcutta childhood is still a wonderful thing. It's a city that (and my wife confirms this) lends itself to make-believe, if you're open to make-believe, and to the kind of illusions precious to children. If you're the more hard-headed kind of child, there's also the rat-race to respond to, given the exacting emphasis the city's secondary education system gives to exams; but, despite this – or because of it – there's ample space for daydreaming.

Putting off Norwich for a year, I see what a nuisance my father has become. Unsurprisingly, he was once the man we all depended upon. The CEO of a major company, a man of calm and integrity, a foil to my mother's impetuousness, he had, after retirement, become my accountant. Six years ago, I had to wrest this responsibility from him gently, and give it to a professional. Today, he spends his spare time (when he's not staring at Bengali soaps, or 'serials' as they're called here, and lying in bed) on the chair in the sitting room, his largely useless walker (since he can hardly walk a step without fear of falling) and his daytime carer by his side – he a sort of chowkidar, a gatekeeper, wearing a polite, abstracted expression. His main mission (as is my mother's) is to protect our daughter from us. The faraway look is misleading; even a whispered reprimand from us to our daughter can stir him to a fury. Equally, my daughter is my father's chowkidar. When he makes a move to get up, she raises the alarm as if the house is on fire. Ordinarily, she's utterly lax, and notices nothing. But it's clear that something deep-seated in her knows my father has poor short-term memory; that he falls almost each time he rises from his chair and, positioning himself against the walker, makes off for somewhere in his low-headed precarious way; knows, too, that he'll have no memory of the fall after twenty minutes. So the house is in a constant state of tension, my daughter preternaturally anxious for my father's welfare, my mostly incoherent father anxious that she may be under attack – from us, her parents and lifelong enemies. 'The mad led by the blind': that's how a well-known city academic, Prof. Sibaji Bandyopadhyay, quoting *King Lear*, once mildly described to me Calcutta's middle class. Also, children leading the old, and vice versa.

Speaking with Sandip Roy confirmed for me what I've long known – that my experiment isn't singular – that all kinds of people (professors of history, gay couples, critics in 'cultural studies', rock guitarists, journalists, bankers) are living here with parents or parents-in-law either because they think *someone* has to, or as a filial duty – some returning to the city to be with them out of a sense of obligation. Naturally, the pressure of obligation or duty is felt most strongly by the only child, perhaps the Bengali only child. This makes Calcutta an odd kind of city at least where a few people are concerned – that they are drawn to it not by work or opportunity, but some other, atavistic concern. Bombay is about money; Delhi about power; Calcutta is about parents – the three cities can't really be compared to one another. Perhaps Banaras is a better analogue of my Calcutta at the moment: a place where people come to be facilitated into the afterlife, while their children and relatives hover there primarily to perform the necessary preparations for that journey. Certainly, it seems a whole bunch of corporate executives, surgeons, doctors, officers in the armed forces, professors, who'd all lived in other parts of the country during their working lives, returned quietly, in the last three decades, to Calcutta after retirement, just as widows, at one time, used to make their way to Banaras, or Kashi, for contemplation and solitude. And at least some of the children of those who've returned follow them to this city to enable their parents to be easeful before they're finally, one day, gone. The other such person I met, besides Sandip Roy, is Devakinandan Chatterjee, whom I've mentioned before in passing, earlier a wealth manager with Standard Chartered Bank in Bombay, now with Citibank, an only son but not an only child, who suddenly moved to Calcutta in 2010 with family because his father was falling down and hurting himself. Of course, he continued to be a wealth manager – but the stakes here are significantly lower. In that sense (at least where the middle class is concerned),

Calcutta is no more a *karmasthal* – the old Sanskrit word for a place where people go traditionally to seek work or employment. It has some other, hidden dimension to it – which makes it not quite Banaras, admittedly, but not quite Bombay or New Jersey either. When I bring up that ancient, forgotten, resonant term to my mother – a term that encompasses so much: life's endeavour; human ambition – she says without hesitation: 'Your karmasthal is East Anglia.' Ah, yes. What I do in Calcutta – writing, music – can't be counted as *work*. 'Calcutta is your *basasthan*,' my mother informs me – that is, my place of habitation. More likely, it's *her* basasthan; for me, it's a place of work, and that work comprises my parents. Not that I can give my parents, or work, much time, because of my writing and music. Still, they are a reason – a compulsion – not to pack our bags and leave. Visiting a city that was not my karmasthal, our visits to our parents tended to grow longer; till we now live here. I have become the figure in the de Chirico painting.

I put to R Sandip Roy's remark that Calcutta's main concern is: 'Will you be eating at home this evening?' She concurs; and adds, 'Also, all the studies we never did at school, and have to now.' My daughter's schoolbooks are scattered around her on the bed. The rat race of secondary education means that the business of gathering knowledge in Calcutta is a traumatic family affair, involving and exhausting everyone at home, like a delinquency, a disability, or a teenage pregnancy. The only one who seems unaffected by this – at least, if our daughter is in any way representative – is the student herself. She alone sees, with a clarity of vision we no longer have, the irrelevance of the present education system. We, instead, are learning up her syllabus in large gulps; going over it with her, but more intent on mastering it ourselves than checking if she's grasped it. We have now perfectly understood balancing equations in chemistry, the valency of elements and metals, we are quite adept at the congruencies of triangles, it wouldn't be an exaggeration to say that the definitions of velocity and force are on our fingertips, we know, of course, that the Andes are fold mountains, in part like the Appalachians, which have a decisive climatic influence on North America. How much of this our daughter knows at the moment is uncertain; but living in this city means we have it by heart. The school itself doesn't dispense education; it holds classes and periodically hosts exams. We, at home, don't dispense education either, but find ourselves getting thoroughly educated. Almost everyone employs private tutors, especially for maths and that increasingly neglected tongue, Bangla; we're no exception. The private tutor is like someone out of another age, country, and genre; he belongs to the world of *Little Dorrit*. He is intensely interesting, either garrulous or shy, and we choose to know little about him. My daughter has had two private tutors for maths, a subject she'll probably never think about again in five years, or at least until she has children of her own. The first is Rajiv, a thin man with a beard, about whom one of my daughter's friends observed: 'He's your maths teacher? He looks like a poet.' Rajiv is in his mid-fifties, and was once a quasi-Naxalite; he now runs a small advertising company. I would put him in the class of 'loquacious' private tutors – he's even played a small but significant role in a well-received art film, where he's a sort of political busybody, a functionary who tries to lord it over a vanishing neighbourhood: someone very unlike himself, and yet a character who's a surprisingly convincing alter ego for Rajiv. The second tutor, Alok, I place in the 'shy' category: highly accomplished, if awkward, he was doing a PhD in maths at what is probably India's leading institution for research in the sciences, the Tata Institute for Fundamental Research. He then placed his doctorate on hold and returned to Calcutta because his father is severely debilitated by back problems, and he's an only child. He's now taken upon himself the task of consolidating my daughter's shaky maths knowledge. It was he who made me think of Dickens; of how uniquely dated and specialised his profession, which we take for granted in India and especially in Calcutta, really is. Many private tutors are exceptional students who, for one reason or another – family; temperament; in some cases, I sense, a resistance to worldliness – haven't made the logical transition to glittering careers. It sometimes seems, when they dutifully appear, that they have no homes (though of course they do); that they're destined to linger and ruminate in others' houses. Their wards' childhoods pass with an unusual rapidity, like the quick, busy frames of the early movies, from month to month, term to term; while their days have, at least in these years of our children's education, a relatively detached stillness.

People begin to arrive in the mornings. The young man, Raja, who cleans the cars in the building, strides in to collect the car keys; the cook rings the doorbell; then the part-time help, Kamala, my father's daytime carer. They're here from different parts of the city. You're careful not to call them *chakor* any more. The word derives from *chakuri* or *chakri*, meaning 'employment'; but it was mainly used to slight and humiliate. But chakor, like 'servant', reflects more poorly on the user today than on the person being alluded to; the preferred term is the neutral and politically acceptable (and slightly anodyne) *kaajer lok* – 'people who work', 'working people'.

The chakor was often addressed as *tui* – the informal second-person pronoun, reserved for children, younger relatives, and best friends. This was the case irrespective of the age of the servant, though children *were* instructed to refer to older retainers as *dada*, or 'older brother', as in 'Laxman dada', while Laxman dada might also, paradoxically, refer to the master's son as *chhoto babu*, or 'young master'. Today, the kaajer lok are addressed as *tumi* – the semi-formal second-person pronoun for equals. However, the kaajer lok mostly address their employers as *aapni* – the formal second-person pronoun, used for superiors or older people, or as a respectful address for all strangers and acquaintances. It has no equivalent in English any more, but does in some European languages, the German *sie* being one. Just as you might address an older kaajer lok as aapni, or, if you're exceptionally liberal or wish to make a point, *all* kaajer lok as aapni, there are some kaajer lok who might, familiarly, address you as *tumi*. In doing so, they might be being friendly, or unmindful, or provocatively democratic. If they do so, however, you don't do anything about it; you don't, for instance, say, 'How dare you address me as tumi?' To do that would be anachronistic; an admission that you're petty and uneducated, as politicians in small towns are, which, for the bhadralok, is a worse thing to be than being powerless. It's a patchwork democracy, heavily weighted against the poor, the people who arrive at your door every morning – the help; the cook; the man who cleans the cars – but the middle class imagines it's also weighted against them. People have a range of demands, the demands of the poor being least attended to; but no one has any rights in this situation – the proper context for rights hasn't been created yet. It would be unfair on the middle class, or the bhadralok, to say they want a return to old-style feudal obeisance from the help, an unqualified servitude; but they do want conscientious work, honesty, long-term commitment, intelligence, and evidence of training in return for a basic salary (which has gone up minutely over the years, but is little more than a small honorarium), two days of paid 'leave' in a month, a Puja bonus and gift, no notion of a minimum wage, no workers' unions and, in effect, no hint of an independent life encroaching upon the middle class's own. And so, the middle class hardly ever gets what it wants. The kaajer lok are unstable, uncommitted, they vanish for days without warning and then come back again one day, and are allowed to resume work after caveats are issued, unless some kind of replacement, who will also flatter to deceive, has been found. The middle class is dependent on this floating, flickering population, a few of whom will always materialise at its door in the morning, but fantasises frequently about living without it – mainly because it can't stand the absence of commitment, the unwillingness to work, the air of being from a place that doesn't accord with normal standards of behaviour and language, and also because it can't bear to raise minimum standards of employment, salaries, and incentives. There's no choice for the middle class, where kaajer lok are concerned, except to live from day to day, and indulge in fantasy and rhetoric.

Strictly speaking, there's no bhadralok any more. Not only its heyday, its distinctive ethos – which produced the poets, novelists, painters, essayists; the Tagore family, Jamini Roy, Gopal

Ghosh, Buddhadeva Bose, Bankimchandra Chatterjee, Kamal Kumar Majumdar, Bibhutibhushan Banerjee, Sudhir Khastgir, Jibanananda Das, Utpal Basu, Purnendu Pattrea; composers like Himangshu Dutta, Atul Prasad, Nazrul, Nachiketa Ghosh, and Salil Chowdhury; film-makers like Paramathesh Barua, Satyajit Ray, Devaki Bose, and Ritwik Ghatak; the scientist Satyen Bose, who collaborated with Einstein in the Bose-Einstein statistics, and after whom the now-celebrated 'boson' is named – that ethos is finished for good. Still, it's possible to be a bhadralok – fleetingly, in a fitful way – in relation to the kaajer lok, and to Calcutta in general: as a sort of anomaly or exception, as a group of people who are around almost by accident.

The poor traditionally live in the *basti*. Basti is an Urdu word, meaning 'neighbourhood'; in Bengali, however, it means 'slum'. I remember the shock I felt when I was seventeen, when I first began to listen to Urdu ghazals, where the poet or singer might be pining for a woman living in a different basti from his own, because the word, with its connotations of squalor and anarchy, familiar to me from my visits to Calcutta, sounded incongruous in the ghazal's fragrant world. These days, the person who comes in the morning as your domestic help doesn't necessarily live in a basti, but often in developments for working-class folk, such as Subhasgram, clusters of houses with poor facilities and inadequate drainage and roadworks, but with shops and a local railway station. The trains are dangerously full in the mornings with commuters making their way to work in South Calcutta – so full, that cooks and maids have sometimes reached us in the tranquillity of our flat in Ballygunge – a posh residential area – with a leg or arm bruised, having fallen off or been pushed off by another commuter on to the platform. These signs – of the wear and tear and abrasions of commuting, of the cook limping dramatically into the apartment and receiving only moderate sympathy from her colleagues and her employer – aren't that unusual.

When a domestic begins to shout in an unseemly way at another domestic, or even at her employer, the word basti invariably makes a reappearance. 'Don't behave as if this is a basti,' the employer will instruct the domestic. 'This is a *bhadra* person's house.' In fact, the word might come up when two middle-class people are shouting unrestrainedly at each other. 'Remember,' one might interrupt the other, 'this is not a basti.' It doesn't matter if neither person has ever seen a basti; it's meant to bring back to them, indirectly, the presence, or the trappings, of that elusive thing, a *bhadra* existence.

Disasters occur in Calcutta, mainly from a stupendous disregard for norms and regulations, and from a mixture of greed and apathy – but not frequently enough for the domestics to arrive late at our doors in the morning. The women come wearing saris meant for the journeys workward and then homeward later in the evening – sometimes saris with atrociously colourful prints – which they discard and change for a drab work-sari after they've entered their small room by the kitchen. All this in six or seven minutes.

The city's not at war with itself, and trains generally run on time, so there's really no excuse for coming late. Despite this, a domestic might walk in an hour after she was due and claim the train was late, a story that may be contradicted by another domestic. Only on bandh or strike days do kaajer lok have an absolute, unarguable reason not to come. In comparison to many other cities, and despite occasional political conflagrations in the outskirts and neighbouring villages, despite 'jungle mahal' further afield (the sovereign mini-states within states where Maoists reign), Calcutta is fairly safe to walk and travel through, and you won't as a rule be robbed or shot or lacerated or raped (though you may be run over by a bus). This is not so much because the police are vigilant, but because the working and homeless people who populate the pavements at any given point of time are, despite their conditions, intrinsically bhadra. On the whole, there's no good reason for domestics to delay reaching, or abscond from, their place of employment – except the obscure compulsions of their personal lives, compulsions which are almost always considered to be fictitious by their employers, and sometimes probably are. The two days of monthly paid leave are given to them reluctantly, and other swathes of time when they disappear without explanation, switching off the mobile phones that all of them have, or simply allowing them to ring endlessly, are viewed with helpless bafflement and outrage. (I've used the word 'they' or 'them' frequently, because it's the other term – *ora* – besides kaajer lok most used to describe domestics.) When they return from their inexplicable absence – citing illness, or a relative's illness or death, or a wedding, or a puja or festival – they're usually accepted once more into the fold, not with open arms as the prodigal son or even one's own son might be, but fairly meekly, with some moral remonstrances that are, on the whole, pretty unintimidating.

I say the city isn't at war with itself, but it is in a state of chafing conflict; the oppositional mode, where kaajer lok are concerned, is passive resistance. Strategy, subtle preparedness, and passive resistance are most in use during festivals. New festivals, paying homage to some unheard-of deity, are invented almost annually by the kaajer lok, in order to fob off the interminable and unrewarding cycle of work in a way that, at least in their own eyes, requires no rationale. Certain dubious middle-class festivals, such as *jamai sasthi*, when the demi-god and star and bane of Bengali society – the son-in-law – is fed and appeased by his wife's parents, have grown in strength and consumerist fervour amongst some sections of the middle class after being appropriated by the free market and advertising; all this is being undone by the fact that jamai sasthi has now been smuggled out of its domain by the kaajer lok, and amplified for their own purposes. For days exceeding the single day of jamai sasthi, domestics fail to reappear, as they're busy celebrating their own jamai sasthi – in an intricate, slow-paced way. Jamai sasthi, as a result, is more or less ruined for the middle class, because you can't flatter and feed the son-in-law without the infrastructure and detail afforded by the hired help. Jamai sasthi, for the middle class now, is a week of dearth and abandonment.

Working people not only lack time for recreation and holidays, they also lack a proper notion of these things, and, at times, they're indistinguishable to them from torture. For days they'll go back to their home or *desh* or *gram* or village or family, the very place whose devastation drove them to Calcutta in the first place, be impeded during their return by a flood or a hurricane or a local election – anything from a natural calamity to a man-made disruption – and return to their employer's apartment looking barely alive. No middle-class person would have undertaken this excursion – they'd simply have severed ties with their home town. Sometimes they insist on embarking on a self-flagellatory pilgrimage – my parents' driver, Mahinder, did this: he went off to the famous Tarakeshwar temple, took a train from Howrah and got off at Sheoraphuli, collected water from the Ganga in two earthen pots which he hung from both ends of a pole resting sideways on his shoulders, then walked forty kilometres barefoot, as is customary, to the temple. He resumed work gaunt as a ghost; not only had he demolished the soles of his feet, he'd contracted gastroenteritis. Despite the awfulness of domestic work, most middle-class people would prefer domestic work to this kind of holiday. For the kaajer lok, *kaaj* or work is often terrible, but the escape from work sometimes seems more destructive. 'Why did you do it?' I asked Mahinder, thinking divine reward might be the attraction. He suspected he was being mocked. 'Oi – for some *bhakti-wakti*' – 'devotion and stuff'. 'Any other reason?' Surely some good fortune? 'No, just bhakti,' he said, sheepish. Should I believe him? To make that trek, but receive no windfall?

❖

The Durga Pujas, the principal festivities of the year, is a period of abeyance and false stability, when passive resistance is applied cautiously, or in stealth. It's akin to a card game; especially to playing poker. The kaajer lok, like everyone else, will receive *notun bastra*, or new clothes, from their employers, as part of the season's distribution of goodwill. Even if they've come to hate their employers, poker-faced, the kaajer lok will play the game till the end of the Pujas, in the interests of the notun bastra, upon receiving which, and the moment they have a better offer from a potential employer, they will show their hand, rise, and leave. Today, notun bastra is passé, and domestics forgo it in favour of a palpable monetary incentive, a Puja bonus, which could be half their salary and thus worth substantially more than a new sari. The drivers, the crème de la crème of the hired help, of course receive a full month's salary as Puja bonus. If, for some reason, you need to hire a driver or a domestic a month and a half leading up to the Pujas, you'll be unsuccessful and have to do without, because the game has begun to be played, and no disaffected staff will reveal their cards and peremptorily move jobs before the bonus has exchanged hands.

The middle class feels it necessarily fares badly at this game of poker, despite holding its cards close to its chest. It also forgets that domestics – besides the fortnightly off-day – have no time for observances and anniversaries: they're chopping onions in the kitchen on Independence Day; they're swabbing the floor on Christmas Eve; they're answering the telephone or doorbell on Republic Day.

Sometimes, when I'm in Norwich during the Pujas, I hear that some of the help have gone missing for a week, and the house is in disarray. The situation is worse with two old people at home, one of whom can no longer walk or talk properly. Helpless in Norwich, I open myself to a sense of penance at my selfishness and to my wife's beleaguerment. This time, I'm in Calcutta, and nothing unexpected happens.

✦ ✦ ✦

Just as there are neither permanent affiliations nor lasting enmities in politics, there are few in the employer–domestic relationship. This is true of our family. Employees who've thrown up their hands in despair and left have returned after months and resumed work; domestics whose services have been terminated because of some tiff or for repeatedly coming late to work, their final salaries paid, their signature or thumbprint received, are re-employed as if nothing had happened. For the employer, in the game of harvesting and hoarding staff that continues well after the Pujas, the returned domestic is a stopgap until a better alternative comes along. Since none does, the domestic becomes a long-term stopgap, her (it's almost unfailingly her) incursion into territory she was recently exiled from tolerated in the knowledge that she'll be discarded when the moment presents itself. The lapsed exile herself reunites with her past employers for being, for now, the least of necessary evils, and will forsake them as soon as it's convenient.

Lakkhi is a case in point. She was our cook long ago, when she was fairly thin and could've been pretty but for her goofy expression. She's quite a good cook in fact – not one of the great Bengali cooks of legend – but, given that culinary skills have receded irreversibly among the bhadralok and the kaajer lok, a good, competent technician. Her language is regally her own: she refers to Aquaguard, the water purifier installed in most kitchens, by her Bengali neologism, *kuaghat*, or, approximately, 'the well on the river bank'; and to vinegar as *bhinikal*, which could be an esoteric kind of tap (given 'kal' is 'tap' in Bengali). She hates cooking, and, though she doesn't say so in so many words, makes no bones about this; but, in a regrettable, circumstantial way, it's what she's spent most of her life doing. In the game of brinkmanship that is employment for the kaajer lok, you probably tend to forget such details. Her husband was a grocer; both a wholesaler and a vegetable-seller in Gariahat Market. Lakkhi left her job because she was arriving increasingly late, and tired, and couldn't stand working in the kitchen any more. The kitchen, especially in April, May, June, and July, is an awful place; which is why cooks, despite being better paid among domestics, are a vanishing breed – the cook must combine the technician's proficiency and a bit of artistic instinct with the archaic tenacity of a slave. Besides, it turned out Lakkhi was working somewhere early in the morning to supplement her income, though she denied it – which is why she was coming late, and, by the time she did, was quite disenchanted by the idea of cooking. Words had to be exchanged.

Outside the context of whatever family and private life she has, and the property she and her husband own in Subhasgram, Lakkhi's work is not that much better than slave labour. Of course, the slave owners of ancient Greece had their own sense of morals and propriety and justice when it came to slaves, and we aren't without morals or propriety when it comes to kaajer lok. And there are reasons why we'll draw the line, and not permit ourselves to be entirely at the mercy of someone like Lakkhi – though, most often, we believe we are, unlike that slave owner in ancient Greece. Comparing ourselves in Calcutta and India to ancient Greece, or even to modern Saudi Arabia, we feel we are somewhat better, that our employees have a range of privileges – though, in times of frustration, we might envy the Greek slave owner. The second time Lakkhi came to work for us was after two years had passed and the heat of her recalcitrance had cooled, while our memory of her delayed arrivals, her loud retorts that made us flinch, her powerful and robust indifference, had transmuted into something pleasant, and seemed preferable to whatever state of instability then ruled the kitchen. Lakkhi was welcomed back discreetly to her rightful place.

She was now a bit heavier, and had lost some of her mad sparkle, as well as a canine tooth. Her slow uncaringness as she walks in, her bodily awkwardness, her evident unawareness of herself as a sexual being, have all come together – why I don't know – to give an impression of honesty – in short, that she is who she is. Besides, her face still has a puritanical symmetry and gleam, so that it's no surprise she never apologises for anything; I can imagine her – roaming in Banaras, her sari loosely tangled around her, as it is in the kitchen; or, back in the eighteenth century, among the early settlers of North America – ploughing forward. Not that there's a way of spotting a dishonest person; nor are the kaajer lok generally any more or less given to dishonesty than the bhadralok. Still – there's been a steady outflow from our apartment over the years, denuding us of bhadralok accoutrements: of decorations, saris, cardigans, shoes, precious jewellery. We know who the most likely culprits are – three people in the last twenty years – but have no proof. Sometimes, with a start, my wife will speculate about what Arati did with the Hobbs cardigan, since no one else could have removed it; and whether straight-backed Chandana, with her soulful gaze, ever wears the long, moss-green East cardigan in Sonarpur in the winter. No, it's most likely they were sold. When a piece of gold jewellery vanishes, my mother mourns, goes into a week-long depression, claims that nothing like this ever happened in her three decades in Bombay, but the police aren't called, the floors are swept, all the usual chores from daytime to evening are performed. I feel helpless, outraged; I also feel a little like the Sheriff of Nottingham did about Robin Hood's activities – except, of course, unlike the Sheriff, I've had the benefit of reading, and being instructed and entertained and illuminated by, the Robin Hood stories.

The Bengali middle class sees itself rather than kaajer lok as primarily responsible for *churi*, or theft. Everything valuable must be kept under lock and key; if it isn't, and if it then disappears, the employer is as much an accomplice as he or she is a victim. Abetment is the primary offence, and it isn't viewed lightly by the bhadralok. On that count, my family have been serial accomplices and abettors. Lakkhi, however, didn't take valuables; she purloined supplies from the storeroom and food from the kitchen. When she protested, in her harried way, about the incredible amounts of oil our kind of cooking consumed, and that she was falling short again, we told her excessive oil was bad for the health, to use it moderately, and went out and bought some more. One evening, R returned early, and found Lakkhi and Arati, the maid who helped around the house, standing right in front of the elevator. They'd shut the door to the flat; so R would have to wait for me to get back with the keys. Lakkhi and Arati rushed into the elevator like obstreperous children, and R, pointing to a bulging carrier bag by one of the elevators, said, 'What's that?' They weren't even aware it existed; indeed, they'd just noticed it: 'We don't know,' they said as the doors closed. R sat on the steps for ten minutes; then thought, 'Wonder what's in that bag?' It was crammed with things from the kitchen and storeroom – two kilograms of Sundrop oil, one kilogram of mustard oil, four kilograms of basmati rice in plastic packets, a one-kilogram packet of moong *daal*, already-opened packets of chana and matar daal, potatoes, onions, garlic, already-opened bottles of ghee, sugar, about three hundred grams of uncooked mutton from the freezer, beginning to thaw, two neatly folded plastic bags, and some bay leaves. So far, we've only felt horror and amusement at the audacity of the operation; now, writing down the list, I feel a self-indulgent wistfulness. How inadequate the provisions seem! Especially since it was the night before Holi – these, the raw materials for the big lunch the next day! But it shocked us. Arati blamed Lakkhi; Lakkhi said it was Arati. 'I can't keep one of you and not the other,' said R. Both had to be dismissed.

After three and a half years, the standards in our kitchen – precarious anyway after Lakkhi's departure – had declined strikingly. A good cook is near impossible to find. People who take up that line of work are conversant with the stereotypical protagonists of Bengali cuisine – daal, *maacher jhol* (fish curry), *kasha mangsho* (dry mutton curry), even the sought-after *malai curry*, made with prawns and coconut milk – and they know the motions of cooking, of vigorously and convincingly scraping the *kadhai* with the spatula; but only have a dim sense of what the food tastes like. This may have to do with Bengal's economic setbacks; yet great artist-cooks were in more plentiful supply when Bengal, in the twentieth century, was as economically devastated as it is today, if not more. Partly it's a symbol of rural and urban Bengal's gradual loss of its past, with its delicate artisanal textures. This food too was delicate. Now it is watery. For there's a thin line separating the delicate from the bloodless, in art as in food. Partly it has to do with the nature of Bengali modernity, which emerged in the nineteenth century as a secular puritanism – evident most clearly in the tenets and practices of Rammohun Roy and Debendranath Tagore's Brahmo Samaj. This puritanism, which rejected the Hindu gods and goddesses and their antics in favour of an immanent radiance, and which, in the realm of the arts, preferred the implicit to the over-the-top, also kept its distance from strong and violent flavours in food. That modernity is on its last legs, as is its food. What was once implicit is now insipid.

For these and other reasons, feelers needed to be sent out to Lakkhi. Besides, R, who works at a research centre from morning to evening, doesn't have time to toil over food and research at once. I, who live in Calcutta when I'm not travelling or in Norwich, and who once honed my culinary skills in England, am presently too lazy to take on the responsibilities of the kitchen. My mother is in her late eighties, and can hardly be expected to rustle up meals. Also, what we spend on Lakkhi's monthly salary and food is roughly what R and I would spend on two or three dinners at decent restaurants. Our approach regarding Lakkhi isn't unique to Calcutta; it's the machinery – cheap labour – on which India, even the world, runs today. I say this not to exculpate myself, but to point out that I'm complicit not in a local mode of exploitation, but in a global arrangement. Lakkhi was doing bits-and-pieces work when we sent out the feelers; she was reluctantly happy to, on a marginally higher salary, take up her rightful position again. Calm came back to the kitchen – the false calm around the returned exile, the resumption of a status quo that conceals inner trouble.

I actually like Lakkhi, and I think she likes us. She takes from us little in comparison to what we take from her; but sometimes she also gives. Her gifts are food she's cooked at home and brought with her when we're still at breakfast, before temperatures have spiked – *taal* fritters, brown outside, white within, with a faint sweet aftertaste; the quintessential *pithé*, cooked in the way my mother abhors, in milk; little trumpet-like flowers from the pumpkin plant that grew from seeds she planted next to her home, which will be deep-fried in a yellow *besan* batter.

If I'm right, then it's not the sort of liking that arises from conversation and shared views. But I remember first experiencing this mutual – what is the opposite of antipathy? – affection after she invited us to her older daughter's wedding in 2004, just after the rains. She'd insisted we must come, and we were intent on going. We saw Subhasgram as in a waking dream – the level-crossing, the railway tracks, the road, the array of built-up houses, the row of bricks that were partly submerged in the undrained monsoon water, and which we negotiated gingerly to reach the porch of Lakkhi's sister-in-law's house – which, signalling the auspicious day, had a light raiment of fairy lights. There, I experienced the onrush of Lakkhi's love, her unexpected hand stroking my arm with a sisterly pressure, her mixture of happiness and sadness when we made our way back, wavering on that line of bricks. She didn't serve us food that evening, but sat beaming beside us as we ate. It was a small room, with folding chairs and long tables on trestles; and, briefly, during the wedding, our old selves – with their distrust and animosities – died. That strange, transcendental mood lasted till we left Subhasgram.

After Lakkhi took up her job for the third time, there was yet another glitch in her narrative of employment in our household. Her husband, the grocer, developed cancer of the mouth: the outcome of dedicated gutka-chewing. Christopher Hitchens, just a few days dead as I write this, said in an interview that death didn't scare him, it was a nothing, an annulment, no surprises there, but that 'a sordid dying' did. 'Cancer can do that to you,' he told Jeremy Paxman sombrely. I think Lakkhi's husband and most (mainly poor) gutka-addicts I know, who use the narcotic as a pick-me-up in the day, are similarly unafraid, and can't not know of its corrosive reputation for causing cancer, but toss it mouthward, without a care for tomorrow. But gutka punishes with a 'sordid dying', and this is what happened very quickly to Lakkhi's husband. She was put on paid leave, but would come anyway to cook for us well after midday. On some days, she'd have to be with him in the government hospital for his treatment. That invariably spelt trouble for us and our lunch. Lakkhi's husband's mouth, in the meanwhile, was out of action; he was being drip-fed by a tube inserted in his throat. I asked Lakkhi if he'd had chemotherapy in the hospital; she didn't think so. She looked a bit vague, exasperated, and out of it. I asked for the doctor's papers. Having promised me she'd bring them, Lakkhi vanished for ten days. We heard soon after that her husband had died. Then, wounded but mildly relieved, Lakkhi, like one who's come back from a rough vacation, took up employment again.

✦ ✦ ✦

There are times when the kaajer lok situation is in chronic disarray, and there's no remedy, and *Shampar baba* – 'Shampa's dad' – must be called. Shampar baba lives in Digha, a seaside resort that's a holiday destination, but is held in vague disrepute. He runs a 'hotel' there; that is, a streetside eatery such as Ramayan Shah's near Mocambo, serving luchi and vegetables for breakfast and fish or vegetables for lunch and dinner to a constituency of about fifty people a day. He's not a professional supplier of domestics, but can occasionally think of someone in his neighbourhood who requires a job, and send them promptly in our direction. Or he'll accompany them himself, usually a diffident girl in her early twenties who's never worked or seen a city before, but might be lately ditched by her spouse, or unable for whatever reason to get married – the choice is always between the devil, the husband, and employment, the choppy ocean – and on arrival, she must come to an agreement on terms in our drawing room. If the terms don't work out, they immediately depart, without ostensible hard feelings, to make the journey back to Digha after having obtained the return fares from one of us. If an agreement is reached, Shampar baba will mutter mantra-like bits of advice and probably reassurances to the diffident girl as he leaves her on the strange, bookshelf- and photograph-lined, decoration-adorned, furnished terrain of our Sunny Park apartment.

My mother is particularly addicted to Shampar baba; because he has a palliative tone on the telephone, and never forgets to promise even if he can't deliver. My mother's never heard him say 'No'; at the very worst and least hopeful it's been, 'Yes, I know someone, Ma, don't worry, she's tied up now but will be free to work in a month.' Who wouldn't want to talk repeatedly to a man who's dispensed with the negative? Only last month, in a thankfully short-lived period of flux, my mother said, 'I've just spoken to Shampar baba, he said it's all right, he'll send someone soon.'

R commented reflectively to me, 'It's strange we still speak of Shampar baba when Shampa herself is no longer around.' That's true – Shampa died this year in May, barely nineteen years old. Shampar baba – whose real name is Nagen – is someone we got to know courtesy of Shampa, who first came to our apartment (I must have been away, because I didn't see her then) when she was fifteen; there was a vacancy, and someone who works in the building asked her to turn up for the job. R and my mother couldn't put her to work, realising she was underage; during the day, my mother made her practise reading, which she'd lost touch with since leaving school. She tells me Shampa read from my daughter's Bengali books in the drawing room, loudly and solemnly. R pricked up her ears when Shampa complained impatiently in the kitchen: 'Stupid cough – wonder when it'll go!' She noticed Shampa got mild recurrent fevers. She and my mother were scared, since our daughter at the time was around ten. R sent Shampa to Dr Lal, our physician, who suspected tuberculosis. This turned out to be true. After having spent ten days in our house, Shampa went back home with her father, while R began to pay for her medication and treatment. TB, in theory, is treatable today, though there's a growing number of drug-resistant mutations.

When Shampa came to visit us two years ago, when I saw her for the first time, the tuberculosis had relapsed, though I noticed no sign of it. I saw a fairly small girl with full lips and dark eyes and a wheatish colour, hair parted in the middle and tied at the back, a familiar smile – probably because she'd seen my pictures earlier on a shelf or wall, and heard me mentioned – and no cough, nothing that remotely brought to mind mortality. No cause for anxiety, then; this was the twenty-first century; people who'd got the flu looked far worse off. The first rebuttal of suspicion was, as is often the case, Shampa's cheerfulness. She was in no mood – and didn't really seem to have the time – to be terminally ill.

At that point, in fact, she probably wasn't. And I think she took the prospect of taking on the role of a domestic in the future – there weren't that many job alternatives for her – robustly, as something that was, for now, being discreetly deferred. Of course, a young girl like Shampa can remain cheery in spite of a possible future of domestic work, because she's expecting, any day, to get married. Pretty and demure working-class girls like Shampa, blithely less than semi-literate, will get snapped up by bridegrooms, vanish, and then be reincarnated as young mothers raising children. Despite the general misery and constraints of these arrangements, I'd say part of Shampa's air of happiness came from the status of the girl child in Bengal – where the daughter isn't, unlike in parts of North India, viewed as a threat to be nipped in the bud. Female foeticide is common in North India, but I sense that rules governing the revealing of the sex of the foetus are followed quite strictly in Calcutta hospitals, whatever other rules are disregarded. And I know many kaajer lok who don't grudge educating their daughters. Not that girls in Punjab and Haryana, who've missed being aborted by a whisker, don't have an air of natural contentment as they grow up, before becoming wives. But my sense is that, while the birth of a daughter almost everywhere in India is a disappointment, it isn't, for people like Nagen, an absolute calamity. Does this have something to do with the Left Front government? I know that they attempted actively to educate people in this regard. At any rate, it was impossible to know the exact cause of Shampa's happiness.

Nevertheless, the news, probably from Nagen, that the illness had relapsed – without too many visible symptoms, as far as I could see – was cause for concern. TB had disappeared from Calcutta and the world, and then it resurfaced here in the eighties, initially as treatable as any minor infection, and then emerging in fatal variants. Was it 'too late' for Shampa? It hardly seemed so. Yet, bantering lightly with her, I was nervous

– mainly for my daughter. Shampa spent no more than one or two or three afternoons with us on that visit, but that felt like one afternoon too many. When I looked upon her, I felt the odd disquiet I'd felt, in 1986, watching my music teacher singing raga Abhogi on the stage, and noticing something about his colour that made me uncomfortable. I'd had a premonition, then – not of death, but of death that could be averted. I had the same hunch when I viewed Shampa. We decided to send her to Dr Nandy, our new physician, with an array of medical reports and X-rays. Dr Nandy wasn't too happy: 'She hasn't been cured,' he said, 'and it's coming back. The treatment hasn't been right.'

Looking for a phone number in a notebook kept in my bedside drawer, I find Shampa's name and contact details in my wife's handwriting, and the following:

Prescription
– Cap R Cinex (600) 1 capsule daily in the morning after b'fast.
– Pyzide (750) 1 tab twice a day after food
– Sthambitol (100 mg) 1 tab daily after food
– Benadon (40) 1 daily

The words are antediluvian – like much of the other information in the notebook, they've become irrelevant; yet they retain an air of pressing importance.

Usually, in the case of tuberculosis as with antiretroviral therapy for HIV, the reason for a setback is simple: an interruption in the regime of medication. In South Africa, where TB is the major killer, larger in scale than AIDS, I'd heard repeated and emollient radio announcements in a taxi, asking patients not to ever stop taking medicine, even for a day, until the course was complete. Some such thing must have happened with Shampa, and from a lack of discipline and organisation rather than from not having access to the medicine. R had paid for Shampa's treatment for more than a year, until Shampar baba told her to stop, because free medication was now available from the district hospital. I'm not exactly sure what occurred later. But I told Shampar baba, after Dr Nandy's diagnosis, that his daughter was in danger, that he must take her to the hospital to find out what was wrong. Shampar baba, in his simple, reassuring style, told me that this was what he intended to do. We said goodbye for the time being to Shampa, who had inherited from her father his conciliatory demeanour, a demeanour of this world, and entirely at home in it, and remote from startlements and anxieties and hints of the afterlife. We couldn't forget her, of course, because she'd call my mother from time to time to chat with her (distance, and a lack of prolonged intermingling – the curse of human beings and of domestics and their employers – ensured they got on well); also, my mother needed habitually to phone Shampar baba, because kaajer lok are forever in flux. Then we heard she was married! She must have healed! We could relax, although our quest for stable and good kaajer lok would of course be eternal. Marriage, as an endorsement, as a long-term enterprise that will brook no distraction, has a weight of finality about it. 'Shampa is married' means 'Shampa is well; the sputum tests are now irrelevant.' There was still, in me, a subconscious undertow of fear; when, holidaying in Bombay, my daughter developed a dry, irritable cough which she unthinkingly displayed everywhere – crossing the street, in restaurants, watching TV – my thoughts telescoped, and my head swam with Shampa's visits. It was ascertained before too long that it was an allergic cough. Peace again: life's full of such inhalations and exhalations. Then, back from a short trip to England in May 2011, I was at home when my mother phoned Shampar baba and he said, *'O chole gechhe, o aar nei'* – 'She's gone, she's no more.' When my mother runs over Shampa's story, her lip quivers – for, at eighty-six, still relatively youthful, she's survived many friends and relations and acquaintances, known many people – real and fictional – who lived and passed into oblivion; as we grow old, we're unsettled not by our need of those who are suddenly absent, but by the coalescing of an old, quite familiar, disappointment.

By the time five or six months had passed from the elections, some people may have wondered when Calcutta would bear the marks of visible change; others would have been surprised if it had. It was too soon. If someone had boarded a time machine in March and been transported forward to November, they, on disembarking, their atoms reassembled, may not have known they were no longer in Marxist Bengal. They might or might not have noticed at once, though, the dim, ghostly racket emanating from the traffic lights: the garbled sound of Tagore songs. This repetitive loop, comprising old recordings by Hemanta Mukherjee, Suchitra Mitra, and others, is what didi – Mamata Banerjee – in one of her early gestures to 'civil society', had prescribed for stressed drivers. Some people felt that listening with half your attention to Tagore songs at a red light subtly heightened, rather than reduced, anxiety. My feeling was Mamata Banerjee was gently – perhaps unwittingly – attempting to simulate, everywhere, the characteristics of a petit bourgeois *para* such as the one she grew up in, in Kalighat; or like my uncle's house in Pratapaditya Road. Here, at any opportunity – usually festivals and public holidays – amateur singers would sing from loudspeakers, as would professional singers of local repute; or, more often, recordings would be played of Hindi film and Tagore songs. One would wake up to that tinny, melodious, intrusive atmosphere; one could nap to it; in the end, when it was gone, one would be disoriented by its lack. Mamata Banerjee would have a deep memory of that ethos – indeed, given she still lives in Kalighat, it must be her perpetual present.

In November, it was reportedly too early for Bengal's future to take shape. And people wanted to know if didi would enter into a dialogue with the Maoists in 'jungle mahal' (an inaccessible region roughly sixty miles north-west of Calcutta, girded by forest), since, at one point, she'd expressed her readiness to hold talks; or whether she'd crush them, as the free market demanded; or if 'jungle mahal' might even be her Vietnam, as it had once threatened to be the Left Front's. Then, well into 'study leave', on 24th November, I woke up to read how Kishenji had been shot dead, in a joint operation in the forests near the Jharkhand border, by the upliftingly named Combat Battalion for Resolute Action (COBRA) and the Central Reserve Police Force, historically lauded for restoring order to difficult areas. Who was Kishenji? I'd never heard of him. He was the Maoists' military leader. In a photo, the lower right side of his face seemed to be missing, probably from close-range gunfire. There was talk about Kishenji having been killed not in a battle, but – as is frequently the case with terrorists-criminals-revolutionaries (the categories are a matter of perspective) – in an 'encounter'; that is, a staged escape or confrontation meant to dispense with the fugitive after his capture. For a few days, there was no official confirmation that the dead man was Kishenji; and, following the confirmation, no public response, unusually, from Ms Banerjee – though, on occasion, it might feel either premature or impossible to exult openly.

When I saw, on TV, Kishenji's mother mourn in her home in Andhra Pradesh, I was struck by how middle-class the family looked, with a dated bhadra socialist air even in grief. Kishenji's name was Mallojula Koteswara Rao. He came from a family of poor village Brahmins, but Kishenji's father was a freedom fighter, and he himself had graduated with a degree in mathematics and then begun to study law. He'd ended up a martyr to the revolution. In all but the final development – revolution and death – his life mimicked one of the classic routes taken in the time of colonialism by the 'great men' of Indian culture, especially of the Bengal Renaissance, and even by men who were born in its wake (I'm thinking of Nirupam Sen): the beginnings in small-town or village poverty; a context of educated utopianism, often created by the father; the emergence into the professions, such as law, or into writing, or into politics and nationalism, and, occasionally, into a kind of greatness. I'd thought the constrictions of independent India had shut down such trajectories in Kishenji's generation (he was a little more than five years older than me); but here, summarised in his life and death, was that trajectory again.

In a room in All Souls College, Oxford, straining to listen to the faltering voice of Prof. Braja Dulal Chattopadhyay as he spoke of the *Ramayana*, I became aware of the timeless lineage of these conflicts now assailing our land. Prof. Chattopadhyay's lecture concerned certain inexplicable actions perpetrated by the virtuous Lord Rama, the repository of Hindu dharma. One of these was the heinous slaying by Rama of Vali, the valiant monkey-king of a forest kingdom, whom he killed with an arrow shot from behind as Vali wrestled with his own brother. Rama's action is attributed to Vali's conflict with this brother, Sugreev, Rama's friend: for, certainly, Rama and Vali had not been antagonists, and the former had no other reason to kill the latter. In fact, as Vali lies dying, he asks Rama: 'What was my crime?'

Prof. Chattopadhyay, if I remember right, pointed out that independent forest kingdoms often sprang up in India, and were seen as a threat to the ethos and sovereignty of the mainland. It was for this reason that Vali would have had to die; because, for Rama, he represented a threat to the norm, to the absolute sway of dharma.

As to how much Bengal would open up again to the world, as it had in the eighteenth century, was a question left hanging in the air. People were trying to shrug off, in a sheepish way, the feeling of having missed the boat that had troubled them until May 2011. For the middle class, international isolation was measured by the number of direct flights there were to London; there was none. Lufthansa, too, providing the last umbilical lifeline to a tarnished but persistently desirable Western capi-talism, announced, in December, the scrapping of its flight to Frankfurt, a punishment for poor business-class activity. Nevertheless, we in Calcutta were still in the year's most para-disial time, heading for another Christmas. It was around now I was reminded, because of an academic paper I happened to read, of Carlo Levi's *Christ Stopped at Eboli*, a record of a year (1935–36) spent under duress in two obscure towns in Southern Italy, Grassano and Aliano, the latter renamed 'Gagliano' in the book. Levi, exiled there by Mussolini, says, 'The title of the book comes from an expression by the people of "Gagliano" who say of themselves, "Christ stopped short of here, at Eboli" which means, in effect, that they feel they have been bypassed by Christianity, by morality, by history itself – that they have somehow been excluded by the full human experience.' I once saw a Penguin Modern Classics edition of this book in Oxford, in 1987; picked it up; put it back again. My memory refreshed and piqued by the paper, I was thinking of Levi's memoir while listening to Rakhi Sarkar, active in the Calcutta art world, married to *Ananda Bazar Patrika*'s Aveek Sarkar, give an impas-sioned account at an event of why she and others had resolved in 2003 to put into motion the idea of KMOMA, or the Kolkata Museum of Modern Art; for the first major Picasso exhibition in India had come to Delhi and Bombay, but bypassed Calcutta for its paucity of museum space and infrastructure. The insult was deep – to a region of the world that had fostered India's first home-grown style in modern art, the Bengal School, and where (it was doubtful if Calcutta itself remembered this) the works of the Bauhaus painters were exhibited in 1922 at the prodding of Tagore – who much admired Paul Klee – and as a consequence of the critic Stella Kramrisch's enterprisingness. I happened to be in Delhi during Picasso's visit there, and, no great admirer of the Spaniard, went obediently from room to room to study again what I'd seen reproduced in encyclopedias and magazines a hundred times. But the hurt hadn't healed in Calcutta, or so it seemed from Rakhi Sarkar's speech. Flippantly, I considered naming the book I was writing *Picasso Stopped at New Delhi* – but remained tempted, at the same time, by the all-purposive, ambiguous *Calcutta*.

I've used the pronoun 'she' of the kaajer lok because they *are*, mainly, women – except the drivers, who are a special breed and a cut above the kaajer lok. Shampa, who was married off hastily before succumbing to TB, experienced marriage for what it is in its first celebratory phase in a working-class woman's life – a rescue and absolvement from a future of domestic work. If the man is sober and relatively well-off – that is, if he owns a small shop or a taxi – it's possible his wife will be spared from becoming part of the immense churning that is kaajer lok. But even if he isn't a destitute alcoholic, she, once the bliss of early married life is over and reality crowds in, might well start work as a maid, especially if the family is ambitious, and wants to give their children an education better than they had. Most often the men aren't sober. This is what adds, in periodic waves, new women to the ranks of the kaajer lok. These days, very few women search for work cold, in the streets, or dependent on their friends' advice, but turn up at one of the several 'centres' in Calcutta that supply houses with domestics and carers. The advantage for the domestic of working via the centre is that they're paid a daily wage rather than a monthly salary, and this works out better for them, as the wage adds up to a more substantial salary than they'd have got as a full-time employee. In return, the centre keeps a small percentage. My father's carer, Kamala, comes to us from one of the smaller and less greedy of these centres, and she has to give to it only ten of the one hundred and ninety rupees she earns daily. In return, she's with my father for a full twelve hours, sometimes nodding off, as she has a punitive routine, and on certain days wakes up at three o'clock in the morning to collect water because of a recurrent drinking water shortage in her area, VIP Nagar. (No problem with running water for bathing, she says; it's the *mishti* or 'sweet' drinking water that's in short supply, and is provided by municipal corporation trucks at dawn, distributed by a pipe three times a week to people who've presumably been lining up with the resolution of shoppers at a sale.) She's here at eight to attend to my father. When she rises and walks about, it's in a scalded tiptoe, like the devout negotiating a bed of coals, an effect created by her corns. My father, whose main aim now is to be left alone, can't stand Kamala; but it's with my mother that she has repeated spats, as once daughter-in-law and mother-in-law did, mysterious, bottled-up outbursts, indicative that each has a strong view on truth and reality, but also of the wearingness of human contact, which rarely ever does credit to human beings.

I recently called the person who runs the centre through which we employ Kamala; he was loath to meet me. 'Let's talk on the phone please,' he said. 'I don't know enough about this business – it's my wife who really runs it. She's away.' His wife had been a nurse at Ruby Nursing Home, and then Divine Nursing Home, and had made good use of the networks she'd built up of carers and nurses when they started the centre in 2009. This man, Debashish Das, had been a manager in a small fertiliser company, then branched out, with the impulse towards freedom common to middle-class Bengalis, into the fertilisers business himself. That venture (as is also often the case with those Bengalis' bright ideas) was a non-starter; unrewarding, with farmers deferring payments, and too demanding. He then got into the private car hire business, first with a Tata Indigo, and then an Indica; it changed Mr Das's life, and became a limited but flourishing trade. This centre for domestics was his latest essay, established upon his wife's contacts, and an enterprise he was pretty confident about. 'There'll always be demand,' he told me.

Supply was ensured too. Cyclone Aila, or Hurricane Aila as it's often known locally, had devastated crops and cultivation in North and South 24 Parganas beyond the city in 2009, the year of Mr Das's centre's inception, and its after-effects still sent a steady trickle of women towards him, and from him eventually to our part of the city. The women from these centres – not Kamala, though, for she's very much a Calcutta person – have the sullen, shell-shocked air of refugees, of people who don't know where they are and what they're doing there. They are unimpressed by upper-middle-class luxury; they're swiftly bored; they've worked in one kind of world all their lives, and are now being asked to comprehend different appetites and demands which make them look despondent and probably feel homesick. 'Women also have to work because their men drink,' said Mr Das. 'They drink and die.' We discussed the adulterated liquor – country liquor or 'hooch' as it's romantically called by newspapers – that claimed, in mid-December, the lives of one hundred and seventy men in a town near the Bihar border. What had struck me was not just the scale of the tragedy, but how little sympathy was expressed in the media for these fatally misguided drinkers.

When a domestic with whom you've had a long-term, rocky relationship – one that goes on and off, on and off – begins to feel restless, there may well be signs, so indecipherable as to be non-existent, that she's about to go again. I'm thinking of Lakkhi's last stint with us – by 'last' I don't mean 'final', but 'most recent'. There's never anything but a cursory finality in one's interaction with a domestic; renewal is usually in the offing.

After Lakkhi's husband's painful demise, she returned distractedly to the fold. In two months, her timings were awry again; midday when it should have been ten o'clock; then later than midday. And she deftly smuggled a little companion into the room adjoining the kitchen. At first, only his voice could be heard – high-pitched, pointed, intermittent, making no kind of sense; then I caught glimpses of his wispy figure.

I realised I'd seen him before. He'd been smaller then – Lakkhi's grandchild, who'd come with her before on a couple of visits. He was still small for a four-year-old, and I was drawn to his high spirits. The boy, whose name was Raja, brought out the vagrant in me; I'd go off in the middle of my writing to investigate his whereabouts.

Raja was flattered by my attention and made a big show of avoiding me. We began to understand, after a week, that his appearances weren't going to be exceptional – they'd be the norm, for he was arriving at our flat every day with his careless-seeming grandmother.

He was very dark: what Bengalis call *kuch kuche kaalo* or 'extremely black' – his late grandfather's complexion, apparently. He had an undernourished, springy agility and bright eyes. Lakkhi had no choice but to bring him along for now. Her younger daughter, Raja's mother, was mentally challenged – that much we knew. She'd been married off six or seven years ago with the usual transactional resolve that Indians have – that life, sociability, and procreation must continue regardless, that marriage is a simple counter to the untoward. Husband and wife produced this child: further evidence of marriage's primordial normalcy. Then, as husbands will, the man vanished. The younger daughter returned to Lakkhi, abstracted and strangely discontented. She had little awareness of or interest in Raja. He, in the meanwhile, had begun to go out on excursions, and Lakkhi found the mother in one place and the boy in another. She fretted; but she had the cooking to do. So she began to bring him to our apartment and deposit him in the kitchen.

He was a clever boy and, once he got over his shyness, full of a specious bravado. It was extraordinary to hear him in the kitchen – disrupting a place of work.

'Are you going to put him in a school?' I challenged Lakkhi. It may have slipped her mind.

'Yes, I'm looking for a place for him, somewhere I can keep him while I'm here,' she said in her characteristic way, suggestive that every decision she has to take, including removing food from the fridge, is onerous.

'A place you can pick him up from on the way back, or a place he can stay in?'

'It would be best to pick him up,' she said, again with that tortured look.

'Then it should be somewhere around here,' I said, gesturing vaguely at the haute bhadralok vicinity of Ballygunge. 'I have a school in mind.'

I had a stealthy feeling my efforts would come to nothing – I've noticed, from a review of past actions, that my attempts to help people are usually oddly thwarted, by a combination of circumstances and probably by an overestimation by me of the wider world's receptivity to my ideas. This prior knowledge didn't keep me from calling Tim Grandage, who lives in my building. I know Tim slightly, but I've been aware that his school for orphaned children – fortuitously located in the very area we live in – is regarded by all as a genuine success. What a good place it would be for Raja, for both disposing of the problem of this boy and giving him a future – and also for giving Lakkhi a relief from chores other than cooking. Tim, however, was in England; he'd be back, I was told by his flat's caretaker, after the Pujas. Ironically, I was just barely getting used to not being in Norwich and embracing the season's new-found calm. Otherwise, now, I'd be teaching students as it grew dark, or sipping on an americano at Starbucks.

'I'll pursue this when my friend returns from England,' I told Lakkhi. She nodded moodily and continued to scrape the *potol*, or rinse the moong pulses, or cut the *chhana* into little squares.

Raja began to lose his shyness. At first, it was an unconscious shedding of inhibition after lunch, when there was a lull in kitchenly activities, and an abnegation of power among those who ruled over the apartment – my parents withdrawing into nap time; I into writing; my daughter not yet back from school. Normally difficult to inveigle from the kitchen, Raja emerged in the drawing room and took over the furniture. He was quickly lost in a daydream; he'd sit on the divan or on the sofa and spend his time in one or the other posture, either with a leg in the air, or half-lying against a cushion. He was a little parody of a despot.

After eight or nine days, he was wholly not in awe of me, and as interested in my whereabouts as I'd been in his – possibly more interested. His new lack of regard and presumptuous four-year-old friendliness were my doing. I had 'encouraged' him. My reasons for fraternising with Raja were selfish; I found him hilarious. Besides, 'all things can tempt me from this craft of verse'. In the midst of writing about the city, I was susceptible to distraction. And now, in a manner of speaking, he was all over me. He was a tough and single-minded taskmaster: just as we demanded timely meals from his grandmother, he wanted constant diversion from me. As with my mother's and R's view of my work, Raja wasn't convinced that a man sitting around with a notebook and pen was seriously occupied. I was most probably doing nothing. His way of hinting to me that he was available was by coming straight to my room after Lakkhi arrived (she was now keeping pretty erratic times), smiling vaguely, and clicking on his palate with his tongue, producing a soft, insinuating sound. When I mimicked this to R, she fell about laughing; but to me it was becoming tiresome, something which I at once looked forward to and dreaded. Familiarity was also beginning to make him provocative, and test how much of the upper hand he could gain. He had to have ownership of the remote control (irrespective of whether the TV was on or not), transporting it, like a courier, from room to room; but he also claimed, in his limited, blithe pidgin, that his TV was bigger than ours. Besides, he had his eyes on the cheap English biro with which I pursue my writing, making off with it on impulse; I hadn't sufficiently appreciated that he had his own pen, and, in our tussle to retrieve our rightful paraphernalia, I'd sometimes take his pen and upset him deeply – but briefly, as he still had no understanding of prolonged deprivation or lack. We became a kind of exasperating drama to the maids, who felt I was ineffectual and said: 'You must holler at him properly.' At the peak of our interfaces, they'd pick him up, and remove him, ignoring his scandalised cries, from my room; but he was like some sort of spring, and in five minutes he'd bounce back, ebullient, making the soft clicking noise in his mouth. I began to lock my door, which I never like doing.

The Pujas ended, I kept calling Tim Grandage's flat and speaking to the caretaker, but Tim showed no signs of returning. Meanwhile, Lakkhi's hours were becoming unacceptable, she was arriving close to late lunchtime, and was unrepentant and had no explanation but, 'I'm thinking of giving up work. I can't take it any more – after all, I'm fifty years old.' 'You're more than fifty,' I informed her. '*I'm* forty-nine.' I was secretly astonished at how old I was. I would probably die one day in Calcutta – which, anyway, was as I'd planned it: that I mustn't, by mistake, die abroad but live and spend and maybe bring to a close the second half of my life in India. It just happened that India, at this point of time, was Calcutta. Maybe most of us, without knowing it, have plans of this kind. I'm reminded of César Vallejo, who states it baldly, as a prophecy: 'I will die in Paris, in a rainstorm, / On a day I already remember.' That second line – 'On a day I already remember' – is shrewd, and it speaks to exactly what I have in mind – that, when it comes to such matters, the future and the past, memory and speculation, are hopelessly mixed up and devoid of chronology. Vallejo actually managed to die in Paris despite being expelled from France in 1930, eight years before his death. But his poem is meant to voice the classic melancholy of the exile with finality – for Vallejo was born in an impoverished Peruvian town. In my case, my aim – whether or not it works out – is to eventually draw my days to a close at home. After twelve years in Calcutta, I realise this notion of 'home' is an invention: that, though I was born in Calcutta, I didn't grow up here, and don't belong here. Each year, I suspect I'll begin to understand this city better, be more at ease with it: and every year I find this is less true.

When I think of Lakkhi's behaviour before and during and after the Pujas, her dishabille entrances, infuriated and infuriating, her grandchild in tow, I wonder if she was telling us, in a sort of code, of her disenchantment. She knew Raja had begun to interrupt my writing and tried to enforce a stricter demarcation for him where kitchen and drawing room and my room were concerned. Then, just as I was warily testing these arrangements, she stopped bringing him. There was no busybody to contend with! I was relieved, because I'd begun to think Raja would be a nuisance for the foreseeable future; but, given the grass is always greener on the other side, I was, in a negligible way, bereft. At times of my choosing, I *wanted* to be interrupted by Raja; just as there are occasions when a cancelled trip answers a secret prayer. 'My friend will be back soon,' I told Lakkhi. 'You should let me know if you still want me to talk to him about the school.' But she'd found a school in Subhasgram, she said, where he'd be looked after night and day: a better deal, given Raja's unmindful – in more than one sense – mother. In this way, I held steadfastly to my own, on the whole unbroken, record – of being unable to intervene positively even when I wanted to.

About a week later, a young, distraught maid who'd just taken up work confessed to us of her own volition that Lakkhi had persuaded her to place a plastic bag with pieces of fish from the freezer behind the fire extinguisher near the lift, half an hour before her departure to Subhasgram, and had, since then, been asking her to do it again. We were gripped by a sense of disbelief at Lakkhi's ingenuity and by a surge of vengefulness. But we knew we needed to strategise – besides, there was a man in the house who was pretty old and had special dietary needs. So we said nothing and only marvelled when Lakkhi came in. But she had her informants and found out she'd been snitched on. Her mood deteriorated. Without the fish being openly discussed, Lakkhi stopped coming, except once, dourly, like one betrayed (as she had been), to collect her dues.

Getting a substitute wouldn't be easy, but we took up the challenge.

A Visit

Twice a year, I'd think, with a start, that I hadn't been to see Mini mashi for months. It was like an email I had to reply to – the memory of it jolted me at the wrong moments: say, after I was in bed, and had switched off the lights. When I woke up, the thought was gone. Then, when there was a lull in the monsoons of 2011, my mother got a phone call saying Mini mashi had had her third stroke, and, increasingly stingy with time though I've become, I knew the journey couldn't be postponed.

These strokes occurred at astrological intervals, every few years. Each time, they took from Mini mashi's learned vocabulary in Bengali a few more words. They were tectonic and decisive, making their presence felt indisputably in her and Shanti mashi's small flat, like a supernatural being. The strokes weren't silent and insidious, like the ones that pursued my father, leaving his face and features unchanged, transforming him from within.

✦

She'd been shifted to the intensive care unit of a nursing home in Shobhabazar, and my mother and I decided we must set out in time to catch the visiting hours. She was my mother's oldest living friend – they had been thick with each other in Sylhet – and they were also very, very distantly related: technically, she *did* qualify as my maternal aunt – or *mashi*.

Shobhabazar is in North Calcutta; so is the narrow lane in which Mini mashi and her elder sister lived doggedly in a government flat, a five-minute walk from the Tagores' house in Jorasanko, two minutes from Mallickbari or the Marble Palace, and not far at all from Mahajati Sadan, the playhouse; an area as littered with the relics of history as Shobhabazar is thriving (besides still being home to the obscure mansions of erstwhile rajas and landlords) with stalls selling wedding cards, saris, dress material – but predominantly wedding cards.

North Calcutta is not just a geographical location; it is, in fact, the other Calcutta. That is, it's approximately what's left of the old or 'black' town – which was, with the exception of a few areas in the south, the great city of the nineteenth century – the environs in which all the cultural innovations of the Bengal Renaissance took place. When people refer to 'Calcutta' or 'Kolkata' today, though, they mean the south, and have meant it for some decades, as urban life flowed and shifted in that direction, and, from the mid-nineties, the merciless property boom extended deeper and deeper southward. No wonder it took me years to visit Mini mashi, on what turned out to be just a few days prior to her death; it wasn't so much the distance, which, by the standards of contemporary cities and their suburbs, is moderate to small (a forty-five minutes' to an hour's drive in the traffic). It may have had to do with this sense of having to push in the opposite direction, of bracing myself to travel against the current.

✦ ✦ ✦

You say, *What's this Renaissance you've kept mentioning? Is it true Bengal had a Renaissance – if that's so, what was its nature? Where are its monuments, its landmarks, its cathedrals? Does it have a Sistine Chapel?*

Reformists like Keshab Chandra Sen, nationalists such as Bipin Chandra Pal, and the Hindu revivalist Swami Vivekananda had begun by the late nineteenth and early twentieth centuries to speak of the *naba jagaran* or 'new awakening' that had occurred in Bengal, and call it, in English, the 'Renaissance'. But the person who probably gave the term its admittedly short-lived academic aura was the Marxist historian Susobhan Sarkar, in his brief tract from 1946, *Notes on the Bengal Renaissance*, where its provenance, characteristics, and canonical moments were duly recorded.

Conventionally, the beginnings of this putative Renaissance might be fixed either at 1814, when Raja Rammohun Roy founded the Atmiyan Sabha with reform in mind, especially on behalf of Hindu widows, who couldn't, at the time, remarry; or in 1828, when he founded the Brahmo Samaj, a unitarian sect that refuted Hinduism's polytheism, turning instead towards an immanent, formless – *nirakaar* – divinity apparently first intuited by humans in the Upanishads and Vedas. But the full-blown effects of this turn would only become palpable from the 1860s onward. It's clear, then, that the Bengalis, in their transition into self-consciousness, went down routes opened up for them by now relatively obscure Orientalist scholars, like the Welshman William Jones, translator of, among other writers and texts, the fourth-century court poet Kalidasa, and the Frenchman Abraham Hyacinthe Anquetil-Duperron, translator of the Upanishads. For these Europeans, the unusual ferment of the time – the late eighteenth century – that brought them into contact with Indian Brahmins and, through them, Indian antiquity had a particular significance: with these hoary, beautiful texts they established the extraordinary lineage of the East, and also proved that the story of humanism – authored by the European Enlightenment – had an ancient and important setting in India, and not just, as had been presumed, in Greece and Rome. For Indians like Roy and Tagore, though, these texts didn't only represent the glory of the Indian past (which they did), or the Indian's place in the larger world (which they did too); they pointed out a way to what India, and they themselves, would be in the foreseeable future. Roy could have been content with the wonder and prestige of Indian antiquity; his great innovation, whether he knew it or not, was to make the Upanishadic heritage a basis and pillar of the secularism we've come to take for granted, to read it, in effect, as a contemporary resource that showed Indians how to be modern. Tagore began to perform a similar innovation with the Sanskrit poet Kalidasa, and with that same Upanishadic tradition, from the 1890s onward: to regard them not just as 'our great tradition', as dead heritage, but as essential to fashioning the modern poem and literature.

We've lost our way. Where exactly is Shobhabazar? We're in Shyambazar, lurching forward steadily in the congestion – *Dada, in which direction is the Naba Jiban Nursing Home?* And, excuse me, Dada, did the Bengal Renaissance really happen? Could you point out its signs?

By the 1960s and 1970s, Marxist critics in Calcutta were ferociously, scathingly, disputing the notion of the Renaissance in Bengal. It was hardly a genuine renaissance, they said; to call it one would be an act of hubris. Their main quarrel was with its bhadralok context: its exclusion of the poor and the minorities – a charge that couldn't be ignored. As a consequence, the idea of the Bengal Renaissance – and the bhadralok himself – has been much reviled: most often by the bhadralok, in an act of expiation.

The English, anyway, had never noticed its existence, though it happened under their noses. For the Englishman, both Indian modernity and the Indian modern were invisible. In a sense, then, Calcutta, to him, was invisible. Kipling, writing in the midst of the Renaissance, populates his magical stories of India with talking wolves, tigers, cheetahs, and orphan Indian children who have no trouble communicating with animals. No one would know, reading Kipling, that Bagheera, Sher Khan, and Mowgli are neighbours and contemporaries of the novelist Bankimchandra Chatterjee and the poet Michael Madhusudan Dutt. In Kipling's universe – and, to a considerable extent, in Britain's – the Renaissance, and Bengali and Indian modernity, might as well have never happened in India's uninterrupted, fabulous time.

This was *not* a renaissance overseen and funded by potentates, as the Italian Renaissance was. It had no Lorenzo de' Medici. It burgeoned, incongruously, in the time of Empire, when the imperial view of culture – when there was one at all – was busy with other things. Which is why it has no monuments; which is why, when I go northward, to Mini mashi's flat, or elsewhere, or, as we did that afternoon, in search of the Naba Jiban Nursing Home (*naba jiban*, 'new life', itself unwittingly echoing the resurgent naba jagaran), the only really grand official buildings are the lapsed colonial institutions on Central Avenue – such as the School of Tropical Medicine – still extant, and symbolic. When, on those journeys, you look for that so-called Renaissance's great buildings, you, of course, see none.

When people visit me in Calcutta, I take them not to see landmarks, but people's houses. These might be the ones found in charming clusters in Bakul Bagan, Paddapukur, or Bhowanipore, built in the twenties, thirties, and forties; or near the Hooghly, in marginal Kidderpore; or up north, where the ancestral mansions are, and which even I haven't properly explored. Each house differs from the other, but there's a family resemblance: the green French windows with slats, the intricate cornices on the balconies, the red stone floors, the stairs rising to the wide terrace where clothes are hung to dry and children hover, and, if the house came up after Independence, the wavy or floral grilles, the flecked tiles, the art-deco type windows with frosted panes. There are no other monuments in Calcutta. When I look at these houses, I feel excited, as I might when rereading one of James Joyce's stories; the pleasure of being surprised, even after repeated encounters, by the new. And the modern is perennially new, no matter what state it's in, and even when it's being dismantled – as many of these houses are, by property scamsters called 'promoters'.

This renaissance wasn't the renaissance of an empire, but of a home-grown bourgeoisie largely unacknowledged by the imperial sovereign; so its theme and subject isn't grandeur, as often seems to be the case in the European Renaissance, in the resplendent, glowing paintings of Titian, in Michelangelo's gigantic, looming, perfectly buttocked David, but the everyday and the desultory, such as you see in the films of Ritwik Ghatak and Satyajit Ray. *This* renaissance is, in many ways, a refutation of that earlier, better-known one, with its epic pretensions. Its protagonist isn't the soldier on horseback, or the gods, or the regent in the hall or garden; it is really the loiterer. Jean Renoir sensed this on his visit to this city in 1949, when he remarked, when describing Calcutta, that 'all great civilisations are based on loitering'.

In the Jewish Museum in Hallesches Tör in Berlin, I realised, on the second floor, that modern man, twentieth-century man – in all his or her unimpressiveness and unintended comedy, in his or her preoccupation with shopping, the arts, the stock market, keeping diaries, borrowing books, going to the cinema, reading newspapers – might be the subject of a memorial, and have these enthusiasms recorded and collections and possessions displayed. That museum, of course, commemorated the sudden, enforced passing of a culture; it paid tribute, on the second floor, to an abortive but, in the end, ordinary world. I was accustomed, in museums, to reluctantly examining the vestiges of great civilisations – portraits of dukes and princes, pictures of dead pheasants in the kitchen, a comb that belonged to an empress, a stone from a palace, a bust of the Buddha or of Zeus. I say 'reluctantly' because I'd never actually been that interested in the crumbling of bygone panoramas, or in the historical or canonical; and it was in the Jewish Museum, on the second floor, that I understood that it was the banality of modern man that gave me most pleasure and most moved me. This explains, to a certain extent maybe, why I introduce visiting friends to neighbourhoods in Calcutta when they ask to see the city. It's here that the particular history I'm speaking of resided, and still persists in an afterlife, and where it will – as is already evident (and probably to the relief of all concerned) – eventually vanish.

The Bengal Renaissance's largely unnoticed state of existence – where the larger world and India's colonial rulers were concerned – might explain its cherishing of secrecy, of looking, and spying, and its air of surreptitious playfulness – its very illegitimacy. And it may also be why, especially, the afternoon was a time of enchantment in Calcutta, pregnant with meaning for the Bengali child, when the adult, the figure of authority, had withdrawn, and the child was granted solitary freedom within a fixed ambit.

Charulata, in Satyajit Ray's eponymous film, diverts herself in the afternoon in an immense nineteenth-century mansion in North Calcutta by opening the slats of the windows and spying on passers-by through binoculars. To be unseen, to look out at the world: for the artist, this is a prized privilege, and, in the late nineteenth century, Calcutta began to feel those possibilities – of being at once known and invisible – precipitously. This was the mood of that anomalous renaissance: the atmosphere – captured in *Charulata*'s opening frames – of afternoon and concealment. 'Freedom consists in not having to make the laws,' said Tolstoy. So with the Bengalis in that age. Isn't that why Tagore constantly mentions *chhuti* (holidays), *khela* (play), and the relief of *kaaj nai* (having no work to do) in his songs – because the colonial world has granted him an odd kind of liberation?

Is that the reason, too, why Calcutta was associated in my mind with play and freedom; or was it because I came here for my holidays? Exactly what kind of experience *is* a holiday?

A holiday is an interruption. It isn't a narrative with a denouement – that's what ordinary life is. A holiday is a break from 'ordinary life'. Part of its enchantment, surely, is that it doesn't follow the rules of narrative that 'ordinary life' does; it's a period of time that's static, unmoving, without the on-and-on progression that our lives generally have – but a period, nevertheless, in which a transformation occurs. A holiday doesn't so much entail a journey to a foreign place as a certain change in mood that causes familiar and everyday things to become foreign. It's this transformation that Calcutta once represented for me.

If I were to rehearse this in generic terms, I suppose what I'm describing is the difference between the poetic and the narrative. For me, the poem is neither rhyme, metre, nor beautiful words strung together, but a period of time in which nothing seems to happen in the conventional sense, but which we're still changed by: a duration in which we're altered. Unlike the novel, the transformation isn't actually dependent on us having come to know a great deal more by the time we've finished reading the poem. Yet we're aware, when we've reached the end of the poem, of a change having taken place.

My holidays in Calcutta were similar to my account of inhabiting a poem, in that I didn't come to know a great deal more during them; in fact, Calcutta, being a break from school, was, for me, a break from knowing.

When I look at my novels, I see that they're mostly – without my having consciously planned them in that way – structured around journeys and visits, rather than stories and plot. My stories aren't about day-to-day life, but breaks and interruptions in the business of living, often caused by a change of venue. The changed venue may or may not cause a transformation (depending on how successful the novel is in its workings, and what its intentions are), but this transformation, if it occurs, probably plays the same role in my novels that plot does in others'. It's an idea of storytelling based – I see now more clearly – on the holiday, rather than on narrative. It must carry with it some residue of the strange, disorienting excitement I felt, as a child, in Calcutta.

◆

My first novel was, in fact, about two trips undertaken by a child to Calcutta: a boy very much like me, who is not, however, at the centre of the novel. At the novel's centre is not even Calcutta, but the holiday itself, which on some level becomes indistinguishable, for the boy, from the city; and for me, the writer, from the novel.

Afternoon Raag, my second novel, was about student life in Oxford: but I see that it treats student life not as something with a proper beginning and end, but as a break from ordinary life; the contrast to ordinary life, with its canonical ambitions and disappointments, seems to be student life's principal definition. Even Oxford, a foreign location for the narrator, is full of foreign locations, like East Oxford, and a mere journey to these brings into effect, in the narrator's mind, a metamorphosis.

In *Freedom Song*, I returned to Calcutta, to explore a number of metamorphoses – political and economic – that had made the city subtly different from itself: fifteen years of Left Front rule, and the departure of industry; the liberalisation of the Indian economy and the ushering in of the free market; the demolition, by right-wing hooligans of the Sangh Parivar, of the Babri Masjid in Ayodhya. Responding to all of this was a young man, Bhaskar, who, instead of taking up a job, had, to the consternation of his family, joined the Communist Party and was doing street-theatre. I wanted to make Bhaskar a Quixote-like figure, in that he'd embrace the codes and tenets of Marxism and be fired by them in a world in which they'd been rendered obsolete, just as Quixote had taken up the dead chivalric codes of the romance novels in all earnestness, unmindful of their complete irrelevance. Perhaps I failed, but my intention was to show that politics and play were inseparable for Bhaskar, just as saving the world, chivalry, and fantasy were for Quixote: and I wished to offer the reader not Bhaskar's life-story, but that charged interruption in the winter in which this confusion occurs.

Freedom Song itself is structured around a trip, or a visit. For it has another story besides Bhaskar's. Two elderly unmarried sisters, Shanti and Mini, schoolteachers, live in North Calcutta. The younger of them, Mini, is troubled by arthritis. Her childhood friend, Khuku, who now lives in South Calcutta, in an apartment in Ballygunge, urges Mini to take a break, and to spend some time with her till her pain subsides. This idea of a change of venue excited not only Mini and Khuku, but primarily myself. It seemed to hold out more promise than plot did. As with Bhaskar, I wouldn't give the reader Mini's life-story, but simply record her stay as if I were recording a change, a transformation. The genre of the novel, for me, wasn't a story; it was created around a visit.

I'd based the characters in *Freedom Song* on people I knew and was even related to; I decided to keep three names unchanged. Khuku, my mother's pet name; and Shanti and Mini. To refer to and in a sense address them by their first names gave me a specific, private joy.

One reason for doing so was the generation these three belonged to, and the kind of women they were. Although they were unlike one another, they shared certain characteristics, such as an immense breadth of knowledge of Bengali literature, of its classic names, like Bankimchandra and Saratchandra and Bibhutibhushan (all referred to with easy familiarity by their first names – as is the Bengali convention), and also its slightly less canonical ones, like Manoj Basu and Premankur Aturthi. They also had a fair knowledge of classical heritage, especially Shanti mashi, who could speak of the *Mahabharata* as if it were a text by Shakespeare, in terms of character, psychology, and conflict. Mini mashi and my mother in particular had a tendency towards laughter; although Mini mashi, having been a schoolteacher, was slightly pedantic, while my mother, never having fared well at school, was less reverent. But they could also be perverse and stubborn; and they were, I think (even Mini mashi, despite her affiliation to a school run by the Sister Nivedita order), completely irreligious, with, shockingly, no regard for any kind of religion or god (this is particularly true of my mother) whatsoever. All in all, they were like some kind of new genre that had emerged in the late nineteenth or early twentieth century – like a film by Ghatak or Renoir, or a painting by Paul Klee, or a poem by Jibanananda Das, or a song by Cole Porter or Himangshu Dutta. They were perennially new. So it felt right to keep, and refer to them by, their first names in the novel, in order to hint at the paradox, in these ageing women, of that youthfulness and surprise. Can the modern ever grow old, and less appealing? For this reason, too, I found it easy to be friends with them in real life – with my mother, with Mini mashi and Shanti mashi – because, once I saw it, I was attracted to that newness in them, that dimension of the strange and delightful, as I was drawn, when I found it, to it in *Mrs Dalloway* and 'At the Bay' and 'Banalata Sen'. They so belonged to the new kind of writing they'd admired while growing up, which had burgeoned in Bengal and other parts of the world, that it was almost logical for me to rediscover them in fiction, in my own writing.

In the late eighteenth and early nineteenth centuries, the North was where the many Bengalis of dubious provenance who made their fortunes out of the growing city, and from their 'import-export' transactions with Englishmen, built their mansions. These great houses, which came up well before the high-thinking bourgeoisie would establish itself in Calcutta in the 1860s, were what most probably gave to the city its appellation, the 'City of Palaces': not palaces, really, but pretentious nouveau riche villas. Some of these were astonishingly ambitious. I am thinking especially of the grand house in Mini mashi's stifling area, the Marble Palace, which the gold trader Raja Rajendra Mallick built in 1835 – a neoclassical mansion with a neighbouring temple and traditional Bengali courtyard, today a kind of museum with a menagerie of exotic birds, a laidback spear-brandishing watchman, two clouded-over paintings apparently by Rubens, two others by Sir Joshua Reynolds, and a startling range of classic, covetable kitsch. In some ways – building fancy homes in a bewildering variety of native and European styles; giving to charity; setting up schools – the Bengali was the Marwari of the early nineteenth century. In fact, early nineteenth-century Calcutta was a lot like what India – even the world – is today: a place of hustlers making good and on the make, of boom and bust (as in Tagore's grandfather 'Prince' Dwarkanath's case, who made a fortune and then died in debt), a place with little time for culture. The difference between popular writing and 'literature' – that is, a kind of writing whose primary concern isn't commercial success – hadn't emerged, just as that distinction has now vanished again; a host of pamphlets and books on scurrilous, contemporary, and vivid themes came out from the *battala* (literally, 'under the banyan tree') press, the verbal counterpart of the Kalighat *pat*. And the North itself, despite its rich, was an impromptu marketplace, trading in commodities, livestock, and even song, women, and stories. We, today, are in the shadow of that great bat, that banyan tree, again; capitalism has transformed our world into the sort of marketplace the North once was; but, as my mother and I go up Central Avenue in the car, I notice North Calcutta itself is more or less untouched by globalisation: no malls, no coffee shop chains.

By the 1870s, some of the sons and grandsons of those very hustlers would become poets, and, running counter to their family's purely material ambitions, while still feeding off their material wealth, bring into existence the 'Renaissance'. In the meanwhile, my mother and I are still headed in that direction. The neighbourhood we are about to enter is described thus by Kaliprasanna Sinha in his great battala offering *Hutom Pyanchaar Naksha* (The Night-Owl's Sketches) from 1860 – the account of the night-time scene is translated by Bankimchandra Chatterjee:

> Fishwerwomen in the decaying Sobha Bazar market are selling – lamps in hand – their stores of putrid fish and salted *hilsa*, and coaxing purchasers by calling out, 'You fellow with the napkin on your shoulder, will you buy some fine fish?' 'You fellow with a moustache like a broom, will you pay four annas?' Some one, anxious to display his gallantry, is rewarded by hearing something unpleasant of his ancestors. Smokers of madat and ganjah, and drunkards who have drunk their last pice, are bawling out, 'Generous men, pity a poor blind Brahman,' and so procure the wherewithal for a new debauch.

We're as good as back in this Calcutta again.

A Visit

The Naba Jiban Nursing Home was in a lane on the right from the direction we were coming from, a lane easy to ignore, but which sucked you in as a drain or crevasse might suck in a trickle of water. It accommodated one car at a time, because a quarter of the lane was taken up by cars parked on the side.

The ground floor of the nursing home was like the ticketing area of a railway station: long-term waiting written on the faces of people hunched in chairs; everyone gathered around reception jostling each other; spontaneous shouting employed as a means of overcoming impediment; the well-to-do quite provincial, with a grim, set-in-stone air of entitlement. My mother and I might as well have arrived from Massachusetts or Bombay, so deceptively privileged and peripheral were we.

Yet we'd reached there just before the visiting hour shrank and vanished. The crowd before reception needed passes to go upstairs. For the ICU, you definitely required a pass; and two were allowed per patient. So my mother had to call Mini mashi's carer's husband, Sripati, a small and reassuring figure – so small and reassuring we might have missed him when he descended into the melee. He handed us two pink cards. We proceeded a few steps to the small lift with collapsible gates, which looked, implausibly, as if it had twenty-five or thirty people striving to enter it. Sripati, despite his unprepossessing looks, ushered us in with a decisive gesture, because he knew the ways of Bombay and Massachusetts weren't respected in these parts. But the liftman too was impressive, and knew how to spot a Massachusetts type, and was determined to treat them like anyone else. This was complicated by the fact that we too were unobtrusively bent on being treated like all the others. My mother's classical Bengali maternal qualities, a mixture of ferocity and warmth, won him over.

When Mini mashi opened her eyes, I noticed she could move her arms and roll her eyes, but not speak, given the tube in her mouth and also what the stroke had accomplished. Both my mother and I spent about ten minutes observing her watch us in a state of agitation, fall asleep, and then wake up and regard us, particularly me, in bafflement and urgency, and work herself to a state from wanting to say something. I calmed her by touching her arm, 'You'll soon be going home, you're getting better,' while noting her sallow complexion, her hair combed back, and the two tiny spots on her left cheek. The doctor-in-charge had said her condition had improved, though she was unstable, owing to the sudden fluctuations in her heartbeat.

Downstairs amidst the throng, we got embroiled in family politics, instructed in whispers by two relatives that Sripati, who'd given my mother news of the stroke, was, with his wife, removing Mini mashi's money, and they might also have their eye on the flat. As we returned southward, it became dark, and my mother and I worried about the two sisters, and decided we should see them again quite soon – Shanti mashi was, at that moment, home in her flat in the CIT Buildings – if we were to solve the Sripati problem, which had been pushed gently in our direction. We'd also been struck by the force of Mini mashi's recognition of me, her startlement, when she opened her eyes. Whoever she'd been expecting to see, it wasn't me.

She died four days later, two days after she was moved back home from the nursing home. My mother and I found that, already, we'd have to return to the North, sooner than we'd presumed, for a last sighting of her childhood friend before she was cremated.

My relatives are East Bengalis, from Sylhet, a province once known for the mystic Sri Chaitanya, its artistic milieu, its enterprisingness, and, after Partition and, even later, post-Bangladesh, its orthodox Muslims (it was a Sylheti mullah who 'issued' a fatwa against the writer Taslima Nasreen), the taxi drivers and pretzel sellers of New York City, and for England's much-maligned, much-loved Indian restaurants. We know now that you put scare quotes around the 'Indian' food in those restaurants not just because the menu was composed in Britain, and replicated in every neighbourhood there, but because its perpetrators were a bunch of loud, indefatigable Sylheti Muslims.

My relatives, located in various parts of the city, had made their way here a little before and during Partition. They were crucial coordinates in my holidays, and set those holidays' tone – of oddity and the absurd. My relatives, mainly on my mother's side, had among them one or two traders and country yokels; but mostly they were engineers, with a few school headmistresses and provincial civil servants in their ranks, and were among the funniest people I knew. They were, I think, cosmopolitans. One sign of the cosmopolitan is their proprietary stake in the world of reading and books; another sign, emerging from the last one, is the tendency to quote constantly; a third sign, probably because it seems their true habitat should be *within* the covers of a book, *inside* a fiction, is that they seldom own property – which adds imperceptibly to their air of not belonging. In my relatives' cases, many of them didn't own property until late in life because of their displacement. Their intrinsic oddness was accentuated by their speaking to one another not in Bengali, but in Sylheti – a dialect and offshoot that was, to me, and particularly to them, a riot. For *korchhi* or 'doing' in Bengali, they'd say *kortesi*; for *hae* or 'yes' they'd say the imbecilic *haw*; for *kano* or 'why' they'd utter the plangent *kané*. 'Chh' sounds would become the sibilant, childish 's'; the 'k' sound approach 'h', as in Arabic. Their jokes were rude, freely and opportunistically making use of farting and shitting – insistently expressing a side less savoury than their lofty Rabindrik or Tagorean loyalties. Naturally, we children enjoyed this humour to a point. One of the things that earned an almost regretful laugh from the elders was the faux-limpid but inadvertently exculpatory line from a Tagore song, *'Tari te pa dei ni ami'*, or 'I didn't step into the boat'. But if the words *pa dei ni* ('didn't step') are said together, as in the song, they merge into *padini*, or the hasty clarification, 'didn't fart'. And Tagore's line becomes indistinguishable from 'I didn't fart in the boat'. I doubt if I'd have entered that dimension of the Bengal Renaissance but for the tastelessness of my uncles and my mother.

Going out now to the government-made flat in the CIT Buildings – a prefabricated socialist structure, like something out of Prenzlauer Berg – was to make yet another Calcutta-type visit. No visit for the emigré – whether it's a family visit or of another kind – is anything but a rehearsal of a past journey to a meeting place, a civilised interregnum in which pleasantries and gifts are exchanged in homage to that first visit in the home town, which was just a simple visit. No visit, later, is what it appears to be, but an echo of that earlier meeting, when we were beginning to know each other, and in lieu of the meeting that will take place when we return to where we then met. I recall Mini mashi and Shanti mashi making their entrance into my uncle's house on Pratapaditya Road before lunch – they must have been in their late forties – with a pot of Bhim Nag yoghurt from their neighbourhood. Even then, some part of me knew that this journey had been made with a previous journey in mind, which had been covered on familiar terrain, and that civilities would be exchanged, jokes laughed at, and the pot of yoghurt given, all in a rehearsed, unencroaching manner, in expectation of the original setting being restored in the future. Till then, *this*, evidently, is where they were.

Acknowledgements

I'd like to thank Peter Straus, my agent, for first suggesting, in 2005, that I write this book, and for not minding too much when I shot down the idea. Having written three novels about Calcutta, I felt reluctant to write about it again, not least because I thought that the city that had once excited me in all kinds of ways had changed permanently. It was when I began to come to terms with that change, and the new city that had resulted from it, that I relented and realised that I had a book to write. For Peter's continuing belief in my work, I'm grateful.

I'm grateful to Sonny Mehta for the same reason, and for commissioning this book. My thanks to Chiki Sarkar and Rosalind Porter for their great enthusiasm and responsiveness, and for bringing a freshness to my life as a published writer. To Diana Cognialese, I remain indebted, as ever, for her intelligence and support.

Jaishree Ram Mohan should be acknowledged for the high standards of her copy-editing. I'd like to thank Maharghya Chakraborty for being my cheerful amanuensis for the manuscript, and my wife for chipping in kindly – and substantially – at the end. Whatever little remained I typed with one finger from my longhand original.

Roughly half of Chapter Five appeared as a *Diary* piece in the *London Review of Books*; my thanks to the editors.

I should also thank Sukanta Chaudhuri, editor of *Calcutta: The Living City* (OUP), from whose pages I've quoted R.K. Dasgupta.

The excerpt quoted from Giorgio Bassani's *The Garden of the Finzi-Continis* (Penguin Modern Classics) is translated by Jamie McKenrick.

I'm grateful to Dwaipayan Bhattacharya and Rudrangshu Mukherjee for helping with information.

To my wife, Rosinka, I'm indebted in ways too various to enumerate; but I'd especially like to say that her discussion of the poet Iswar Gupta, quoted in these pages, can be found in her critical study of poetry in nineteenth-century Bengal, *The Literary Thing: History, Poetry, and the Making of a Modern Cultural Sphere* (OUP). This book and her work in general have been an invaluable, irreplaceable resource.

The book was written roughly between August 2009 and December 2011, and is a personal record of that time. Needless to say, whatever has happened in West Bengal and its capital since then is, given the period *Calcutta* covers, beyond the book's parameters.

18 August 2012